Disclaimer: The information presented is purely to share my experience and for entertainment
purposes. As always, check with a doctor before making any fitness or nutrition changes. The
author disclaims liability for any damage, mishap, or injury that may occur from engaging in any
activities or ideas from this site. All information posted is merely for educational and
informational purposes. It is not intended as a substitute for professional advice. Should you
decide to act upon any information in this book, you do so at your own risk. The content
displayed in the book is the intellectual property of the author. You may not reuse, republish, or
reprint such content without our written consent.

Table of Contents

Introduction 17

Breakfast..18

    Breakfast Bread Balls 18

    Morning Nutella Toasts 18

    Aromatic Morning Casserole...19

    Light Ham Casserole 19

    Sweet Oatmeal 19

    Quinoa with Pistachios..20

    Pumpkin Butter..20

    Homemade Raspberry Honey Yogurt 20

    Chocolate Oatmeal with Cinnamon 21

    Salty Zucchini Oatmeal 21

    Granola Crumble 21

    Quinoa-Oatmeal Mix 22

    Oatmeal-Pumpkin Pie 22

    Tomato Omelette 22

    Spicy Breakfast Frittata...23

    Green Quiche 23

    Cheesy Frittata 24

    Walnut Cinnamon Rolls 24

    Huevos Ranchero...25

    Veggie Omelette...25

    Mexican Casserole 26

    Vanilla Oats with Honey 26

    Breakfast Ham Toasts..26

    Butter Grits 27

    Sausage Casserole 27

    Cottage Cheese Pudding 27

    Poppy Breakfast Bread 28

    Western Omelette 28

    Herbed Breakfast Potatoes 28

    Breakfast Vanilla Pancake 29

Slow Cooker Strawberry Porridge 29

Monkey bread 30

Scrambled Eggs 30

Bacon Wrapped Eggs 30

Breakfast Jam 31

Sweet Potatoes with the Peanuts 31

Creamy Millet 32

Spinach Muffins 32

Breakfast Peach Butter 32

Breakfast Baby Carrots 33

Muffins with Crunchy Bacon 33

Sausage Rolls 33

Slow Cooker Meatballs 34

Delicious Eggplant Pate with Breadcrumbs 34

Red Beans with the Sweet Peas 35

Nutritious Burrito Bowl 35

Quinoa Curry 35

Ham Pitta Pockets 36

Breakfast Meatloaf 36

Breakfast Sweet Pepper Rounds 36

Breakfast Cauliflower Hash 37

Bread Pudding with Dried Apricots 37

Breakfast Bread Boats 37

Mushroom Casserole with Cheddar Cheese 38

Roasted Pumpkin Cubes 38

Soft Cabbage with Onion 38

Bread Crumb Meatballs 39

Creamy Chicken Strips 39

Lunch 40

Chicken Salad with Vegetables 40

Pot Pie 40

Noodle Soup 41

Zucchini Noodle Soup 41

White Bean Soup 42

Onion Soup 42

Slow Cooker Mac 42

Chickpea Stew 43

Lunch Chili 43

Panade 43

Fish-Pasta Casserole 44

Enchilada Soup 44

Bacon Rigatoni 45

Stuffed Potatoes 45

Hominy Stew 45

Sweet Pulled Pork Sandwiches 46

Caramelized Zucchini with Chicken Cubes 46

Lunch Ragout 46

Stuffed Plums 47

Stuffed Tomatoes 47

Avocado Cups 47

Cottage Cheese Dumplings 47

Chicken and Egg Noodle Soup 48

Soft Cauliflower Florets 48

Pumpkin Soup 48

Pappardelle 49

Date Pudding with Ham 49

Spicy Vegetable Casserole 49

Cauliflower Cutlets 50

Meatloaf with Eggs 50

Polenta Dumplings 51

Garlic Jacket Potatoes 51

Mushroom Stew 51

Stuffed Peppers 52

Cheese Pie 52

Carrot with Honey Gravy 52

Rice Apple Cups 53

Lunch Salsa Layer Pie 53

Lunch Gratin 53

Rice Casserole 54

Layered Pie 54

Lentil Salad 55

Spaghetti Salad 55

Couscous Salad 56

Quinoa Salad 56

Lunch Chicken Wraps 56

Nutritious Lunch Wraps 57

Butternut Squash Soup 57

Eggplant Bacon Wraps 57

Mexican Warm Salad 58

Hot Chorizo Salad 58

Stuffed Eggplants 58

Light Lunch Quiche 59

Chicken Open Sandwich 59

Onion Lunch Muffins 59

Tuna in Potatoes 60

Banana Lunch Sandwiches 60

Parmesan Potato with Dill 60

Light Taco Soup 61

Slow Cooker Risotto 61

Lemon Orzo 61

Veggie Bean Stew 62

Carrot Soup with Cardamom 62

Cod Chowder 62

Sweet Corn Pilaf 63

Zucchini Lasagna 63

Mediterranean Vegetable Mix 63

Spaghetti Cottage Cheese Casserole 64

Meatballs with Coconut Gravy 64

Fresh Dal 64

Side Dishes 65

    Parsley Cauliflower Rice 65

    Butter Couscous 65

    Butternut Squash Noodles 65

    Slow Cooker Tomatoes 66

    Red Beans 66

    Quinoa Stuffed Bell Peppers 66

    Lentil Chili 67

    Side Dish Jambalaya 67

    Dumplings 67

    Mashed Potato with Garlic 68

    Broccoli Hash 68

    Aromatic White Rice 68

    Cheesy Brussels Sprouts 69

    Fragrant Garlic Cloves 69

    Turmeric Chickpea 69

    Creamed corn 70

    Tomato Cabbage Petals 70

    Barbecue Beans 70

    Slow Cooker Spinach with Nuts 71

    Cheese Mushrooms 71

    Spicy Marinated Sweet Peppers 71

    Paprika Carrot with Sesame Seeds 72

    Almond Milk Asparagus 72

    Sweet Corn with Jalapeno Rub 72

    Herbed Sweet Potato 73

    Soy Sauce Green Peas 73

    German Potato Salad 73

    Slow Cooker Greens 74

    Tender Turnips 74

    Creamy Artichoke Dip 74

    Soft Millet with Dill 75

    Glazed Vegetables 75

Balsamic Beets 75

Chili Orange Squash 76

Slow Cooker Tamale Side Dish 76

Easy Corn Pudding 76

Tender Red Onions 77

Fragrant Applesauce 77

Wild Rice with Berries 77

Sweet Pumpkin Wedges 78

Scalloped Potatoes 78

Mayo Eggplant Cubes 78

Turmeric Buckwheat 79

Mashed Sweet Potato 79

Cornbread Pudding 79

Glazed Yams 80

Zucchini Pate 80

Red Cabbage with Onions 80

Broccoli Stuffing 80

Slow Cooker Shallots 81

Lemon-Garlic Mushrooms 81

Paprika Potato Strips 81

Macaroni with Cream Cheese 82

Baked Potato with Mushrooms 82

Jalapeno Side Dish 82

Slow Cooker Ramen 83

Refried Beans 83

Slow Cooker Fennel 83

Butter Artichokes 84

Coriander Rainbow Carrots 84

Creamy Parsnips 85

Sliced Eggplants with Mayo Sauce 85

Party Macaroni Side Dish 85

Rosemary Hasselback Potatoes 86

Asian-Style Asparagus 86

Mac Cups 86

Baked White Onions 87

Tomato Okra 87

Slow Cooker Corn Salad 87

Smashed Red Potatoes 88

Snacks 89

Banana Bread 89

Energy Bars with Quinoa 89

Pecan Snac 89

Bacon Sausages 90

Wrapped Sausages 90

Chili Scrolls 90

Jalapeno Taquitos 91

Spaghetti Fritters 91

Corn Fritters 91

Slow Cooker Meatballs with Sesame Seeds 92

Slow Cooker Cheese Dip 92

Cinnamon Pecans 92

Snack Chicken Wings 93

Cocktail Meatballs with Tomato Sauce 93

Hamburger Dip 93

Sugar Sausages 94

Sugared Pecans 94

Snack Party Mix 94

Boiled Peanuts 95

Kielbasa 95

Semi-Sweet Meatballs 95

Beer and Chicken Logs 96

Slow Cooker Taquitos 96

Snack Hot Dogs 96

Pita Bites 97

Chocolate nuts 97

Slow Cooker Fudge 97

Nutella Granola 98

Oatmeal-Raisin Bars 98

Chicken Nachos 98

Meat Balls with Cheese 99

Bean Dip 99

Cayenne Pepper Shrimp 99

Marsala Mushrooms 100

Rosemary Fingerling Potatoes 100

Chili Pepper Dip 100

Snack Chickpeas 101

Shiitake Mushroom Bites 101

Veggie Potato Cups 101

Chicken Butter Balls 102

Spicy Nuts 102

Spinach Cream Cheese Dip 103

Mozzarella Tomatoes 103

Dill Muffins 103

Peanut Chicken Strips 104

Pork Cheese Rolls 104

Glazed Turkey Strips 104

Spicy Apple Chutney 105

Potato Dip with Cheddar Cheese 105

Creamy Apple Wedges with Peanuts 106

Egg Muffins 106

Carrot Fritters 106

Garlic Bacon Slices 107

Salty Peanut Bombs 107

Crunchy Zucchini Sticks 107

Pitta Pockets with Sweet Pepper 108

Garlic Dip 108

Sausage Dip 108

Marinated Chili Peppers 109

Poultry 110

Chicken Pita Pockets 110

Jerk Chicken Meal 110

Chicken Rice with Lemon 111

Poultry Burrito Bowl 111

Asian Chicken Bowl 112

Italian Style Chicken 112

Thai Bowl...112

Teriyaki Chicken 113

Stuffed Chicken with Tomatoes..113

Chicken Liver Pate..114

Chicken Soup with Tortillas..114

Ground Turkey Soup...115

Chicken Tikka Masala 115

Turkey Minestrone 116

Slow Cooker French Chicken...116

Turkey Chili 117

Chicken Cream Soup..117

Chicken Paella..118

Chicken and Biscuits 118

Glazed Chicken Breast...119

Balsamic Chicken...119

Barbecue Chicken Slices 120

Honey Chicken 120

Spicy Peanut Butter Chicken...120

Onion Chicken 121

Creamy Chicken 121

Bourbon Chicken 121

Latin Style Chicke...122

Chicken Pot Pie 122

Curry Chicken...123

Whole Chicken Stuffed with Soy Beans...123

Fennel Chicken...124

Moscow Chicken...124

Chocolate Chicken Mash...124

Chicken Adobo 125

Chicken-Dumplings Mix 125

Thyme Whole Chicken..126

Lime Chicken Drumsticks..126

Sesame Chicken Wings 126

African Chicken 127

Butter Chicken Wings...127

Soy Sauce Chicken..127

Puerto Ricco Chicken 128

Pomegranate Turkey...128

Orange Duck Fillets..129

Delightful Chicken Mole...129

Chicken-Potato Casserole..129

Sweet Curry Chicken Strips...130

Incredible Chicken Continental...130

Chicken Stew with Pumpkin..130

Hawaiian Chicken 131

Apple Chicken Balls 131

Ginger Turkey..131

Lemon Sauce Pulled Chicken 132

Tomato Chicken...132

Slow Cooker Poultry Mix..132

Parmesan Chicken Fillet..133

Tender Chicken Cacciatore 133

Coca Cola Chicken...134

Horseradish Chicken...134

Meat...135

Beef Shank 135

Lamb Tagine 135

Corned Beef..135

Beer Brats...135

Cilantro Meat Bowl...136

Sausage Stew...137

Cuban-Style Beef..137

Sausage Gravy..137

Boeuf Bourguignon...138

Bacon Jam..138

Ham Soup...138

Beef Goulash..139

Sweet Pork Goulash..139

Pork Chops with Peppers...139

Amazing Swedish Meatballs...140

Turmeric Lasagna...140

Beef Roast..140

Shallot Beef..141

Honey Ribs...141

Mango Pulled Pork...141

Spicy Pulled Pork for Sandwiches..142

Parsley Barbecue Meatballs...142

Cranberry Meatballs...142

Lasagna Soup...143

Pork Shepherd Pie..143

Cheesy Ground Pork...144

Italian Beef Roast with Grapes..144

Beef Stroganoff..144

Stuffed Pork Chops...145

Pork Strips with Mushrooms..145

Slow Cooker French Beef Stew..145

Country Style Pork..146

Beef Ratatouille..146

Pepperoncini Beef..146

Curry Lamb..147

Honey Pulled Pork..147

Delightful Pulled Pork Nachos...147

Garlic Beef Mash..148

Beef Strips in Bread Crumbs..148

Pork and Barley Soup..148

Hungarian Tender Beef..149

Thyme Lamb..149

Lamb Meatballs...149

Stuffed Lamb with Onions...150

Lamb Shoulder..150

Lamb Stew...151

Lamb Casserole...151

Garlic Lamb...152

Rosemary Lamb..152

Lamb and Apricot Tagine 152

Greek Style Lamb with Olives...153

Succulents Lamb...153

Moroccan Lamb..153

Lemon Lamb Fillet..154

Indian Pork..154

Lamb Meatballs...154

Lime Zest Pork..155

Lamb Leg in Red Wine..155

Mongolian Beef...156

Mexican Lamb...156

Fish 157

Slow Cooker Salmon 157

Cod Fillets 157

Tilapia in Sour Cream 157

Scallops with Cherry Sauce...158

Fish Stew 158

Seafood Stew 159

Fish Chowder...159

Asparagus Tilapia...159

Delightful Shrimp Scampi..160

Jamaican Fish Stew...160

Ginger Trout...160

Clams in Almond Milk Sauce..161

Mango Milkfish...161

Garlic Mussels...161

Balsamic Catfish...162

Chili Salmon Cubes..162

Tomato Shrimp...162

Tuna Salpicao...163

Miso Trout...163

Asian Style Catfish..163

Soy Sauce Calamari...164

Ginger Squid...164

Parsley Seabass...164

Salmon in Coconut Milk...165

Seabass Cutlets...165

Fish Sticks...165

Turmeric Shrimp Soup...166

Cayenne Pepper Snapper...166

Salmon Pie...167

Slow Cooker Rosemary Trout..167

Garlic Sole...167

Tuna Dip...168

Cream Tuna Casserole...168

Stuffed Trout..169

Mushroom and Seabass Ragout..169

Salmon Miso Soup..170

Sweet Shrimps with Fresh Dill...170

Orange Fish...171

Salmon Chili...171

Slow Cooker Fish Cakes..172

Trout Croquettes...172

Thai Fish Cakes...173

Harissa Cod...173

Trout Piccata 175

Salmon Fingers 175

Lime Flounder 175

Snapper with Mushrooms 176

Carp Soup 176

Spicy Perch 176

Stuffed Squid 177

Halibut with Peach 177

Glazed Sesame Salmon 178

Japanese Style Cod Fillet 178

Slow Cooker Crab 179

Light Lobster Soup 179

Flounder Casserole 180

Fish Tacos 180

Dill Crab Cakes 180

Desserts 181

Easy Chocolate Cake 181

Fruit Cobbler 181

Ginger Giant Cookies 181

Sweet Monkey Bread 182

Pecan Brownies 182

Peanut Muffins 182

Spoon Cake 183

Lemon Curd 183

Pumpkin Cake Bombs 183

Fragrant Cinnamon Apples 184

Cherry Pudding 184

Almond Dump Cake 184

Apple Pie Dip 185

Fudge Cake 185

Classic Apple Pie 185

Charlotte 186

Cinnabons Pie 186

Walnut Pudding Cake 187

Carrot Muffins 187

Baked Apple Slices 187

Simple Lava Cake 188

Caramel Cake 188

Tapioca Pudding 188

Super Tasty Banana Dip 189

Sweet Wild Rice 189

Coconut Pie 189

Bread Cake with Oranges 190

Strawberry Pavlova 190

Blueberry Bread Pudding 190

Cocoa Bars 191

Peach Caramel 191

Apples with Granola Filling 191

Orange Upside down Cake 192

Oatmeal Crumble 192

Brewed Coffee Pie 192

Vanilla Cream Pie 193

Graham Cookies Bars 193

Chopped Strawberry Pie 193

Citron Bars 194

Sweet Apple Butter 194

Cocoa Candies 194

Summer Melon Pudding 195

Latte Cake 195

Peach Crisp 195

Milk-Chocolate Fondue 195

Raspberry Sponge 196

Puff Pastry Pears Boards 196

Banana Foster 196

Vanilla Crème Brulee 197

Tangerine Pie 197

Lemon Pie with Cardamom..197

Caramel Apples...198

Raisin Bars..198

Cocoa Rice Pudding..199

Cheesecake..199

Thick Hot Chocolate...199

Indian Pudding...200

Huge Coffee Cinnamon Roll...200

Slow Cooker Figs..200

Poppy Sweet Pie...201

Conclusion 202

Introduction

If you have never heard of a slow cooker, you definitely need to check out this essential kitchen appliance. To give you a basic overview, the slow cooker has a ceramic container, where you place all of your ingredients. The slow cooker bowl sits inside a metal holder which is the heater for the appliance. Now, a slow cooker doesn't fry food or bake it necessarily but it heats it slowly and maintains a low temperature, allowing the food inside the bowl to cook slowly, absorbing all the flavors of the ingredients and breaking down all the tough proteins in any meats to give you tender, juicy foods. Sounds great, right?

The slow cooker technology means cooking the food slowly at low temperatures between (LOW) 170F/77C and (HIGH) 280F/138C. Due to such a low temperature, the products in the slower cooker do not burn, do not boil and do not require constant stirring. The food inside is evenly cooked from all sides due to the heating elements installed at the bottom and sides of the device. All you need to do is plug it in, add your ingredients and you are ready to go!

The method of cooking in the slow cooker is rather easy as well. Almost every meal essentially involves placing the food in the slow cooker bowl, closing the lid and selecting the appropriate mode- High or Low. The slow cooker is completely safe and the heat sources are securely contained inside the machine. You can turn it on, walk away and not worry about it for hours!

One more advantage of the slow cooker is that many versions will automatically turn off when the cooking cycle is complete. No need to worry about food over cooking when you have this convenient feature! The slower cookers also do not need full sealing to cook properly. You can open the lid, check the cooking process, or add the necessary ingredients to the dish as it cooks. It will continue to function properly!

This special kitchen tool allows you to prepare any food that needs long-term cooking such as meat, poultry, roasts, stuffed peppers, cereals, etc. Using the slow cooker for cooking these tougher dishes will make them come out fantastically and with very little effort.

The slow cooker is also the perfect tool for the cooking different jams and jellies, cooking fruits slowly and allowing them to naturally turn into soft jelly.

There are many kinds of slow cookers so it is important to choose one that will be perfect exactly for you. The first thing you should pay attention to is its capacity. Think about how big you need your slow cooker to be and purchase one that is sized correctly for you. You should also think about features you want. Do you need a lid that locks so you can take the bowl and the lid out and transport them easily? Do you need the slow cooker to turn off after a set amount of time? Think about all of this when purchasing your new favorite piece of kitchen equipment.

You are likely ready to use your slow cooker now and dying to try some of these amazing dishes. Wait no longer! Plug in that slow cooker and start creating some fantastic foods.

Breakfast

Breakfast Bread Balls

Prep time: 35 minutes | Cooking time: 87 minutes | Servings: 7

Ingredients:

- 10 oz. flour
- ½ teaspoon salt
- 1 teaspoon brown sugar
- 1 teaspoon fresh yeast
- 1 cup plain yogurt
- 1 teaspoon cinnamon
- 1 teaspoon vanilla extract
- ½ cup white sugar
- 1 tablespoon butter
- 3 tablespoon powdered sugar

Directions:

Preheat the whey until it is room temperature. Add the fresh yeast and brown sugar. Whisk the mixture until the yeast is dissolved. Add the 5 oz. of the flour and stir it until smooth. Leave the dough for 10 minutes in a warm place. Then add the salt, cinnamon, vanilla extract, white sugar, and remaining flour. Knead until a smooth dough forms. Let sit for 15 minutes in a warm place to let the dough to rise. Cut the dough into 7 pieces and roll into balls. Cover the slow cooker bowl with the baking paper and place the dough balls into the slow cooker. Cook the balls on HIGH for 90 minutes. When the time is done – open the slow cooker lid and check if the surface of the balls is golden brown. If they have browned, remove the breakfast balls from the slow cooker. Serve the cooked balls with the butter and sprinkle the balls with the powdered sugar then serve.

Nutrition: calories 223, fat 4.9, fiber 2, carbs 39.13, protein 5

Morning Nutella Toasts

Prep time: 15 minutes | Cooking time: 2 hours | Servings: 6

Ingredients:

- 10 cups French bread, chopped
- 1 tablespoon cinnamon
- 4 tablespoon Nutella
- ¼ cup brown sugar
- 3 banana
- 1 teaspoon vanilla extract
- 3 tablespoon butter
- 2 eggs
- ½ cup milk

Directions:

Combine the Nutella, vanilla extract, butter, and milk in the big bowl. Crack the eggs into the mix and blend, using a hand mixer if needed. When the mix is a homogeneous mass – it is done. Put the chopped bread in the slow cooker and add the nutella mix. Stir it carefully and close the lid. Cook on the high for 1.5 hours. Meanwhile, slice the bananas and mix them with the brown sugar. After 1.5 hours – open the lid of the slow cooker and stir the mixture up carefully. Add the sliced bananas and stir it again. Cook the dish for 30 minutes more. When the time is done – transfer the dish to a serving bowl and serve it warm.

Nutrition: calories 461, fat 18.3, fiber 5, carbs 64.76, protein 11

Aromatic Morning Casserole

Prep time: 15 minutes | Cooking time: 7 hours | Servings: 8

Ingredients:

- 7 oz. Cheddar cheese
- 4 oz. potatoes
- 1 carrot
- 1 teaspoon thyme
- 1 teaspoon salt
- 1 teaspoon oregano
- 1 sweet yellow pepper
- 8 eggs
- 8 oz. ham
- 5 oz. milk
- 1 tablespoon flour
- 1 cup chopped white onion

Directions:

Shred the cheddar cheese. Combine the salt, oregano, and thyme together in a shallow bowl. Peel the potatoes and chop into tiny cubes. Peel the carrot and grate it. Beat the eggs in a separate bowl then add the milk, flour and spice mixture. Combine the chopped potato with the white onion and grated carrot. Put the vegetable mixture in the slow cooker. Add the whisked egg mix and sprinkle the dish with the shredded cheese. Cut the ham into the strips. Sprinkle the casserole with the ham strips and close the lid. Cook the dish on LOW for 7 hours. When the time is done and the casserole is cooked – serve the dish immediately.

Nutrition: calories 269, fat 14.2, fiber 1, carbs 16.16, protein 19

Light Ham Casserole

Prep time: 15 minutes | Cooking time: 5 hours | Servings: 12

Ingredients:

- 7 oz. ham
- 10 eggs
- 1 cup chopped parsley
- 1 cup milk
- 1 teaspoon salt
- 6 oz. Romano cheese
- 1 teaspoon turmeric
- 1 teaspoon paprika
- 1 tomato

Directions:

Chop the ham into the small cubes then crack the eggs into a bowl and whisk them well. Add the milk, salt, and turmeric. Whisk the mixture carefully again. Then slice Romano cheese and tomato. Add the chopped parsley to the whisked egg mixture. Place the ham cubes in the slow cooker. Then make a layer of sliced cheese. After this, add the sliced tomato and pour the egg mix on top. Close the slow cooker and cook on HIGH for 5 hours. When the casserole is cooked – remove it from the slow cooker and cut into the serving pieces. Enjoy the casserole warm!

Nutrition: calories 200, fat 13, fiber 0, carbs 4.52, protein 16

Sweet Oatmeal

Prep time: 10 minutes | Cooking time: 2 hours | Servings: 5

Ingredients:

- 3 cup oatmeal
- 1 cup water
- 2 cup milk
- 1/3 teaspoon salt
- 1 tablespoon brown sugar
- ¼ cup white sugar
- 1 teaspoon vanilla extract
- 1 tablespoon butter, chopped into pieces
- ¼ teaspoon ground ginger

Directions:

Combine the water with the milk and salt. Add the brown sugar and white sugar. Stir the mixture carefully until the sugar is dissolved. After this, add vanilla extract and ground ginger. Stir gently. Add the oatmeal and mix everything together. Add butter and pour the mixture into the slow cooker. Close the lid and cook on HIGH for 2 hours. When the time is done, remove the cooked sweet oatmeal from the slow cooker and stir it carefully. Serve the dish immediately.

Nutrition: calories 217, fat 8.9, fiber 3, carbs 28.94, protein 7

Quinoa with Pistachios

Prep time: 8 minutes | Cooking time: 3.5 hours | Servings: 4

Ingredients:

- 1/3 cup pistachios
- 2 cup quinoa
- 2 cup chicken broth
- 1 teaspoon salt
- ¼ teaspoon ground black pepper
- 5 tablespoon cream cheese
- 1 teaspoon garlic powder

Directions:

Crush the pistachio carefully and mix them with the cream cheese. In a separate bowl, combine the quinoa with the salt, ground pepper and garlic powder. Transfer the quinoa mixture to the slow cooker. Add the chicken broth and stir it gently. Close the slow cooker lid. Set the slow cooker on HIGH and cook the quinoa for 3 hours. Add the cream cheese mixture and stir it into the quinoa carefully. Close the slow cooker lid and cook the dish for 30 minutes more on HIGH. When the time is done, stir the cooked dish one to more time to make it homogenous. Serve the quinoa in the bowls.

Nutrition: calories 436, fat 15.4, fiber 7, carbs 59.36, protein 16

Pumpkin Butter

Prep time: 10 minutes | Cooking time: 4 hour | Servings: 8

Ingredients:

- 1 pound pumpkin puree, canned
- 4 tablespoon honey
- 1 tablespoon cinnamon
- 1 oz. clove
- 1/3 teaspoon ground cardamom
- ¼ teaspoon salt
- ½ cup brown sugar
- 3 tablespoon lemon juice
- 1 tablespoon orange zest
- ¼ teaspoon vanilla extract

Directions:

Place the pumpkin puree in the slow cooker and add honey, cinnamon, clove, salt, sugar, orange zest, vanilla and lemon juice. Whisk everything together well and then place the lid on the slow cooker. Cook the dish on the HIGH for 3 hours. Open the slow cooker and stir in the ground cardamom. Keep the lid open and cook the dish for 1 hour more. Stir gently. Cook the dish until you get the desired thick texture. Transfer the cooked pumpkin butter into jars. Chill well and serve or keep the pumpkin butter in the fridge for up to 2 weeks.

Nutrition: calories 415, fat 27.8, fiber 4, carbs 31.96, protein 17

Homemade Raspberry Honey Yogurt

Prep time: 15 hours | Cooking time: 7 hours | Servings: 4

Ingredients:

- 4 cup milk
- 1 cup Greek yogurt
- 1 cup raspberries
- 2 tablespoon honey

Directions:

Pour the milk into the slow cooker and cook it on LOW for 7 hours. After this, chill the milk till it reaches 100 degrees F. Add the Greek yogurt and stir the mixture. Then, let the milk mixture sit covered for 10 hours more at room temperature. When the milk has thickened, transfer it to a piece of cheesecloth. Put the cheesecloth in a colander and leave for 5 hours to remove the whey. Meanwhile, wash the raspberries carefully and slice them. Combine the sliced raspberries with the honey and stir it gently. When the time is done, transfer the cooked yogurt into the serving bowls. Add the honey-raspberry mixture and serve.

Nutrition: calories 266, fat 8.2, fiber 2, carbs 36.89, protein 13

Chocolate Oatmeal with Cinnamon

Prep time: 10 minutes | *Cooking time:* 3 hours 10 minutes | *Servings:* 5

Ingredients:

- 3 oz. white chocolate
- 1 tablespoon ground cinnamon
- 1 teaspoon vanilla extract
- 1/3 cup heavy cream
- 3 cup almond milk
- 3 cup oatmeal
- ½ cup white sugar
- ¼ teaspoon ground cloves

Directions:

Pour the almond milk and heavy cream in the slow cooker bowl. Add the ground cinnamon, vanilla extract and ground cloves. After this, add the oatmeal and stir the mixture gently. Add the white sugar and close the lid. Cook the oatmeal on LOW for 3 hours. Meanwhile, grate the chocolate. After 3 hours, add the grated white chocolate to the oatmeal and stir carefully until the white chocolate is melted. Close the lid and cook the oatmeal for 10 minutes more on HIGH. When the time is done, transfer the cooked breakfast to serving bowls.

Nutrition: calories 354, fat 15.5, fiber 5, carbs 50.52, protein 6

Salty Zucchini Oatmeal

Prep time: 15 minutes | *Cooking time:* 3 hours | *Servings:* 7

Ingredients:

- 6 oz. zucchini
- 1 teaspoon butter
- 4 cup oatmeal
- 5 cup water
- 1 teaspoon salt
- ¼ teaspoon ground white pepper
- 1 tablespoon sour cream
- 1 tablespoon tomato paste
- 5 oz. Feta cheese

Directions:

Wash the zucchini carefully and grate it. Sprinkle the grated zucchini with the salt and ground white pepper and toss together. Add tomato paste and sour cream and mix. Transfer the grated zucchini mixture to the slow cooker and cook for 4 hours on HIGH. Then add oatmeal and water and stir the mixture. Close the slow cooker lid and cook the oatmeal for 3 hours on LOW. Meanwhile, chop Feta cheese roughly. When the time is done, open the slow cooker lid and toss in the butter. Mix the oatmeal carefully to mix in the butter. Place the cooked dish in the bowls and sprinkle it with the chopped cheese then serve.

Nutrition: calories 175, fat 6.5, fiber 3, carbs 24.03, protein 7

Granola Crumble

Prep time: 15 minutes | *Cooking time:* 4.5 hours | *Servings:* 4

Ingredients:

- 3 tablespoon maple syrup
- 2 tablespoon apple juice
- ¼ teaspoon salt
- 4 green apples
- 7 oz. granola
- ¼ teaspoon ground cardamom
- 1 tablespoon butter

Directions:

Peel the green apples and cut them into halves. Remove the seeds from the apples and chop into the small pieces. Place the chopped green apples in the slow cooker and add salt, apple juice, maple syrup, ground cardamom, and butter. Add the granola and stir everything together well. Close the slow cooker lid and cook the Granola Crumble for 4.5 hours on LOW. When the crumble is done, transfer it to serving bowls and let cool slightly then serve.

Nutrition: calories 427, fat 18.7, fiber 6, carbs 62.48, protein 5

Quinoa-Oatmeal Mix

Prep time: 15 minutes | Cooking time: 4 hours | Servings: 5

Ingredients:

- 2 cup quinoa
- 1 cup oatmeal
- 1 cup almond milk
- 1 cup coconut milk
- 1 cup whole milk
- 4 tablespoon condensed milk
- 1 tablespoon butter
- ¼ teaspoon salt
- ¼ teaspoon clove

Directions:

Combine the oatmeal and quinoa together in the slow cooker bowl. Then add the almond milk, coconut milk, and whole milk and stir gently. Add the condensed milk, salt, and clove into the slow cooker and stir again. Close the lid and cook the mixture on HIGH for 4 hours. When the time is done, open the slow cooker lid and mix in the butter.

Nutrition: calories 494, fat 20.8, fiber 7, carbs 65.28, protein 14

Oatmeal-Pumpkin Pie

Prep time: 15 minutes | Cooking time: 3 hours | Servings: 6

Ingredients:

- 7 oz. oats
- 12 oz. milk
- 4 tablespoon coconut milk
- 7 oz. pumpkin puree
- 4 tablespoon brown sugar
- 1/3 tablespoon vanilla extract
- 2 tablespoon pumpkin pie spice
- 1/4 teaspoon salt
- ¼ tablespoon olive oil
- ¼ cup walnuts

Directions:

Combine the oats with the milk inside the slow cooker bowl. Add the pumpkin puree into the slow cooker as well and then add the brown sugar and vanilla extract. Sprinkle the mixture with the pumpkin spices, salt, and olive oil. Mix the oat mixture carefully and close the lid. Set the slow cooker on LOW for 3 hours. Mix the cooked dish carefully with and transfer it to the serving bowls. Sprinkle the cooked dish with the coconut milk.

Nutrition: calories 322, fat 16, fiber 12, carbs 45, protein 15

Tomato Omelette

Prep time: 10 minutes | Cooking time: 2 hours | Servings: 7

Ingredients:

- 8 eggs
- ½ cup milk
- 1/3 cup broccoli
- 1 cup tomato
- 1 teaspoon olive oil
- ¼ teaspoon salt
- 1/3 teaspoon paprika
- 1/3 cup fresh dill
- 1 teaspoon turmeric

Directions:

Wash the fresh dill and chop it. Add the chopped dill and eggs to a bowl and whisk together. Chop the broccoli and tomatoes and add the vegetables to the egg mixture as well. Add the milk and whisk again. Spray the slow cooker vessel with the olive oil to grease the inside. Pour the egg mixture into the slow cooker and close the lid. Cook the omelet on HIGH for 2 hours. When the time is done and the omelet is ready, remove it from the slow cooker, slice and serve.

Nutrition: calories 170, fat 12.3, fiber 1, carbs 3.25, protein 11

Spicy Breakfast Frittata

Prep time: 15 minutes | Cooking time: 1.5 hour | Servings: 10

Ingredients:

- 1 cup spinach
- 1 teaspoon chili flakes
- 1 teaspoon cayenne pepper
- 1 teaspoon salt
- 1 teaspoon olive oil
- 12 eggs
- 1 teaspoon ground white pepper
- 1 teaspoon butter
- ½ white onion
- ½ cup sour cream

Directions:

Beat the eggs in a large bowl. Add sour cream and mix with the help of the hand mixer for 1 minute. Then chop the onion and spinach. Combine the chili flakes, cayenne pepper, salt, and ground white pepper in a shallow bowl. Add the spices to the whisked eggs. After this, add the chopped onion and spinach and stir it carefully. Then spread the slow cooker vessel with the butter and add the egg mixture. Close the lid and cook the frittata on HIGH for 1.5 hours. When the Frittata is cooked, cut it into serving pieces and enjoy the Frittata warm.

Nutrition: calories 182, fat 13.7, fiber 0, carbs 2.81, protein 11

Green Quiche

Prep time: 20 minutes | Cooking time: 5 hours | Servings: 9

Ingredients:

- 7 oz. uncooked pie crust dough
- 1 tablespoon flour
- 2 tablespoon butter
- 2 yellow onions, chopped
- 2 green peppers, chopped
- 7 eggs
- 1 cup spinach
- ½ cup parsley
- 1 cup fresh dill
- 8 oz. Cheddar cheese
- 1 teaspoon salt
- 1 teaspoon ground black pepper
- 1 teaspoon paprika
- 5 oz. broccoli
- 8 oz. ham
- 1 tablespoon mayonnaise

Directions:

Cover the slow cooker bowl with parchment paper. Toss the butter into a skillet and melt. Add the diced onion and chopped green peppers. Sauté the vegetables for 5 minutes and stir the mixture frequently. Then chop the spinach, parsley, and fresh dill. Separate the broccoli into small florets and beat the eggs in the mixer bowl. Add the mayonnaise, paprika, ground black pepper, broccoli and salt and stir together. Shred Cheddar cheese and combine it with the flour. Add the flour and cheese mix to the egg mix and blend together. Roll the piecrust to about ¼ inch thick and transfer it to the covered slow cooker vessel. Push the crust slightly up the sides of the bowl, making it look like it was in a pie pan. Add the sautéed veggies, egg mix and ham. Cook the quiche for 5 hours on HIGH. Chill well then slice and serve.

Nutrition: calories 340, fat 20.4, fiber 2, carbs 21.84, protein 18

Cheesy Frittata

Prep time: 15 minutes | Cooking time: 4 hours | Servings: 15

Ingredients:

- 6 oz. Romano cheese
- 7 oz. Parmesan cheese
- 6 oz. Cheddar cheese
- 13 eggs
- 1 teaspoon salt
- 1 onion
- 1 sweet red pepper
- 1 carrot
- ½ cup green peas
- 1 teaspoon paprika
- ½ teaspoon ground white pepper
- 1/3 teaspoon lemon juice
- ½ teaspoon olive oil
- 3 tablespoon fresh dill

Directions:

Peel the carrot and onion and chop. After this, cut the sweet red pepper into the medium squares. Combine all the prepared vegetables together and sprinkle them with the salt, paprika, and ground white pepper. Add the green peas and lemon juice. After this, add the fresh dill and stir the mixture carefully. Then crack the eggs into a bowl and stir. Grate all of the cheeses and add into the egg mixture. Spray the slow cooker bowl with the olive oil and pour the egg mixture in. Add the chopped vegetables and close the slow cooker lid. Cook Frittata on HIGH for 4 hours. When the dish is done, remove it from the slow cooker and serve immediately.

Nutrition: calories 248, fat 16.5, fiber 1, carbs 7.34, protein 17

Walnut Cinnamon Rolls

Prep time: 20 minutes | Cooking time: 4.5 hours | Servings:6

Ingredients:

- 10 oz. puff pastry
- 1 tablespoon almond flour
- 1 cup walnuts
- ½ teaspoon salt
- 5 tablespoon brown sugar
- 2 tablespoon ground cinnamon
- 1 teaspoon vanilla
- 3 tablespoon butter
- 2 egg yolks

Directions:

Combine the butter, vanilla, ground cinnamon, and brown sugar together. Add the salt and whisk the mixture carefully. Crush the walnuts and combine them with the almond flour. After this, roll the puff pastry to be about ¼ of an inch thick and spread the brown sugar mixture across he dough carefully. Cover the puff pastry with the crushed walnuts and roll the puff pastry up. Cut the dough into 6 pieces and form into medium buns. Then, whisk the egg yolks and brush the buns with the yolks. Cover the slow cooker bowl with parchment and put the prepared buns inside. Close the slow cooker lid and cook the dish on HIGH for 4.5 hours. When the buns are golden brown, they are cooked. Remove the prepared buns from the slow cooker and serve them immediately.

Nutrition: calories 436, fat 34.1, fiber 3, carbs 28.02, protein 7

Huevos Ranchero

Prep time: 25 minutes | Cooking time: 5 hours | Servings: 5

Ingredients:

- 5 oz. chorizo, chopped
- 1 tablespoon olive oil
- 8 oz. Cheddar cheese, shredded
- 5 eggs
- 5 tortilla
- ½ teaspoon salt
- ½ teaspoon thyme

- ½ teaspoon ground black pepper
- ½ teaspoon paprika
- ½ cup black beans, cooked
- 3 tomatoes
- 1 white onion, chopped
- 1 sweet green pepper, chopped

Directions:

Pour the olive oil into a pan and add the chopped vegetables. Add the salt, thyme, ground black pepper, paprika, and cooked black beans. Chop the tomatoes and add them to the vegetable mixture too. Sauté everything together for 10 minutes. Transfer the mix to the slow cooker. Layer the tortillas on top and sprinkle the mix with the shredded cheese. Pour in the beaten eggs. Sprinkle the dish with paprika and chorizo. Close the slow cooker lid and cook the dish for 5 hours on HIGH. When the dish is cooked, the egg yolks may still runny which is okay. Transfer the prepared breakfast into the serving plates gently to not damage it and serve.

Nutrition: calories 531, fat 30.4, fiber 3, carbs 36.7, protein 27

Veggie Omelette

Prep time: 20 minutes | Cooking time: 5 hours | Servings: 8

Ingredients:

- 7 oz asparagus, chopped
- 8 eggs
- ½ cup heavy cream
- 1 teaspoon salt
- 1 teaspoon paprika

- 1 teaspoon ground black pepper
- 2 bell peppers, chopped
- 5 oz broccoli, chopped
- 1 tomato, chopped

Directions:

Put the vegetables in the slow cooker and sprinkle the mixture with the salt, paprika, and ground black pepper. Close the slow cooker lid and cook the vegetables on HIGH for 2 hours. Meanwhile, whisk the eggs and the heavy cream. Chop the tomato and add it to the egg mixture and stir. When the veggies are cooked, open the slow cooker and stir the vegetables. Pour the egg mixture into the slow cooker bowl with the veggies and close the lid. Cook the omelet on HIGH for 3 hours more. When the vegetarian omelet is done, let it cool briefly. Sprinkle the prepared dish with the chopped fresh dill if desired. Enjoy

Nutrition: calories 59, fat 4, fiber 2, carbs 4.06, protein 3

Mexican Casserole

Prep time: 15 minutes | Cooking time: 7 hours | Servings: 8

Ingredients:

- 1 cup sweet corn
- 1 chili pepper
- ½ cup tomato paste
- 1 onion
- 7 oz. Cheddar cheese
- 2 tablespoon sour cream
- 7 oz. chorizo

- 1 teaspoon salt
- 1 teaspoon cayenne pepper
- 1 tablespoon minced garlic
- 3 teaspoon onion powder
- 4 corn tortillas
- 5 egg

Directions:

Chop the chili pepper and combine it with the tomato paste. Dice the onion. Chop chorizo sausages and cut the tortillas into the strips. Then, crack the eggs into the bowl and whisk. Add the minced garlic, onion powder, cayenne pepper, salt, sour cream and sweet corn in the whisked egg mixture. Then pour the mix into the slow cooker. Add the chorizo sausages and tortilla strips. Cut Cheddar cheese into the cubes and add in the slow cooker too. After this, add the tomato paste mixture and diced onion. Stir the mix carefully and close the slow cooker lid. Cook the dish on LOW for 7 hours. When the casserole is cooked, serve while warm and

Nutrition: calories 317, fat 18.7, fiber 2, carbs 21, protein 17

Vanilla Oats with Honey

Prep time: 10 minutes | Cooking time: 2.5 hours | Servings: 5

Ingredients:

- 3 tablespoon raw honey
- 3 tablespoon almond flakes
- 1 teaspoon vanilla extract
- 3 cup whole milk

- 3 cup oats
- ¼ teaspoon salt
- ½ teaspoon ground anise
- 1 teaspoon butter

Directions:

Pour the whole milk and vanilla extract in the slow cooker. Add the sal and, ground anise and mix. After this, add the oats and butter. Close the slow cooker lid and cook the oats for 1 hour on HIGH. Open the slow cooker lid and stir the oats. Then add the raw honey and mix. Close the slow cooker lid and cook the dish for 1.5 hours more on HIGH. When the time is over and the dish is cooked, transfer it to the serving bowls and sprinkle with the almond flakes.

Nutrition: calories 323, fat 9.6, fiber 9, carbs 67, protein 14

Breakfast Ham Toasts

Prep time: 15 minutes | Cooking time: 3 hours | Servings: 6

Ingredients:

- 5 egg
- ¼ cup fresh parsley
- 1 teaspoon salt
- 10 oz. ham
- 2 tablespoon butter
- 6 tablespoon heavy cream

- 1 teaspoon sugar
- 1 teaspoon paprika
- 1 teaspoon oregano
- 4 oz. bacon, chopped
- 1 teaspoon minced garlic
- 10 oz. white bread

Directions:

Chop the white bread into the tiny cubes. After this, beat the eggs in a large bowl. Add salt, heavy cream, butter, sugar, paprika, oregano, and minced garlic. Cut the ham into strips and combine it with the chopped bacon. Add the mixture to the eggs and stir it with the help of a fork. After this, chop the parsley and add to the egg mixture. Then stir the mix very carefully well combined. Pour it into the slow cooker bowl along with the bread cubes. Close the slow cooker lid and cook the dish on HIGH for 3 hours. When the dish is cooked, transfer it to a big plate and cut into servings.

Nutrition: calories 427, fat 25.2, fiber 5, carbs 27.69, protein 24

Butter Grits

Prep time: 10 minutes | Cooking time: 6 hours | Servings: 3

Ingredients:

- 2 cups grits
- 1/3 teaspoon salt
- 6 cup water
- 3 tablespoon butter

Directions:

Combine the grits with 2 cups of the water and let soak for 1 hour. After this, strain the grits in a colander. Put the strained grits in the slow cooker and add the remaining water. Add salt and stir the mixture gently. Close the slow cooker lid and cook the dish on HIGH for 6 hours. When the time is done, add the butter and mix. Transfer the hot cooked grits into bowls and serve.

Nutrition: calories 263, fat 19.3, fiber 1, carbs 21.7, protein 3

Sausage Casserole

Prep time: 25 minutes | Cooking time: 4.5 hours | Servings: 7

Ingredients:

- 8 oz. sweet potato, peeled and sliced
- 2 red onion, chopped
- 12 oz. sausage, chopped
- 1 teaspoon butter
- 1 carrot, peeled and chopped
- 10 oz. Parmesan cheese
- 1 cup fresh dill
- ¼ cup milk
- 3 eggs
- 1 teaspoon salt
- ½ teaspoon paprika
- 1 tablespoon chives

Directions:

Beat the eggs in a large bowl and add the milk, salt, paprika, and chives. Whisk well and then slice Parmesan and chop the fresh dill. Make the layer of the sliced sweet potato in the bottom of the slow cooker. After this, add the sliced Parmesan and fresh dill. Sprinkle the mix with the chopped carrot and onions. Add the chopped sausages and pour the egg-milk mixture. Add the butter and close the slow cooker lid. Cook the dish on HIGH for 4.5 hours. When the time is done, serve it immediately.

Nutrition: calories 550, fat 35.6, fiber 5, carbs 34, protein 26

Cottage Cheese Pudding

Prep time: 25 minutes | Cooking time: 6 hours | Servings: 8

Ingredients:

- 2-pound cottage cheese
- 3 tablespoon sour cream
- ½ cup brown sugar
- 9 eggs
- 4 tablespoon raisins
- 1 teaspoon vanilla extract
- 1 tablespoon butter
- 3 tablespoon semolina flour

Directions:

Transfer the cottage cheese to a blender and blend it for 1 minute. Beat the eggs into the blended cottage cheese. Add brown sugar and sour cream and continue to blend for 3 minutes on high speed. Add butter and vanilla extract. Pulse the mixture for 30 seconds. Remove the fluffy cottage cheese mix from the blender and transfer it to a big bowl. Add raisins and semolina and mix carefully. Transfer the cottage cheese to the slow cooker vessel and cook on HIGH for 6 hours. The cottage cheese pudding will be a light brown color. Remove the cooked dish from the slow cooker and serve.

Nutrition: calories 325, fat 15.4, fiber 0, carbs 27.57, protein 18

Poppy Breakfast Bread

Prep time: 20 minutes | Cooking time: 5 hours | Servings: 7

Ingredients:

- 3 tablespoon poppy seeds
- 1 teaspoon baking soda
- 1 tablespoon lemon juice
- 8 oz. cottage cheese
- 3 egg
- 3 tablespoons milk
- 2 tablespoons water
- ½ cup flour
- 4 tablespoons sugar
- 2 tablespoons butter
- ½ teaspoon olive oil
- 1 teaspoon ground cardamom

Directions:

Sift the flour into a bowl. Add baking soda, lemon juice, sugar, poppy seeds, and ground cardamom and mix. After this, add the cottage cheese, water, and milk. Beat the eggs into the flour mixture and add olive oil. Knead the dough well until you get a soft and little bit sticky dough. After this, form a round ball with the dough and place it in the slow cooker bowl. Close the slow cooker lid and cook the bread for 5 hours on HIGH. When the time is done, let the bread chill until room temperature. Cut the bread into the servings. Sprinkle the dish with the powdered sugar if desired.

Nutrition: calories 189, fat 10.4, fiber 1, carbs 16.24, protein 8

Western Omelette

Prep time: 20 minutes | Cooking time: 4 hours | Servings: 14

Ingredients:

- 7 oz. potato, frozen, chopped
- 6 oz. ham, cooked, chopped
- 1 white onion, chopped
- 1 tablespoon chives, chopped
- 1 sweet yellow pepper, chopped
- 7 oz. Cheddar cheese, shredded
- 15 eggs
- 6 oz. milk
- 1 teaspoon salt
- 1 teaspoon ground black pepper
- 1 teaspoon paprika

Directions:

Beat the eggs in the large bowl. Sprinkle the whisked egg mixture with the milk, salt, ground black pepper, and paprika. Add the chopped ham, sweet pepper, potatoes, and diced onion in the slow cooker. Add everything to the slow cooker and sprinkle with the cheese. Close the slow cooker lid and cook Western Omelette on LOW for 4 hours. Serve the omelet immediately.

Nutrition: calories 205, fat 12.4, fiber 1, carbs 8.52, protein 15

Herbed Breakfast Potatoes

Prep time: 15 minutes | Cooking time: 6 hours | Servings: 8

Ingredients:

- 3-pound finger potatoes
- 2 tablespoon fresh rosemary
- 4 oz. bacon
- 1 teaspoon salt
- 1 teaspoon thyme
- 1 teaspoon fresh coriander
- 1 tablespoon butter
- 2 teaspoon heavy cream

Directions:

Wash the finger potatoes very carefully and do not peel them. Chop the fresh rosemary and combine it with the salt and thyme. Chop the fresh coriander leaves and add them to the rosemary mixture. Then chop the bacon and combine it with the finger potatoes. Place the mixture in the large bowl and sprinkle with the spice mixture. Toss everything together and transfer to the slow cooker. Add butter and heavy cream and close the lid. Cook the dish on LOW for 6 hours. When the potatoes are cooked, serve them hot.

Nutrition: calories 193, fat 6.3, fiber 4, carbs 30.76, protein 5

Fruit Muesli

Prep time: 20 minutes | Cooking time: 6 hours | Servings: 8

Ingredients:

- 1-pound oats
- 2 cup bran
- 2 tablespoons shredded coconut
- 6 tablespoons brown sugar
- 1 tablespoon butter
- 1 teaspoon vanilla extract
- 3 tablespoons raisins

- 3 tablespoons dried apricots
- 3 tablespoons prunes
- 1 tablespoon walnuts
- 1 tablespoon sesame seeds
- 3 tablespoons cherries
- 5 cups milk

Directions:

Combine the coconut, brown sugar, vanilla extract, and raisins together. Chop the dried apricots and prunes. Crush the walnuts and slice the cherries. Combine all the prepared ingredients together in the bowl. Put the prepared fruit mixture in the slow cooker. Add the oats and bran. Pour the milk in the slow cooker bowl and stir the mix together. Close the slow cooker lid and cook the muesli on LOW for 6 hours. When the time is done, mix the cooked dish with a wooden spatula and transfer to serving bowls. Serve the dish immediately.

Nutrition: calories 431, fat 17.8, fiber 16, carbs 80.05, protein 19

Breakfast Vanilla Pancake

Prep time: 15 minutes | Cooking time: 4 hours | Servings: 8

Ingredients:

- 2-pounds biscuit mix
- 1 cup milk
- 6 egg
- 6 oz. cream, whipped

- 7 tablespoon white sugar
- 1 teaspoon vanilla extract
- ½ teaspoon ground cardamom
- ½ cup strawberries

Directions:

Crack the eggs into large bowls and whisk them up with the help of the hand mixer. Add milk and cream and whisk again. Then add white sugar, vanilla extract, ground cardamom and biscuit mix. Mix until smooth. Cover the slow cooker bowl with the foil inside. Pour the prepared pancake batter in the slow cooker and flatten it with the help of the spatula. Close the slow cooker lid and cook the pancake on HIGH for 4 hours. When the time is done, remove the cooked pancake from the slow cooker. Slice the strawberries and sprinkle the prepared pancake with the sliced strawberries then cut it into serving pieces.

Nutrition: calories 466, fat 19.2, fiber 0, carbs 57.93, protein 15

Slow Cooker Strawberry Porridge

Prep time: 15 minutes | Cooking time: 5 hours | Servings: 6

Ingredients:

- 2 cup strawberries
- 1 tablespoon raw honey
- 2 tablespoon powdered sugar

- 1 cup oatmeal
- 1 cup milk
- 1 teaspoon vanilla sugar

Directions:

Place the strawberries in a blender and add the raw honey, milk, oatmeal, and vanilla sugar. Pulse the mixture for 20 seconds. Pour the prepared mixture into the slow cooker and close the lid. Cook the dish on LOW for 5 hours. When the time is done, sprinkle the dish with the powdered sugar and mix. Transfer the dish to bowls and serve the dish warm. Add fresh fruits if desired.

Nutrition: calories 92, fat 1.9, fiber 2, carbs 17.52, protein 2

Monkey bread

Prep time: 20 minutes | Cooking time: 2 hours | Servings: 6

Ingredients:

- 12 oz. biscuit rolls
- 1 tablespoon ground cinnamon
- 3 oz. white sugar
- 1 teaspoon vanilla extract
- 4 tablespoon butter
- 1 egg white
- 4 tablespoon brown sugar

Directions:

Cut the biscuit rolls into the small cubes. Then put the ground cinnamon and white sugar in the bowl. Stir the mixture with the help of the form gently. After this, melt the butter in the microwave oven. Add the ground cinnamon mixture in the melted butter and whisk till sugar is dissolved. After this, separate the biscuit roll cubes into 2 parts and place the first part in the slow cooker vessel. Then sprinkle the layer of the biscuit cubes with the melted butter mixture and add the second part of the biscuit rolls. Close the slow cooker lid and cook the dish for 2 hours on HIGH. Meanwhile, whisk the egg white till the strong peaks and add the brown sugar. Continue to whisk the egg white for 1 minute more – the icing is cooked. When the monkey bread is done – remove it from the slow cooker and chill well. Spread the surface of the monkey bread with the icing.

Nutrition: calories 313, fat 16.8, fiber 3, carbs 34.14, protein 7

Scrambled Eggs

Prep time: 25 minutes | Cooking time: 2 Hours | Servings: 9

Ingredients:

- 8 eggs
- ½ cup spinach
- ½ cup cherry tomatoes
- 1 teaspoon dried oregano
- 1 teaspoon salt
- 3 tablespoon butter
- 1 teaspoon minced garlic
- 5 oz. Cheddar cheese
- ½ cup milk

Directions:

Beat the eggs in a bowl and add the shred Cheddar cheese. Then pour in the milk and sprinkle the mixture with the dried oregano, salt, and minced garlic. Chop the spinach and cut the cherry tomatoes into the halves. Add the vegetables to the egg mixture and stir it gently. Grease the slow cooker bowl with the butter carefully. Pour the egg mixture into the bowl and close the lid. Cook the eggs on HIGH for 2 hours. Open the lid and scramble the eggs with a fork to break them up. When the scrambled eggs are cooked – transfer them to plates.

Nutrition: calories 187, fat 14.3, fiber 0, carbs 3.55, protein 11

Bacon Wrapped Eggs

Prep time: 15 minutes | Cooking time: 2 hours | Servings: 6

Ingredients:

- 7 oz. bacon, sliced
- 1 teaspoon salt
- 6 eggs, hard boiled, peeled
- ½ cup cream
- 3 tablespoon mayonnaise
- 1 tablespoon minced garlic
- 1 teaspoon ground black pepper
- 4 oz. Parmesan cheese, shredded
- 1 teaspoon dried dill

Directions:

Preheat a skillet and add the sliced bacon with the salt and ground black pepper. Cook it for 1 minute on the medium heat from the each side. The bacon should be crunchy but still flexible. Combine the cream and mayonnaise together. Add the minced garlic and dried dill. Put the cream mixture in the slow cooker bowl. After this, wrap the peeled eggs in the prepared sliced bacon. Put the wrapped eggs in the slow cooker. Cover the eggs with a layer of the shredded cheese and close the slow cooker lid. Cook the dish on HIGH for 2 hours. When the time is over – serve the wrapped eggs with gravy.

Nutrition: calories 381, fat 31, fiber 1, carbs 8.07, protein 19

Apple Breakfast Frittata Pie

Prep time: 15 minutes | Cooking time: 3 hours | Servings: 8

Ingredients:

- 7 oz. mozzarella, sliced
- 10 eggs
- 1 cup milk
- 3 tablespoon flour
- 1 teaspoon salt
- 1 teaspoon chili flakes
- ½ cup cherry tomatoes, chopped
- 1 red sweet pepper
- 1 yellow sweet pepper
- 1 apple
- 1 teaspoon butter

Directions:

Crack the eggs into the bowl and mix them up with the help of the hand mixer. After this, pour the milk into the mixture. Add the flour, salt, chili flakes, and butter. Then peel the apple and chop it. Add the chopped apple to the egg mixture. Remove the seeds from the sweet peppers and chop them into the small pieces. Whisk the egg mixture with the flour until it has dissolved and then add the chopped vegetables. Then pour the egg mixture into the slow cooker and make a layer of the sliced mozzarella on top. Close the slow cooker lid and cook frittata pie for 3 hours on LOW. Cut the prepared dish into the slices.

Nutrition: calories 252, fat 13.7, fiber 2, carbs 11.25, protein 21

Breakfast Jam

Prep time: 20 minutes | Cooking time: 4 hours | Servings: 6

Ingredients:

- 1 cup white sugar
- 1 cup strawberries
- 1 tablespoon gelatin
- 3 tablespoon water
- 1 tablespoon lemon zest
- 1 teaspoon lemon juice
- ½ cup blueberries

Directions:

Wash the strawberries and blueberries carefully. Transfer the ingredients to a food processor and blend for 3 minutes or until the mixture is smooth. After this, add the white sugar, lemon zest, and lemon juice. Pulse the mixture for 30 seconds more. Then pour the liquid into the slow cooker and cook it on HIGH for 1 hour. Meanwhile, combine water with the gelatin and stir it carefully. Add the prepared gelatin mixture in the slow cooker and whisk it carefully. After this, close the lid and cook the jam for 3 hours more on HIGH. When the time is over – chill the prepared dish well and serve with toast.

Nutrition: calories 163, fat 8.3, fiber 2, carbs 20.48, protein 3

Sweet Potatoes with the Peanuts

Prep time: 15 minutes | Cooking time: 6 hours | Servings: 8

Ingredients:

- 2 tablespoon peanut butter
- ¼ cup peanuts
- 1-pound sweet potato
- 1 garlic clove, peeled and sliced
- 2 tablespoon lemon juice
- 1 cup onion, chopped
- ½ cup chicken stock
- 1 teaspoon salt
- 1 teaspoon paprika
- 1 teaspoon ground black pepper

Directions:

Wash the sweet potatoes and peel them. Cut the sweet potato into the strips and mix with the peanut butter, lemon juice, salt, paprika, and ground black pepper. Put the sweet potato strips in the slow cooker. Sprinkle the sweet potatoes with the sliced garlic clove and chopped onions. Cove the bowl and cook the dish on the LOW for 6 hours. Crush the peanuts and when the dish is cooked – sprinkle it with the crushed peanuts and serve immediately.

Nutrition: calories 376, fat 22.4, fiber 6, carbs 39.36, protein 5

Creamy Millet

Prep time: 8 minutes | Cooking time: 4 hours 10 minutes | Servings: 6

Ingredients:

- 3 cup millet
- 6 cup chicken stock
- 1 teaspoon salt
- 4 tablespoon heavy cream
- 5 oz. bacon, chopped

Directions:

Put the millet and chicken stock in the slow cooker bowl and mix. Add salt and chopped bacon. Close the slow cooker lid and cook the dish on HIGH for 4 hours or until the millet absorbs all the liquid. Then add the heavy cream and mix. Cook the dish on HIGH for 10 minutes more. Mix carefully one more time and transfer the millet in the serving plates.

Nutrition: calories 572, fat 17.8, fiber 9, carbs 83.09, protein 20

Spinach Muffins

Prep time: 20 minutes | Cooking time: 2.5 hours | Servings: 8

Ingredients:

- 1 cup spinach
- 5 tablespoon butter
- 1 cup flour
- 1 teaspoon salt
- ½ teaspoon baking soda
- 1 tablespoon lemon juice
- 1 tablespoon sugar
- 3 eggs

Directions:

Wash the spinach carefully and put it in a food processor. Blend the spinach until you get smooth mass. After this, transfer the spinach mixture to a big bowl. Beat in the eggs and whisk the mixture until homogenous. Add the salt, baking soda, lemon juice, sugar, and flour. Mix the dough until smooth. Place a muffin liners inside a few small glass jars that wil fit inside the slow cooker. Then fill ½ of every muffin liner with the batter and place them in the slow cooker. Close the slow cooker lid and cook the muffins for 2.5 hours on high. Chill the muffins and remove them carefully from the glass jars.

Nutrition: calories 172, fat 6.1, fiber 1, carbs 9.23, protein 20

Breakfast Peach Butter

Prep time: 15 minutes | Cooking time: 8 hours | Servings: 8

Ingredients:

- 15 oz. peach, pitted, peeled and cubed
- 2 cup sugar
- ¼ teaspoon salt
- 1 tablespoon ground cinnamon
- 1 teaspoon fresh ginger
- 5 tablespoon lemon juice

Directions:

Place the peach cubes in a blender and blend well until smooth. Put the blended peaches in the slow cooker. Add the sugar and salt. Peel the fresh ginger and grate into the slow cooker. After this, add the ground cinnamon and mix the mixture carefully. Close the slow cooker lid and cook the dish for 8 hours on LOW. When the time is up, open the slow cooker lid and add the lemon juice. Stir the peach butter carefully and let it chill. Transfer into glass jars and serve it with bread slices.

Nutrition: calories 141, fat 0.1, fiber 1, carbs 37.03, protein 0

Breakfast Baby Carrots

Prep time: 10 minutes | Cooking time: 8 hours | Servings: 6

Ingredients:

- 2 teaspoon fresh dill
- 1-pound baby carrot
- 1 teaspoon honey
- 1 teaspoon paprika
- 1 teaspoon ground ginger
- 3 tablespoon butter
- ½ teaspoon salt
- 2 eggs

Directions:

Chop the dill and combine it with the paprika and honey. Add the ground ginger and salt. Beat the eggs in a bowl and add the raw honey mixture into the eggs and stir it. After this, melt the butter and add it to the egg mixture too. Wash the baby carrot carefully and toss in the slow cooker. Pour the egg mixture into the slow cooker and stir it carefully. Close the slow cooker lid and cook the dish on LOW for 8 hours. Stir the dish frequently during the cooking. When the time is over and the baby carrot are soft, remove from the slow cooker and serve immediately.

Nutrition: calories 128, fat 9.2, fiber 3, carbs 8.36, protein 4

Muffins with Crunchy Bacon

Prep time: 15 minutes | Cooking time: 4.5 hours | Servings: 9

Ingredients:

- 1 cup flour
- 6 tablespoon butter
- 3 eggs
- 1 teaspoon salt
- ½ tablespoon apple cider vinegar
- 1 teaspoon baking powder
- 5 oz. bacon, chopped

Directions:

Melt the butter and combine it with salt, apple cider vinegar, and baking powder. Then preheat a skillet and toss the chopped bacon in. Roast the chopped bacon until it is crunchy. Stir the bacon frequently. After this, add the crunchy bacon into the melted butter mixture. Whisk the eggs and pour the liquid into the bacon mixture. Sift the flour over the batter and whisk the dough together. After this, put muffin liners into small glass jars and fill the muffin papers with the batter ½ the way up the paper. Then pour 1 cup of water in the bottom of the slow cooker and place the glass jars with the muffins batters in the bowl as well. Close the slow cooker and cook the muffins on HIGH for 4.5 hours. Chill the muffins and serve them.

Nutrition: calories 211, fat 15.7, fiber 1, carbs 12.13, protein 6

Sausage Rolls

Prep time: 20 minutes | Cooking time: 3 hours | Servings: 11

Ingredients:

- 1-pound puff pastry
- 2 tablespoon flour
- 1 tablespoon mustard
- 1 egg
- 10 oz. breakfast sausages
- 1 teaspoon paprika
- 1 tablespoon mayo

Directions:

Roll the puff pastry and sprinkle it with the flour. Cut the puff pastry into the long thick strips. Beat the egg in the bowl and spread the puff pastry strips with the paprika, mayo, and mustard. Then wrap every sausage in the puff pastry strips to make the sausage rolls. Then brush every sausage roll with the whisked egg. Cover the slow cooker bowl with parchment and put the sausage rolls on top of the paper. Close the slow cooker and cook the dish for 3 hours on HIGH. When the time is up, check if the sausage rolls are cooked; they should have the light golden color. Then remove the prepared sausage rolls from the slow cooker and chill them for at least 10 minutes. Serve the dish!

Nutrition: calories 311, fat 21.8, fiber 1, carbs 20.49, protein 8

Slow Cooker Meatballs

Prep time: 20 minutes | Cooking time: 4 hours | Servings: 9

Ingredients:

- 2-pound ground pork
- 1 tablespoon dried parsley
- 1 teaspoon dried dill
- 1 teaspoon paprika
- 1 teaspoon salt
- 1 egg
- 1 tablespoon semolina
- ½ cup tomato juice
- 3 tablespoons flour
- 1 tablespoon minced garlic
- 1 teaspoon onion powder
- 1 teaspoon sugar
- 1 teaspoon chives
- 1 oz. bay leaves

Directions:

Beat the egg in a big bowl and add the ground pork. After this, sprinkle the meat mixture with the dried parsley and dried dill. Then add salt and paprika. Add semolina and minced garlic. Sprinkle the mixture with the onion powder and mix it carefully. Then make the mix into medium balls. Cover a tray with parchment and transfer the meatballs to the tray. Cook them for 3 minutes in a preheated 365 F oven. Then transfer the meatballs to a slow cooker. Whisk the tomato juice and flour together in a separate bowl. Add chives, sugar, and bay leaf and stir. Pour the tomato juice liquid in the slow cooker to try to cover the meatballs. Close the slow cooker lid and cook the meatballs for 4 hours on LOW.

Nutrition: calories 344, fat 22.4, fiber 1, carbs 6.87, protein 28

Delicious Eggplant Pate with Breadcrumbs

Prep time: 27 minutes | Cooking time: 6 hours | Servings: 15

Ingredients:

- 5 medium eggplants
- 2 sweet green pepper
- 1 cup bread crumbs
- 1 teaspoon salt
- 1 tablespoon sugar
- ½ cup tomato paste
- 2 yellow onion
- 1 tablespoon minced garlic
- ¼ chili pepper
- 1 teaspoon olive oil
- 1 teaspoon kosher salt
- 1 tablespoon mayonnaise

Directions:

Peel the eggplants and chop them. Sprinkle the chopped eggplants with the salt and let sit for 10 minutes. Meanwhile, combine the tomato paste with the kosher salt and sugar. Add minced garlic and mayonnaise. Whisk carefully. Then, peel the onions and chop. Spray the slow cooker bowl with the olive oil. Add the chopped onions. Strain the chopped eggplants to get rid of the eggplant juice and transfer the strained eggplants into the slow cooker bowl as well. After this, add the tomato paste mixture. Chop the chili pepper and sweet green peppers and add them in the slow cooker too. Stir the mixture inside the slow cooker carefully and close the lid. Cook the dish for 6 hours on LOW. When the time is done, transfer the prepared mix into a bowl and blend it until smooth with the help of the hand blender. Sprinkle the prepared plate with the bread crumbs.

Nutrition: calories 83, fat 0.8, fiber 7, carbs 18.15, protein 3

Red Beans with the Sweet Peas

Prep time: 21 minutes | Cooking time: 6 hours | Servings: 5

Ingredients:

- 1 cup red beans, dried
- 3 chicken stock
- 3 tablespoon tomato paste
- 1 onion
- 1 teaspoon salt
- 1 chili pepper
- 1 teaspoon sriracha
- 1 tablespoon butter
- 1 teaspoon turmeric
- 1 cup green peas

Directions:

Soak the red beans in water for 8 hours in advance. After this, strain the red beans and put them in the slow cooker. Add the chicken stock, salt, and turmeric. Close the slow cooker lid and cook the red beans for 4 hours on HIGH. Meanwhile, peel the onion and slice it. Combine the sliced onion with the tomato paste, sriracha, and butter. Chop the chili pepper and add it to the onion mixture. When the time is done, open the slow cooker lid and add the onion mixture. Stir it very carefully and close the slow cooker lid. Cook the dish for 1 hour more on Low. Stir the red beans mixture carefully again and add the green peas. Cook the dish on LOW for 1 more hour. After this, stir the dish gently and serve.

Nutrition: calories 190, fat 3.1, fiber 8, carbs 31.6, protein 11

Nutritious Burrito Bowl

Prep time: 18 minutes | Cooking time: 7 hours | Servings: 6

Ingredients:

- 10 oz. chicken breast
- 1 tablespoon chili flakes
- 1 teaspoon salt
- 1 teaspoon onion powder
- 1 teaspoon minced garlic
- ½ cup white beans, canned
- ¼ cup green peas
- 1 cup chicken stock
- ½ avocado, pitted
- 1 teaspoon ground black pepper

Directions:

Put the chicken breast in the slow cooker. Sprinkle the chicken breast with the chili flakes, salt, onion powder, minced garlic, and ground black pepper. Add the chicken stock. Close the slow cooker lid and cook the dish for 2 hours on HIGH. After this, open the slow cooker lid and add the white beans and green peas. Mix and close the lid. Cook the dish for 5 hours more on LOW. When the time is done, remove the meat, white beans, and green peas from the slow cooker. Transfer the white beans and green peas in the serving bowls. Shred the chicken breast and add it to the serving bowls too. After this, peel the avocado and chop it. Sprinkle the prepared burrito bowls with the chopped avocado.

Nutrition: calories 192, fat 7.7, fiber 5, carbs 15.66, protein 16

Quinoa Curry

Prep time: 20 minutes | Cooking time: 9 hours | Servings: 7

Ingredients:

- 8 oz. potato
- 7 oz. cauliflower
- 1 cup onion, chopped
- 7 oz. chickpea, canned
- 1 cup tomatoes, chopped
- 13 oz. almond milk
- 3 cup chicken stock
- 8 tablespoon quinoa
- 1/3 tablespoon miso
- 1 teaspoon minced garlic
- 2 teaspoon curry paste

Directions:

Peel the potatoes and chop them. Put the chopped potatoes, onion, and tomatoes into the slow cooker. Combine the miso, chicken stock, and curry paste together. Whisk the mixture until the ingredients are dissolved in the chicken stock. Pour the chicken stock in the slow cooker too. Separate the cauliflower into the florets. Add the cauliflower florets and the chickpeas in the slow cooker. Add the almond milk, quinoa, and minced garlic. Close the slow cooker lid and cook the dish on the LOW for 9 hours. When the dish is cooked, chill it and then mix it gently. Transfer the prepared curry quinoa in the bowls.

Nutrition: calories 262, fat 4.6, fiber 7, carbs 44.31, protein 12

Ham Pitta Pockets

Prep time: 14 minutes | Cooking time: 1.5 minutes | Servings: 6

Ingredients:

- 6 pita breads, sliced
- 7 oz. mozzarella, sliced
- 1 teaspoon minced garlic
- 7 oz. ham, sliced
- 1 big tomato, sliced
- 1 tablespoon mayo
- 1 tablespoon heavy cream

Directions:

Preheat the slow cooker on HIGH for 30 minutes. Combine the mayo, heavy cream, and minced garlic. Spread the inside of the pita bread with the mayo mixture. After this, fill the pitta bread with the sliced mozzarella, tomato, and ham. Wrap the pita bread in foil and place them in the slow cooker. Close the slow cooker lid and cook the dish for 1.5 hours on HIGH. Then discard the foil and serve the prepared pita pockets immediately.

Nutrition: calories 273, fat 3.3, fiber 2, carbs 38.01, protein 22

Breakfast Meatloaf

Prep time: 18 minutes | Cooking time: 7 hours | Servings: 8

Ingredients:

- 12 oz. ground beef
- 1 teaspoon salt
- 1 teaspoon ground coriander
- 1 tablespoon ground mustard
- ¼ teaspoon ground chili pepper
- 6 oz. white bread
- ½ cup milk
- 1 teaspoon ground black pepper
- 3 tablespoon tomato sauce

Directions:

Chop the white bread and combine it with the milk. Stir then set aside for 3 minutes. Meanwhile, combine the ground beef, salt, ground coriander, ground mustard, ground chili pepper, and ground black pepper. Stir the white bread mixture carefully and add it to the ground beef. Cover the bottom of the slow cooker bowl with foil. Shape the meatloaf and place the uncooked meatloaf in the slow cooker then spread it with the tomato sauce. Close the slow cooker lid and cook the meatloaf for 7 hours on LOW. Slice the prepared meatloaf and serve.

Nutrition: calories 214, fat 14, fiber 3, carbs 12.09, protein 9

Breakfast Sweet Pepper Rounds

Prep time: 10 minutes | Cooking time: 3 hours | Servings: 4

Ingredients:

- 2 red sweet pepper
- 7 oz. ground chicken
- 5 oz. Parmesan
- 1 tablespoon sour cream
- 1 tablespoon flour
- 1 egg
- 2 teaspoon almond milk
- 1 teaspoon salt
- ½ teaspoon ground black pepper
- ¼ teaspoon butter

Directions:

Combine the sour cream with the ground chicken, flour, ground black pepper, almond milk, and butter. Beat eggs into the mixture. Remove the seeds from the sweet peppers and slice them roughly. Place the pepper slices in the slow cooker and fill them with the ground chicken mixture. After this, chop Parmesan into the cubes and add into the sliced peppers. Close the slow cooker lid and cook the dish for 3 hours on HIGH. When the time is done make sure that the ground chicken is cooked and the cheese is melted. Enjoy the dish immediately.

Nutrition: calories 261, fat 8.9, fiber 1, carbs 19.15, protein 26

Breakfast Cauliflower Hash

Prep time: 17 minutes | Cooking time: 8 hours | Servings: 5

Ingredients:
- 7 eggs
- ¼ cup milk
- 1 teaspoon salt
- 1 teaspoon ground black pepper
- ½ teaspoon ground mustard

- 10 oz. cauliflower
- ¼ teaspoon chili flakes
- 5 oz. breakfast sausages, chopped
- ½ onion, chopped
- 5 oz. Cheddar cheese, shredded

Directions:
Wash the cauliflower carefully and separate it into the florets. After this, shred the cauliflower florets. Beat the eggs in a bowl and whisk. Add the milk, salt, ground black pepper, ground mustard, chili flakes, and chopped onion into the whisked egg mixture. Put the shredded cauliflower in the slow cooker. Add the whisked egg mixture. Add the shredded cheese and chopped sausages. Stir the mixture gently and close the slow cooker lid. Cook the dish on the LOW for 8 hours. When the cauliflower hash is cooked, remove it from the slow cooker and mix up.

Nutrition: calories 329, fat 21.8, fiber 2, carbs 10.31, protein 23

Bread Pudding with Dried Apricots

Prep time: 21 minutes | Cooking time: 5 hours | Servings: 9

Ingredients:
- 10 oz. French bread
- 6 tablespoons dried apricots
- 10 oz. milk
- 3 eggs, beaten
- 4 tablespoons butter
- ½ teaspoon salt

- 1 teaspoon vanilla sugar
- ½ teaspoon ground nutmeg
- ½ teaspoon ground cardamom
- ¼ cup whipped cream
- 4 tablespoons brown sugar

Directions:
Preheat the milk and melt the butter then combine. Add the salt, vanilla sugar, ground nutmeg, ground cardamom, and brown sugar. Mix until the brown sugar is melted. Chop French bread and put it in the slow cooker. Chop the dried apricots and add them in the slow cooker too. After this, whisk the eggs in a separate bowl. Combine the whisked eggs with the milk liquid. Add whipped cream and stir it carefully. Then sprinkle the chopped bread with the milk liquid. Stir it carefully until the bread starts to dissolve. After this, close the slow cooker lid and cook the dish on the HIGH for 5 hours. When the pudding is cooked, let it cool briefly. Serve it!

Nutrition: calories 229, fat 11.5, fiber 1, carbs 24.3, protein 8

Breakfast Bread Boats

Prep time: 15 minutes | Cooking time: 5 hours | Servings: 4

Ingredients:
- 6 oz. baguette
- 7 oz. breakfast sausages
- 3 tablespoons whipped cream
- 1 teaspoon minced garlic
- 1 teaspoon onion powder

- 4 oz. ham
- 6 oz. Parmesan
- 3 tablespoons ketchup
- 2 oz. green olives

Directions:
Cut the baguette into the halves and remove the flesh from the bread. Chop the breakfast sausages into the tiny pieces. Shred Parmesan cheese and combine it with the chopped sausages. Add the minced garlic, onion powder, and ketchup. Add the whipped cream. After this, shred the ham and add it to the prepared mixture. Fill the baguette with the sausage mixture. Place the dish in the slow cooker and close the lid. Cook the dish on LOW for 5 hours. When the time is over, remove the dish from the slow cooker and cut every baguette half into 2 part. Serve the cooked dish hot!

Nutrition: calories 483, fat 17.2, fiber 2, carbs 47.06, protein 35

Mushroom Casserole with Cheddar Cheese

Prep time: 18 minutes | Cooking time: 8 hours | Servings: 5

Ingredients:

- 8 oz. mushrooms
- 1 cup cream
- 1 carrot
- 6 oz. Cheddar cheese, shredded
- 7 oz. chicken fillet
- 1 teaspoon butter
- 1 teaspoon fresh rosemary
- 1 teaspoon salt
- ½ teaspoon coriander

Directions:

Slice the mushrooms and put them in the slow cooker. After this, peel the carrot and grate it. Make the layer of the grated carrot in the bottom of the slow cooker. Cut the chicken fillet into the strips and sprinkle them with the fresh rosemary and coriander. Place the chicken strips in the slow cooker. Add the butter and sprinkle the casserole mixture with salt. Add the shredded cheese and pour in the cream. Close the lid and cook the casserole for 8 hours on LOW. When the casserole is cooked – transfer it to the serving plates.

Nutrition: calories 405, fat 19.2, fiber 6, carbs 49.93, protein 15

Roasted Pumpkin Cubes

Prep time: 10 minutes | Cooking time: 10 hours | Servings: 4

Ingredients:

- 2 tablespoons lemon juice
- 3 tablespoons honey
- 1 tablespoon ground cinnamon
- 1 tablespoon brown sugar
- 1 tablespoon lemon zest
- 2 tablespoons water
- 1-pound pumpkin

Directions:

Peel the pumpkin and cut it into the big cubes. Combine the honey, ground cinnamon, brown sugar, lemon zest, and water together in the bowl. Stir it carefully. Sprinkle the pumpkin cubes with the sugar mixture and stir. Transfer the pumpkin cubes into the slow cooker and close the lid. Cook the pumpkin cubes on LOW for 10 hours. When the pumpkin cubes are cooked, transfer them to the serving plates. Sprinkle the pumpkin cubes with the remaining juice and serve immediately.

Nutrition: calories 81, fat 0.2, fiber 2, carbs 21.84, protein 1

Soft Cabbage with Onion

Prep time: 17 minutes | Cooking time: 4.5 hour | Servings: 5

Ingredients:

- 6 oz. ground chicken
- 10 oz. cabbage
- 1 white onion
- ½ cup tomato juice
- 1 teaspoon sugar
- ½ teaspoon salt
- 1 teaspoon ground black pepper
- 4 tablespoons chicken stock
- 2 garlic cloves

Directions:

Wash the cabbage carefully and chop. After this, combine the tomato juice, sugar, salt, ground black pepper, and chicken stock together. Peel the onion and slice it. Put the cabbage and the sliced onion in the slow cooker. Sprinkle the mixture with the tomato juice mixture and stir carefully. Peel the garlic cloves and cut into 4. After this, add the garlic cloves in the slow cooker and close it. Cook the dish on the HIGH for 4.5 hours. When all the ingredients are cooked, remove from the slow cooker.

Nutrition: calories 91, fat 3.1, fiber 2, carbs 9.25, protein 8

Bread Crumb Meatballs

Prep time: 15 minutes | Cooking time: 7 hours | Servings: 8

Ingredients:

- 1 cup bread crumbs
- 2 tablespoon sour cream
- 9 oz. ground chicken
- 7 oz. ground pork
- 1 teaspoon onion powder
- 1 onion, chopped
- 1 teaspoon ketchup
- ¼ teaspoon olive oil

Directions:

Combine the sour cream, ground chicken, ground pork, onion powder, chopped onion and ketchup in a big bowl. Mix the meat mixture well. After this, put the bread crumbs in the large bowl. Make several balls from the meat mixture and toss them in the bread crumbs. Coat the meatballs with the bread crumbs carefully. Spray the inside of the slow cooker with the olive oil. Place the prepared meatballs in the slow cooker and close the lid. Cook for 7 hours on LOW.

Nutrition: calories 116, fat 5, fiber 0, carbs 4.08, protein 14

Creamy Chicken Strips

Prep time: 23 minutes | Cooking time: 8 hours | Servings: 7

Ingredients:

- 1 cup cream
- 2-pound chicken breast, skinned, boneless
- 1 teaspoon chili powder
- 3 tablespoons flour
- 1 teaspoon oregano
- 1 teaspoon ground white pepper
- 1 teaspoon sriracha
- 6 oz. asparagus
- 1 teaspoon sage

Directions:

Cut the chicken breast into the strips. Combine the chili powder, flour, oregano, ground white pepper, and sage together in a shallow bowl. Mix the mixture up and sprinkle the chicken strips with the spices. After this, pour the cream in the slow cooker. Chop the asparagus roughly and put the vegetables in the slow cooker. Add the sriracha and stir. Place the chicken strips in the slow cooker. Do not mix the ingredients. Close the slow cooker lid and cook the dish for 8 hours on LOW. Let the prepared dish cool briefly and serve it with the creamy gravy.

Nutrition: calories 311, fat 18.8, fiber 1, carbs 5.71, protein 29

Lunch

Chicken Salad with Vegetables

Prep time: 15 minutes | Cooking time: 5 hours | Servings: 5

Ingredients:

- 12 oz. chicken breast, boneless, skinless
- 3 oz. white onion
- 4 oz. celery
- ¼ cup fresh parsley
- 2 cup chicken stock
- 1 tablespoon chives
- 1 cup green grapes
- 1 teaspoon salt
- 1 teaspoon ground black pepper
- 1 oz. bay leaf
- 4 tablespoons mayonnaise
- ¼ teaspoon sugar

Directions:

Chop the chicken breast roughly and put it in the slow cooker. Chop the celery and combine it with the chives then add both to the slow cooker. Peel the onion, and cut it into 4 parts and place in the slow cooker as well with the chicken stock. Close the slow cooker lid and cook the chicken for 5 hours on HIGH. Meanwhile, wash the green grapes and cut them into the halves. Add the mayonnaise, sugar, ground black pepper, salt, and halved green grapes into a big bowl. Chop the parsley and add to bowl too. When the chicken is cooked, remove it from the chicken stock and shred with a fork. Then add the shredded chicken to the mayonnaise mixture and toss. Serve the salad immediately.

Nutrition: calories 236, fat 9.9, fiber 3, carbs 19.6, protein 18

Pot Pie

Prep time: 18 minutes | Cooking time: 7 hours | Servings: 12

Ingredients:

- 1-pound chicken fillet
- 6 medium potatoes, peeled, chopped
- 8 oz. baby carrots, chopped
- 3 tablespoons chives
- 1 cup cream
- 3 bouillon cubes
- 2 cups water
- 1 teaspoon minced garlic
- 1 teaspoon salt
- 1 cup mix vegetables, frozen
- 6 oz. dry biscuit mix
- 1/3 teaspoon chili flakes

Directions:

Chop the chicken fillet and put it in the slow cooker. Place the fresh vegetables in the slow cooker too. Add chives, minced garlic, salt, and chili flakes. Add the bouillon cubes and water and close the lid. Cook the mixture on HIGH for 4 hours. Meanwhile, combine the biscuit mix with the cream and whisk it. After 4 hours, add the frozen vegetables to the slow cooker and pour in the cream mixture. Close the slow cooker and cook the dish for 3 hours more on HIGH. When the time is done and the pot pie is cooked, serve it immediately.

Nutrition: calories 337, fat 10.5, fiber 6, carbs 52.31, protein 10

Noodle Soup

Prep time: 20 minutes | Cooking time: 6 hours 40 minutes | Servings: 12

Ingredients:

- 16 oz. chicken breast
- 1 teaspoon salt
- 1 teaspoon chili flakes
- 1 teaspoon coriander
- ½ teaspoon ground black pepper
- 1 teaspoon oregano
- 1 teaspoon rosemary
- 2 green sweet pepper
- 1 large white onion
- 1 teaspoon minced garlic
- 6 oz. spaghetti
- 10 cup chicken stock
- 1 teaspoon chives
- 3 oz. celery, chopped

Directions:

Put the chicken breast in the slow cooker. Sprinkle it with the salt, chili flakes, coriander, ground black pepper, oregano, minced garlic and rosemary. Add the chicken stock. Peel the onion and dice it. Chop the sweet peppers and add them to the slow cooker. Add the diced onion and stir the mixture with the help of the spatula. After this, close the slow cooker lid and cook the chicken for 6 hours on LOW. When the time is done remove the chicken breast from the slow cooker and shred it well. Return the shredded chicken breast back to the slow cooker and add chives. Add celery and spaghetti. Close the slow cooker lid and cook the dish for 40 minutes on HIGH. When the soup is cooked, stir it gently and ladle into the serving bowls.

Nutrition: calories 166, fat 6.1, fiber 1, carbs 13.38, protein 14

Zucchini Noodle Soup

Prep time: 10 minutes | Cooking time: 3 hours 25 minutes | Servings: 8

Ingredients:

- 1 pound green zucchini
- 1 carrot
- 1 onion
- 8 cups chicken stock
- 2 red potatoes
- 3 oz. bacon, roasted
- 1 teaspoon salt
- 1 teaspoon ground black pepper
- ½ teaspoon paprika
- ½ cup fresh dill

Directions:

Peel the carrot and cut it into the strips. Then peel the onion and chop it. Pour the chicken stock into the slow cooker. Add carrot strips and chopped onion. After this, add ground black pepper, salt, and paprika. Chop the fresh dill. Peel the potatoes and cut them into the cubes. Add the red potato cubes in the slow cooker too. Stir gently and close the slow cooker lid. Cook the soup mixture on HIGH for 3 hours. Meanwhile, wash the green zucchini carefully and make the noodles from them with the help of the spiralizer. When the time is done, add the zucchini noodles in the slow cooker and cook the soup on HIGH for 25 minutes more. Stir the cooked soup gently and serve it.

Nutrition: calories 216, fat 6.8, fiber 3, carbs 29.3, protein 11

White Bean Soup
Prep time: 22 minutes | Cooking time: 12 hours | Servings: 7

Ingredients:

- 1 teaspoon canola oil
- 1 tablespoon garlic, chopped
- 3 oz. white onion
- 6 oz. celery stalk
- 2 cups white beans
- 6 cups water
- 1 teaspoon salt
- 1 tablespoon tomato paste
- 1 teaspoon ground black pepper
- ½ teaspoon rosemary
- 1 carrot
- 1 teaspoon turmeric

Directions:

Combine the canola oil with the chopped garlic. Dice the white onion and chop the celery stalk. Put the prepared vegetables in the slow cooker. Add white beans, tomato paste, ground black pepper, rosemary, and turmeric. Peel the carrot and chop it. Add the chopped carrot in the slow cooker and add the water. Close the slow cooker lid and cook the soup on LOW for 12 hours. Blend the mixture for 20 seconds with a hand mixer and add salt. Stir the soup gently and ladle it into the serving bowls.

Nutrition: calories 231, fat 1.9, fiber 10, carbs 40.8, protein 14

Onion Soup
Prep time: 10 minutes | Cooking time: 8 hours 15 hours | Servings: 6

Ingredients:

- 7 oz. Gruyere cheese, shredded
- 5 cup chicken stock
- 1-pound white onion, peeled and diced
- 1 teaspoon salt
- 1 teaspoon ground black pepper
- 1 tablespoon butter
- ½ teaspoon apple cider vinegar
- 6 oz. French bread, toasted

Directions:

Put the diced onion in the slow cooker. Add salt, ground black pepper, butter, and apple cider vinegar. Pour the chicken stock in the slow cooker and stir the mixture gently. Close the slow cooker lid and cook the soup on LOW for 8 hours. Meanwhile, chop toasted French bread roughly. When the time is done, ladle the soup into the serving bowls. After this, preheat the oven to 365 F. Put the chopped toasted bread in the bowls with soup and add the grated cheese. Place the bowls with onion soup in the preheated oven and cook until the cheese is melted and the surface of the soup gets light brown color. Then remove the prepared soup from the oven and serve it immediately.

Nutrition: calories 416, fat 20.1, fiber 3, carbs 39.55, protein 20

Slow Cooker Mac
Prep time: 10 minutes | Cooking time: 4 hours 7 minutes | Servings: 6

Ingredients:

- 8 oz. Cheddar cheese, shredded
- 7 oz. macaroni
- 7 oz. milk
- 1 cup almond milk
- ½ teaspoon paprika
- 1 teaspoon salt
- 1 teaspoon oregano
- 1 teaspoon cilantro
- ½ teaspoon onion powder

Directions:

Combine the almond milk, milk, paprika, salt, oregano, cilantro, and onion powder together in the slow cooker. Add the macaroni and mix. After this, close the slow cooker lid and cook the macaroni on LOW for 4 hours. Stir the macaroni every 2 hours. When the time is over and macaroni absorbs all the liquid – cover the macaroni with the shredded cheese and close the slow cooker lid. Cook the dish for 7 minutes more on the HIGH. When the macaroni is cooked and the cheese is melted, stir the mixture gently. Transfer the prepared dish in the serving plates.

Nutrition: calories 231, fat 5.5, fiber 1, carbs 34.47, protein 11

Chickpea Stew

Prep time: 14 minutes | Cooking time: 8 hours | Servings: 8

Ingredients:

- 7 oz. chickpea, canned
- 1 teaspoon paprika
- 1 teaspoon salt
- 1 teaspoon ground black pepper
- 1 teaspoon powdered chili
- 5 tablespoons tomato puree
- 2 garlic cloves, peeled and sliced
- ½ teaspoon ground ginger
- 1 yellow sweet pepper
- 5 oz. pumpkin
- 5 cup beef broth

Directions:

Combine the paprika, salt, ground black pepper, powdered chili, and ground ginger together in a bowl. After this, put the canned chickpea in the slow cooker. Add tomato puree. Slice the sweet pepper and add it in the slow cooker too. Chop the pumpkin into the small cubes and add to the slow cooker. Sprinkle the slow cooker ingredients with the spice mixture and add beef broth. Close the slow cooker lid and cook the chickpea stew for 8 hours on LOW. When the chickpea stew is cooked, mix it up gently. Put the prepared dish on the serving plates.

Nutrition: calories 199, fat 5.4, fiber 7, carbs 28.74, protein 11

Lunch Chili

Prep time: 16 minutes | Cooking time: 9 hours | Servings: 12

Ingredients:

- 8 oz. ground beef
- ½ cup sweet corn
- ½ cup green peas
- 1 teaspoon salt
- ½ cup tomato juice
- 2 cup chicken stock
- 1 onion, chopped
- 1 cup sweet pepper, chopped
- 1 teaspoon minced garlic
- 1 teaspoon ground paprika
- ½ teaspoon ground ginger
- ½ cup fresh dill
- 1 carrot, chopped
- ½ chili
- 1 teaspoon thyme
- ¼ teaspoon olive oil
- 1 cup red beans, canned

Directions:

Place the chopped carrot, chopped sweet pepper, chopped onion, green peas, sweet corn, and ground beef in the slow cooker and mix. Combine the salt, minced garlic, ground paprika, ground ginger, and thyme. Sprinkle the slow cooker mixture with the spices. Add chicken stock and tomato juice. Chop the chili pepper and add it to the slow cooker. Then add olive oil and red beans. Mix the chili mixture gently and close the slow cooker lid. Cook the chili for 9 hours on LOW. When the chili is cooked serve the dish warm and

Nutrition: calories 154, fat 6.6, fiber 4, carbs 16.18, protein 8

Panade

Prep time: 15 minutes | Cooking time: 7 hours | Servings: 14

Ingredients:

- 13 oz. bread, toasted
- 1 cup white onion, chopped
- 1 tablespoon minced garlic
- 2 cups black beans
- 8 oz. mozzarella
- 8 cups chicken stock
- 1 teaspoon butter
- 4 oz. chicken sausages
- 1 teaspoon cayenne pepper

Directions:

Chop the bread roughly. Toss the chopped onion, minced garlic, black beans, chicken stock, butter, and cayenne pepper in the slow cooker. Chop the chicken sausages and add them in the slow cooker too. Stir the mixture gently and close the slow cooker lid. Cook the dish for 5 hours on HIGH. Meanwhile, cut Mozzarella cheese into the strips. When the time is done, sprinkle the dish with the chopped toasted bread and mozzarella strips. Close the slow cooker lid and cook Panade for 2 hours more on HIGH. When the dish is cooked, mix it gently and serve hot.

Nutrition: calories 196, fat 5.2, fiber 3, carbs 24, protein 13

Fish-Pasta Casserole

Prep time: 19 minutes | Cooking time: 9 hours | Servings: 6

Ingredients:

- 10 oz. salmon
- 5 oz. pasta
- 1 cup heavy cream
- 2 cups chicken stock
- ½ teaspoon fresh rosemary
- 1 teaspoon salt
- ½ teaspoon coriander
- 8 oz. mozzarella, sliced
- 1 cup carrot, chopped
- 1 cup onion, diced
- ½ cup sweet corn
- 3 tablespoons tomato paste
- ¼ teaspoon cayenne pepper

Directions:

Chop the salmon and sprinkle the fish with the fresh rosemary, salt, and coriander. Combine the chopped carrot and diced onion. Combine cayenne pepper with the tomato paste and mix it. After this, separate the onion mixture into 3 parts. Separate the salmon into 2 parts. Then make the layer of the onion mixture in the slow cooker. Spread it with the tomato paste mixture gently. After this, sprinkle with the salmon mixture. Then make the layer of the onion mixture again. Spread the onion layer with the tomato paste mixture. Then make the layer of the pasta. Make the layer of the salmon and sprinkle it with the last layer of the onion mixture. Pour the chicken stock and heavy cream. Then sprinkle the casserole with sliced mozzarella. Close the slow cooker lid and cook the casserole for 9 hours on LOW. When the casserole is cooked – let it cool well. Serve it!

Nutrition: calories 291, fat 12.1, fiber 3, carbs 20.29, protein 26

Enchilada Soup

Prep time: 25 minutes | Cooking time: 8 hours | Servings: 9

Ingredients:

- 17 oz. chicken fillets, cubed
- 6 tablespoon enchilada sauce
- 1 tablespoon onion powder
- 8 cups chicken stock
- 1 tablespoon tomato paste
- 7 oz. black bean, canned
- 1 cup tomatoes
- 4 oz. corn kernel
- 1 jalapeno pepper
- 1 tablespoon garlic clove, sliced
- 1 cup fresh cilantro, chopped
- 1 tablespoon lemon juice

Directions:

Sprinkle the chicken pieces with the lemon juice. Place the meat in the slow cooker and add the onion powder, enchilada sauce, tomato paste, canned black beans, sliced garlic, and chopped fresh cilantro. Then slice the jalapeno pepper and chop the tomatoes. Add the vegetables in the slow cooker and pour the chicken stock. Close the slow cooker lid and cook the soup on LOW for 8 hours. When the soup is cooked, let it rest for 20 minutes. Shred the chicken with a fork if desired. Ladle the prepared soup in the serving bowls.

Nutrition: calories 251, fat 10.6, fiber 3, carbs 26.47, protein 13

Bacon Rigatoni

Prep time: 25 minutes | *Cooking time:* 4 hours | *Servings:* 6

Ingredients:

- 7 oz. bacon
- 10 oz. rigatoni
- 1 cup heavy cream
- 1 cup chicken stock
- 5 oz. fresh parsley
- 1 teaspoon salt
- 1 teaspoon paprika
- 1 teaspoon butter
- 4 oz. Parmesan cheese
- 1 tablespoon tomato sauce
- 1 tablespoon chives

Directions:

Chop the bacon into the tiny pieces and place it in the slow cooker bowl. Cook the bacon on HIGH for 1 hour. Meanwhile, chop the fresh parsley and combine it with the salt, heavy cream, butter, paprika, tomato sauce, and chives. Shred Parmesan cheese. When the bacon is done, stir pour the cream mixture into the pot along with the chicken stock. Add the rigatoni and cook on high for 3 hours. Stir the rigatoni every 1.5 hours. Add the chives into the slow cooker 15 minutes before the time is ended. Mix the dish carefully then sprinkle the dish with the shredded cheese and let it sit with the lid closed for 10 minutes to melt the cheese. Serve the dish hot.

Nutrition: calories 327, fat 25.6, fiber 3, carbs 13.03, protein 14

Stuffed Potatoes

Prep time: 16 minutes | *Cooking time:* 8 hour | *Servings:* 4

Ingredients:

- 5 oz. Parmesan cheese
- 4 oz. Cheddar cheese
- 4 big potatoes
- 3 tablespoons cream cheese
- 1 teaspoon minced garlic
- 1 teaspoon chives
- 1 teaspoon fresh dill, chopped
- 1 teaspoon paprika
- 1 teaspoon butter
- ½ teaspoon salt

Directions:

Wash the potatoes carefully then let dry. Whisk the cream cheese with the minced garlic. Add paprika and salt and whisk until fluffy. After this, slice the Cheddar cheese and Parmesan cheese. Make the medium crosswise cuts in the potatoes. Fill the potatoes with the sliced cheese. Then wrap the bottom of the potatoes in the foil to make a holder. Spread the potatoes with the whisked cream cheese mixture generously. Sprinkle the potatoes with the chives and fresh dill. Place the uncooked wrapped potatoes in the slow cooker. Close the slow cooker lid and cook for 8 hours on LOW. Serve the cooked meal hot.

Nutrition: calories 529, fat 17, fiber 8, carbs 74, protein 22

Hominy Stew

Prep time: 24 minutes | *Cooking time:* 9 hours | *Servings:* 8

Ingredients:

- 10 oz. hominy, canned
- 1-pound pork chop
- 3 cup chicken stock
- 3 tablespoon salsa Verde
- 1 jalapeno pepper
- 7 oz. corn tortilla
- 6 tablespoons cream
- 1 teaspoon salt
- ½ teaspoon ground ginger
- 1/3 cup fresh parsley

Directions:

Chop the pork and put it in the slow cooker. Add strained hominy. Sprinkle the mixture with the salsa Verde, cream, salt, and ground ginger. After this, slice the jalapeno pepper and chop the fresh parsley. Add the prepared ingredients to the slow cooker then pour the chicken stock in as well and close the slow cooker lid. Cook the dish on LOW for 9 hours. Meanwhile, chop tortilla roughly and heat them for 10 minutes in the oven. When the stew is cooked – transfer it to the serving bowls. Serve the stew with the prepared tortillas.

Nutrition: calories 256, fat 10.6, fiber 3, carbs 20.43, protein 19

Sweet Pulled Pork Sandwiches

Prep time: 18 minutes | Cooking time: 6 hours | Servings: 6

Ingredients:

- 1-pound pork fillet
- 3 cups water
- 1 onion
- 2 garlic cloves
- 6 cinnamon buns
- 1 teaspoon salt
- ½ teaspoon ground black pepper
- 1 teaspoon onion powder
- 3 tablespoons tomato paste
- 1 tablespoon garlic sauce
- 1 cup lettuce

Directions:

Rub the pork fillet with the ground black pepper and onion powder. Place the meat in the slow cooker. Add the water and salt. After this, peel the onion and garlic cloves and add to the slow cooker too. Add the tomato paste, stir and close the slow cooker lid. Cook the meat on HIGH for 6 hours. When the meat is cooked, strain the meat and shred it carefully with a fork. Then, cut the cinnamon buns into 2 parts and spread each bun part with the garlic sauce gently. Then top with the lettuce and pulled pork. Serve them immediately.

Nutrition: calories 518, fat 30.9, fiber 2, carbs 36.19, protein 23

Caramelized Zucchini with Chicken Cubes

Prep time: 25 minutes | Cooking time: 6 hours | Servings: 6

Ingredients:

- 2 tablespoons brown sugar
- 1 teaspoon salt
- 1-pound chicken fillets
- 3 zucchinis, chopped
- ½ cup chicken stock
- 1 tablespoon fresh cilantro
- 1 teaspoon onion powder
- ½ teaspoon ground black pepper
- 1 carrot
- 1 tablespoon butter

Directions:

Cut the chicken fillets into cubes. Sprinkle the chicken cubes with the salt, ground black pepper, and onion powder. Toss the chicken fillet mixture in the slow cooker. Add the chicken stock and close the slow cooker lid. Cook the chicken cubes for 4 hours on HIGH. Meanwhile, melt the brown sugar and pour over the zucchini. Peel the carrot and grate it. Add the grated carrot to the zucchini mixture and stir. After 4 hours, open the slow cooker lid and mix the chicken gently. Add the carrot-zucchini mixture and close the lid. Cook the dish for 2 hours on HIGH. Then serve the prepared lunch immediately.

Nutrition: calories 233, fat 13, fiber 2, carbs 19.93, protein 10

Lunch Ragout

Prep time: 15 minutes | Cooking time: 9 hours | Servings: 10

Ingredients:

- 7 oz. ground beef
- 6 oz. red cabbage, sliced
- 1 cup carrot, chopped
- 1 cup yellow onion, chopped
- 6 oz. tomato sauce
- 1 cup chicken stock
- 4 medium potatoes
- 1 tablespoon sugar
- 1 teaspoon salt
- 1 teaspoon ground black pepper
- 1 teaspoon chili pepper
- 1 teaspoon cilantro
- 5 oz. celery stalk
- 3 garlic cloves, peeled
- 1 teaspoon butter
- 5 oz. Monterey Jack cheese, shredded

Directions:

Pour the chicken stock and tomato sauce in the slow cooker. Add the sliced red cabbage. After this, add chopped onion and carrot. Add peeled garlic cloves, salt, sugar, ground beef, ground black pepper, cilantro, chili pepper, and butter. Then chop the celery stalk and peel the potatoes. Chop the potatoes and transfer them to the slow cooker. Mix well and close the slow cooker lid. Cook the ragout for 9 hours on LOW. When the ragout is cooked, transfer it to the serving plates and sprinkle with the shredded cheese.

Nutrition: calories 292, fat 12.1, fiber 5, carbs 35.06, protein 11

Stuffed Plums

Prep time: 15 minutes | Cooking time: 3 hours | Servings: 4

Ingredients:

- 1-pound big plums, pitted
- 1 tablespoon pistachio, crushed
- 3 tablespoons cream cheese
- 3 oz. ground chicken
- 2 oz. Parmesan, shredded
- 1 teaspoon tomato sauce
- ¼ teaspoon oregano

Directions:

Separate the plums into the halves and remove the small amount of the flesh from the fruits. Then combine the crushed pistachio, cream cheese, ground chicken, shredded Parmesan and tomato sauce together. Add the oregano and mix well. Fill the plum halves with the cream cheese mixture and connect 2 plum halves together so the filling is sealed inside. Then wrap each stuffed plum in the foil. Place the wrapped plums in the slow cooker and close the lid. Cook the dish for 3 hours on HIGH. When the dish is cooked – remove from the slow cooker and chill. Discard the foil and serve the lunch.

Nutrition: calories 181, fat 6.9, fiber 2, carbs 19.89, protein 11

Stuffed Tomatoes

Prep time: 21 minutes | Cooking time: 4 hours | Servings: 5

Ingredients:

- 5 large tomatoes
- 1 cup rice, cooked
- 4 oz. ground pork
- 1 egg
- 1 teaspoon salt
- ½ teaspoon ground black pepper
- ½ teaspoon fresh dill
- ½ cup heavy cream
- ¼ cup chicken stock
- ½ onion, chopped
- ½ teaspoon cayenne pepper

Directions:

Wash the tomatoes carefully and cut the tops off. Then remove the flesh from the tomatoes. In a separate bowl, beat the egg with the cooked rice. Add the ground pork, salt, ground black pepper, fresh dill, and chopped onion. Sprinkle the mixture with the cayenne pepper and mix it up carefully. Then fill the prepared tomatoes with the rice filling and cover them with the tomato tops like a hat. Pour the chicken stock and heavy cream in the slow cooker. Add the prepared stuffed tomatoes and close the slow cooker lid. Cook the dish on LOW for 4 hours. When the stuffed tomatoes are cooked, transfer them gently to the serving plates. Be careful not to crush them as they will be fragile! Enjoy the dish immediately or chill to serve cold.

Nutrition: calories 229, fat 13.5, fiber 8, carbs 21.44, protein 14

Avocado Cups

Prep time: 25 minutes | Cooking time: 3 hours | Servings: 2

Ingredients:

- 1 avocado, pitted
- 5 oz. chicken, canned
- 1 tablespoon fresh parsley
- 1 tablespoon fresh cilantro
- 1 teaspoon fresh dill
- ½ teaspoon ground coriander
- ½ teaspoon cayenne pepper
- 1 teaspoon tomato sauce
- ½ teaspoon olive oil
- ¼ teaspoon minced garlic
- ½ carrot

Directions:

Cut the avocado into halves and remove the meat. Shred the canned chicken meat with a fork and combine it with the fresh parsley, cilantro, and dill. Sprinkle the shredded chicken mixture with the ground coriander, cayenne pepper, and minced garlic. Peel the carrot and grate it then add the grated carrot to the chicken mixture. Add the tomato sauce and mix. Sprinkle the avocado halves with the olive oil. Then fill the avocado with the chicken mixture. Put the avocado halves in the slow cooker and cook on LOW for 3 hours. When the dish is cooked, serve it immediately.

Nutrition: calories 288, fat 21.9, fiber 8, carbs 11.72, protein 15

Cottage Cheese Dumplings

Prep time: 21 minutes | Cooking time: 1 Hour | Servings: 5

Ingredients:

- ½ cup flour
- ½ cup cottage cheese
- 2 tablespoons sugar
- ½ teaspoon vanilla sugar
- 1 egg
- 6 tablespoons water
- ¼ teaspoon salt

Directions:

Sift the flour into the big bowl. Blend the cottage cheese until fluffy. Combine the cottage cheese with the sugar and vanilla sugar. Beat the egg into the cottage cheese and sprinkle the mixture with salt. Then combine the cottage cheese mix with the flour and knead the soft to a non-sticky dough. Then make a log from the dough and cut the log into 5 balls. Pour the water into the slow cooker and add the cottage cheese balls. Cook the dish on HIGH for 1 hour. When the time is over, stir the cooked dumplings with a wooden spatula gently. Sprinkle the prepared dumplings with sour cream if desired.

Nutrition: calories 103, fat 2.6, fiber 0, carbs 14.94, protein 5

Chicken and Egg Noodle Soup
Prep time: 10 minutes | Cooking time: 5 hours | Servings: 3

Ingredients:

- 8 oz. egg noodles
- 1 cup chicken soup, canned
- 1 teaspoon butter
- 1-pound chicken breast
- 1 tablespoon paprika

Directions:

Put the chicken breast in the slow cooker and add the paprika. Pour the canned chicken soup in as well and close the slow cooker lid. Cook the dish for 5 hours on HIGH. After this, remove the chicken breast from the slow cooker and shred it carefully with a fork. Place the shredded chicken breast back in the slow cooker and add the egg noodles. Close the slow cooker lid and cook the dish on HIGH for 10 minutes more. When the dish is cooked, transfer it to serving bowls and add the butter on the top of every bowl. Serve the dish immediately.

Nutrition: calories 424, fat 18.2, fiber 2, carbs 24.57, protein 39

Soft Cauliflower Florets
Prep time: 25 minutes | Cooking time: 8 hours | Servings: 5

Ingredients:

- 2-pound cauliflower head
- ¼ cup flour
- 2 eggs
- 1/3 cup heavy cream
- 1 teaspoon salt
- 1 cup water
- 1 teaspoon ground black pepper
- ½ teaspoon turmeric
- 1 teaspoon garlic powder

Directions:

Wash the cauliflower head and separate it into medium florets. Pour water in the slow cooker and add the cauliflower florets. After this, close the slow cooker lid and cook the vegetables for 2 hours on HIGH. Meanwhile, whisk the flour with the heavy cream in a mixing bowl. Crack the eggs into the separated bowl and mix them with a hand mixer. After this, add the mixed eggs in the heavy cream liquid. Add the salt, ground black pepper, turmeric, and garlic powder. When the cauliflower is cooked, remove the florets from the slow cooker and get rid of the water. Coat the florets with the heavy cream liquid well. Then transfer the cauliflower florets back to the slow cooker and close the lid. Cook the dish for 6 hours more on HIGH. Serve the prepared dish hot.

Nutrition: calories 154, fat 7.4, fiber 4, carbs 15.93, protein 8

Pumpkin Soup
Prep time: 12 minutes | Cooking time: 3.5 hour | Servings: 8

Ingredients:

- 1-pound pumpkin, peeled chopped
- 2 potatoes, peeled, cubed
- 5 oz. carrot, shredded
- 1 onion, peeled, diced
- 3 cup water
- 1 teaspoon cinnamon
- ¼ teaspoon nutmeg
- 1 teaspoon cilantro
- 1 teaspoon oregano
- ½ tablespoon salt
- 1 cup cream

Directions:

Put all the prepared veggies in the slow cooker vessel. Add water, salt, and cream. Stir the vegetables gently and close the lid. Cook the soup on HIGH for 3 hours. After this, add oregano, cilantro, cinnamon, and nutmeg and cook the dish for 2 minutes more. Then blend the soup with a hand blender until you get the creamy texture. Cook the soup for 30 minutes more on LOW. Then ladle the prepared lunch in the serving bowls or keep the soup in the fridge.

Nutrition: calories 468, fat 33.8, fiber 7, carbs 28.68, protein 20

Pappardelle

Prep time: 17 minutes | Cooking time: 4 hours | Servings: 6

Ingredients:
- 9 oz. pappardelle
- 4 oz. Parmesan cheese
- ¼ chili pepper
- 7 oz. ground chicken
- 1 tablespoon tomato paste
- 1 teaspoon salt
- 1 teaspoon butter
- ½ teaspoon ground black pepper
- 4 cups chicken stock
- 2 teaspoons fresh cilantro, chopped

Directions:

Chop the chili pepper and combine it with the chopped fresh cilantro. Add the tomato paste and salt. Add the ground chicken and ground black pepper. Mix carefully and then place in the slow cooker. Close the slow cooker lid and cook the dish for 3 more hours on HIGH. After this, add the pappardelle and chicken stock. Mix gently and cook the dish on HIGH for 1 hour more. When the time is done, place the prepared dish in the serving dish and add the butter.

Nutrition: calories 253, fat 11.4, fiber 1, carbs 20.02, protein 17

Date Pudding with Ham

Prep time: 23 minutes | Cooking time: 9 hours | Servings: 7

Ingredients:
- 8 oz. biscuits
- 1 cup milk
- 4 eggs
- 6 oz. ham
- 6 oz. dates, pitted
- 1 teaspoon cayenne pepper
- ½ teaspoon salt
- 2 tablespoon sugar
- 1 teaspoon butter
- 2 tablespoon semolina

Directions:

Cut the dates and ham into the strips and combine the ingredients together. Chop the biscuits and combine them with the milk. Beat the eggs in a separate bowl then add the cayenne pepper, salt, sugar, and semolina and stir again. Pour the whisked egg mixture over the biscuits and stir carefully. Transfer the ham and date strips to the slow cooker and pour in the biscuit mix. Close the lid and cook the dish on LOW for 9 hours. When the pudding is cooked – cut it into the servings.

Nutrition: calories 328, fat 11.5, fiber 3, carbs 44.3, protein 14

Spicy Vegetable Casserole

Prep time: 20 minutes | Cooking time: 8 hours | Servings: 6

Ingredients:
- 3 oz. turnip
- 1 teaspoon cayenne pepper
- 1 teaspoon sriracha
- 4 tablespoons heavy cream

- 1 teaspoon salt
- ½ teaspoon chili flakes
- 1 teaspoon butter
- 2 potatoes
- 1 cup onion, sliced
- 2 carrots
- 1 can red beans
- 1 cup chicken stock
- 4 tortillas

Directions:

Prepare the vegetables: peel the turnip, potatoes, and carrot. Cut the vegetables into the same size pieces. Spread the tortilla with the butter. Combine the salt, chili flakes, heavy cream, cayenne pepper, and sriracha together. Pour the mixture into the slow cooker vessel. Add the prepared vegetables then layer the onions on top. Cover the casserole with the tortilla and close the slow cooker lid. Cook the casserole for 8 hours on LOW.

Nutrition: calories 319, fat 7.4, fiber 7, carbs 53.46, protein 11

Cauliflower Cutlets

Prep time: 16 minutes | Cooking time: 3.5 hours | Servings: 7

Ingredients:

- 2 eggs
- 4 tablespoons semolina
- 1 tablespoon flour
- 1 teaspoon salt
- ½ teaspoon olive oil
- ½ teaspoon paprika
- 1-pound cauliflower
- 2 oz. onion, chopped

Directions:

Beat the eggs in the bowl and whisk with a fork. After this, wash the cauliflower and chop it roughly. Place the chopped cauliflower in the food processor and blend it until you get a smooth mixture. Combine the blended cauliflower with the whisked eggs. Add flour, semolina, salt, paprika, and chopped onion. Knead into a non-sticky dough. Form medium cutlets from the cauliflower dough. Spray the slow cooker bowl with the olive oil. Place the cauliflower cutlets in the slow cooker and close the lid. Cook the dish for 3.5 hours on HIGH. When the cauliflower cutlets are cooked, chill slightly and serve the dish!

Nutrition: calories 82, fat 3, fiber 2, carbs 9, protein 5

Meatloaf with Eggs

Prep time: 15 minutes | Cooking time: 5 hours | Servings: 6

Ingredients:

- 10 oz. ground beef
- 3 eggs, boiled, peeled
- 1 egg, beaten
- 1 teaspoon salt
- ½ teaspoon ground black pepper
- 1 tablespoon dried dill
- 3 tablespoons ketchup
- 1 teaspoon almond flour
- 1 teaspoon chili flakes

Directions:

Combine the salt, ground black pepper, dried dill, chili flakes, and almond flour in the shallow bowl. Combine the spice mixture and ground beef together and stir well. Add the beaten egg and mix with your hands. Shape the meatloaf from the ground beef mixture and transfer it to the slow cooker. Press the peeled boiled eggs into the meatloaf and flatten the surface of the loaf. Cover the outside of the meatloaf with the ketchup and close the slow cooker lid. Cook the dish for 5 hours on HIGH. Chill the cooked dish and slice it.

Nutrition: calories 259, fat 20.9, fiber 1, carbs 4.23, protein 13

Polenta Dumplings

Prep time: 16 minutes | Cooking time: 65 minutes | Servings: 6

Ingredients:

- ½ cup polenta
- ½ cup flour
- 1 teaspoon salt
- 4 oz. Parmesan
- ½ cup milk
- 2 eggs
- ¼ teaspoon ground ginger
- ½ cup water
- 1 onion, roasted

Directions:

Combine polenta and flour together. Beat the egg into the mixture. Add salt, milk, and ground ginger. After this, grate Parmesan and add it to the flour mixture too. Knead into a soft dough. Make 6 balls from the soft dough. Pour water in the slow cooker and heat for 20 minutes on HIGH. Then add the dough balls and close the slow cooker. Cook the dumplings for 45 minutes on HIGH. Strain the dumpling and place them in the big serving bowl. Sprinkle the dish with the roasted onion. Serve the dish immediately.

Nutrition: calories 190, fat 5, fiber 1, carbs 22.62, protein 13

Garlic Jacket Potatoes

Prep time: 11 minutes | Cooking time: 7 hours | Servings: 6

Ingredients:

- 2-pound potatoes
- 1 cup heavy cream
- 1 tablespoon minced garlic
- 1 teaspoon garlic powder
- ½ teaspoon salt
- 1 tablespoon fresh dill
- 1 teaspoon butter

Directions:

Rub the non-peeled potatoes with the butter and place them in the slow cooker. Combine the heavy cream with the minced garlic, garlic powder, salt, and fresh dill. Whisk the heavy cream well. Sprinkle the potatoes with the whisked heavy cream and close the slow cooker. Cook the jacket potatoes for 7 hours on low. Stir the potatoes during the cooking occasionally. Serve the prepared potatoes with the heavy cream sauce.

Nutrition: calories 198, fat 8.3, fiber 4, carbs 28, protein 4

Mushroom Stew

Prep time: 18 minutes | Cooking time: 10 hours | Servings: 7

Ingredients:

- 1-pound mushrooms
- 7 oz. pork chop
- 1 tablespoon salt
- 2 tablespoons flour
- ½ cup tomato juice
- 3 tablespoons sour cream
- 1 cup chicken stock
- 1 large onion
- 1 teaspoon sugar
- 2 carrots
- 1 cup green peas
- 1 teaspoon garlic

Directions:

Slice the mushrooms and place them in the slow cooker. Add the pork chop and green pepper. Peel the onion and carrots. Cut the carrots into the strips and chop the onion. Add the vegetables to the slow cooker. After this, add the sour cream, chicken stock, sugar, and garlic. Combine the tomato juice with the flour and stir it until well blended. Add the tomato juice mixture in the slow cooker too. When all the ingredients are added, stir the stew carefully and close the lid. Cook the meal for 10 hours on LOW. When the stew is cooked, you can serve it immediately or keep in the fridge not more than 3 days.

Nutrition: calories 316, fat 5.1, fiber 10, carbs 59.71, protein 16

Stuffed Peppers

Prep time: 22 minutes | Cooking time: 7.5 hours | Servings: 5

Ingredients:

- 1 tomato
- 1 cup wild rice, cooked
- 4 oz. ground chicken
- 2 oz. mushroom, sliced
- ½ onion, sliced
- 1 teaspoon salt
- 1 teaspoon turmeric
- 1 teaspoon curry
- 1 cup chicken stock
- 2 teaspoons tomato paste
- 1 oz. black olives
- 5 red sweet pepper

Directions:

To prepare the sweet peppers, cut off the top and remove the seeds. After this, toss the cooked wild rice in the bowl. Add sliced mushrooms, onion, salt, turmeric, curry, and ground chicken. Chop the tomatoes and add them to the rice mixture too. Then pour chicken stock and tomato paste in the slow cooker. Whisk the liquid gently. Fill the prepared sweet peppers with rice mix. Add black olives to the slow cooker, close the lid and cook the stuffed peppers for 7.5 hours on LOW. Enjoy the dish with the gravy.

Nutrition: calories 232, fat 3.7, fiber 5, carbs 41.11, protein 12

Cheese Pie

Prep time: 18 minutes | Cooking time: 3.5 hours | Servings: 6

Ingredients:

- 1 teaspoon baking soda
- 1 tablespoon lemon juice
- 1 cup flour
- 1 cup milk
- 1 teaspoon salt
- 5 oz. Cheddar cheese, shredded
- 5 oz. Parmesan cheese, shredded
- 2 eggs
- ½ teaspoon oregano
- 1/3 teaspoon olive oil

Directions:

Sift the flour into the bowl. Add baking soda, salt, all shredded cheeses, and oregano. After this, beat the eggs in a separated bowl. Add milk, lemon juice, and mix the liquid. Then combine the liquid mixture and dry mixture together. Use a hand mixer to make a nice smooth dough. Spray the slow cooker with the olive oil inside and place the dough inside as well. Close the slow cooker lid and cook the pie on high for 3.5 hours. Check if the pie is cooked and cut it into the serving pieces.

Nutrition: calories 288, fat 13.7, fiber 1, carbs 24.23, protein 16

Carrot with Honey Gravy

Prep time: 20 minutes | Cooking time: 2.5 hours | Servings: 4

Ingredients:

- 3 tablespoons mustard
- 2 tablespoons honey
- 1-pound carrot
- 1 teaspoon white sugar
- 1 teaspoon cinnamon
- ½ teaspoon salt
- 2 teaspoons butter
- 2 tablespoons water

Directions:

Peel the carrots and slice them. Place the sliced carrot in the slow cooker and sprinkle with the cinnamon, white sugar, water, and salt. Mix gently and close the slow cooker lid. Cook the carrot for 2 hours on HIGH. Meanwhile, whisk the mustard, honey, and butter together. When the time is done, sprinkle the carrot with the mustard-honey sauce and stir. Cook the carrot for 30 minutes more on LOW.

Nutrition: calories 99, fat 2.7, fiber 4, carbs 19.27, protein 1

Rice Apple Cups

Prep time: 15 minutes | Cooking time: 6 hours | Servings: 4

Ingredients:

- 4 red apples
- 1 cup white rice
- 3 tablespoons raisins
- 1 onion, diced
- 7 tablespoons water
- 1 teaspoon salt
- 1 teaspoon curry
- 4 teaspoons sour cream

Directions:

Prepare the apples for the filling: scoop the seeds and ½ of the flesh from the apples to make the shape of "cups". Then combine the raisins, diced onion, white rice, salt, and curry. Mix the ingredients together. Fill the prepared apple "cups" with the rice mixture. Put the sour cream on the top of every apple "cup". Pour the water into the slow cooker. Place the apples in the slow cooker and close the lid. Cook the dish on LOW for 6 hours. When the apples are done, cool them until they are just warm and ready to eat.

Nutrition: calories 317, fat 1.3, fiber 7, carbs 71.09, protein 4

Lunch Salsa Layer Pie

Prep time: 15 minutes | Cooking time: 7 hours | Servings: 6

Ingredients:

- 8 tortillas
- 7 oz. ground beef
- 7 oz. salsa
- 5 oz. red beans, canned
- 5 oz. Cheddar cheese, shredded
- 3 tablespoons tomato sauce
- ¼ tablespoon salt

Directions:

Place 2 tortillas in the bottom of the slow cooker bowl. Combine ground beef, tomato sauce, shredded cheese, and salt together in a separate bowl. Mix then place inside the slow cooker. Layer in 4 more tortillas and cover them with the canned red beans. Then make the last layer of the remaining tortillas and sprinkle the top with the salsa. Close the slow cooker lid and cook the pie for 7 hours on LOW. Let the prepared pie chill very well then cut the pie into servings.

Nutrition: calories 433, fat 16, fiber 6, carbs 53, protein 19

Lunch Gratin

Prep time: 25 minutes | Cooking time: 5 hours | Servings: 7

Ingredients:

- 1-pound potato
- 2 white onions
- 1 cup chicken stock
- 7 oz. ground beef
- 1 teaspoon ground black pepper
- 1/3 cup tomato juice
- 1 teaspoon paprika
- 1 teaspoon salt
- ½ teaspoon cayenne pepper
- 1 teaspoon cilantro

Directions:

Peel the potato and slice it. Separate the sliced potato into two piles. Then combine the ground beef with the ground black pepper. Peel the onions and slice them. Make a layer using 1 part of the sliced potato in the slow cooker. Then spread the potato layer with the ground beef and sliced onions. Start a second layer of sliced potatoes and sprinkle with the salt, cayenne pepper, and cilantro. Add the tomato juice and chicken stock and close the slow cooker lid. Cook the gratin for 5 hours on HIGH.

Nutrition: calories 175, fat 9.1, fiber 2, carbs 16.72, protein 7

Rice Casserole

Prep time: 16 minutes | Cooking time: 8 hours 10 minutes | Servings: 6

Ingredients:

- 1 cup white rice
- 5 oz. broccoli
- 4 oz. cauliflower
- 1 cup Greek Yogurt
- 1 cup chicken stock
- 6 oz. Cheddar cheese, shredded
- 1 teaspoon onion powder
- 2 yellow onions
- 1 teaspoon paprika
- 1 tablespoon salt
- 2 cups water
- 1 teaspoon butter

Directions:

Wash the cauliflower and broccoli carefully and chop them. Place the chopped vegetables in the slow cooker. Add the chicken stock and water. Combine the onion powder, paprika, and salt together in a shallow bowl. Add rice to the slow cooker then sprinkle the mixture with the spice mix. Peel the onion, slice it and sprinkle the casserole mixture with the sliced onion then close the slow cooker lid. Cook the casserole on LOW for 8 hours. When the time is completed, toss the butter on top of the casserole and sprinkle it with the shredded cheese. Close the lid and cook the dish on HIGH for more 10 minutes. Mix the prepared casserole and serve immediately.

Nutrition: calories 229, fat 4.2, fiber 3, carbs 36.27, protein 12

Layered Pie

Prep time: 25 minutes | Cooking time: 6 hours | Servings: 8

Ingredients:

- 2 sweet potatoes
- 2 red potatoes
- 6 oz. Parmesan, shredded
- 1 cup sweet corn
- 1 teaspoon salt
- 1 teaspoon paprika
- 1 teaspoon curry
- 2 red onions
- 1 cup flour
- 1 teaspoon baking soda
- ½ teaspoon apple cider vinegar
- 1 cup Greek Yogurt
- 3 tomatoes
- ¼ teaspoon butter

Directions:

Peel the sweet potatoes, red potatoes, and onions. Slice the peeled vegetables. Combine the curry, paprika, and salt together. Sprinkle the prepared vegetables with the spices. Spread the slow cooker bowl with butter inside. Make a layer of the sliced red potatoes in the slow cooker. Then make the layer of the sweet potatoes and sliced onions. Sprinkle the layers with the sweet corn. Slice the tomatoes and make the layer of the tomatoes in the slow cooker too. Then combine the baking soda, apple cider vinegar, flour, and Greek Yogurt. Whisk the mixture. Pour the whisked liquid into the slow cooker. Then sprinkle with a layer of the shredded cheese and close the slow cooker lid. Cook the layered pie on HIGH for 6 hours. When the pie is cooked, transfer it carefully to the serving plate and cut into the serving slices.

Nutrition: calories 272, fat 1.9, fiber 4, carbs 51.34, protein 14

Lentil Salad

Prep time: 15 minutes | Cooking time: 7 hours | Servings: 5

Ingredients:

- ¼ chili pepper
- 1 red onion
- ½ cup lentils
- ¼ cup rice
- ¼ teaspoon minced garlic
- 1 teaspoon chili flakes
- ¼ teaspoon ground ginger
- ½ teaspoon ground thyme
- 1 teaspoon salt
- 2 cups chicken stock
- 3 tablespoon sour cream
- 1 cup lettuce

Directions:

Peel the onion and slice it. Chop the chili pepper. Put the chopped chili pepper and sliced onion in the slow cooker. Add lentils and rice. Sprinkle the mixture with the minced garlic, chili flakes, and ground ginger. Add salt, ground thyme and the chicken stock and mix gently. Close the slow cooker lid and cook the dish on HIGH for 7 hours. Meanwhile, tear the lettuce and toss it in a salad bowl. When the lentils are done, remove them from the slow cooker and let cool slightly. Transfer the warm lentils to the salad bowl. Add sour cream and toss.

Nutrition: calories 84, fat 3.3, fiber 2, carbs 11.29, protein

Spaghetti Salad

Prep time: 15 minutes | Cooking time: 5.5 hours | Servings: 6

Ingredients:

- 1-pound chicken breast
- ½ cup onion
- 6 oz. spaghetti
- 3 cups chicken stock
- 1 cup heavy cream
- 2 tablespoons mayo
- 1 teaspoon minced garlic
- 1 teaspoon paprika
- ½ teaspoon salt
- ½ teaspoon ground black pepper
- 1 teaspoon sesame oil
- 1 tablespoon flax seeds
- 1 teaspoon sesame seeds
- 1 cup lettuce
- 2 sweet red peppers

Directions:

Rub the chicken breast with the paprika, salt, and ground black pepper and place in the slow cooker. Add minced garlic and chicken stock. Close the slow cooker lid and cook the dish for 4 hours on HIGH. Remove the cooked chicken and shred it with a fork. Return the chicken back to the slow cooker. Add heavy cream, sesame seeds, and spaghetti. Mix gently and close the slow cooker lid. Cook the dish on HIGH for 1.5 hours more or till the spaghetti is cooked. Meanwhile, slice the onion and chop the red sweet pepper. Chop the lettuce roughly and place all the vegetables in a large salad bowl. Add the mayo and toss. When the spaghetti is cooked – add the sesame oil to the mixture and stir it. Transfer the hot spaghetti mix to the salad bowl and toss. Enjoy the salad warm.

Nutrition: calories 312, fat 17.9, fiber 2, carbs 16.37, protein 22

Couscous Salad

Prep time: 20 minutes | Cooking time: 4 hours | Servings: 5

Ingredients:

- 1 cup couscous
- 1 green sweet pepper
- 2 garlic cloves
- 1 cup beef broth
- 1 teaspoon chives
- ½ cup cherry tomatoes
- 1 zucchini
- 7 oz. halloumi cheese
- 1 teaspoon olive oil
- 1 teaspoon paprika
- ¼ teaspoon ground cardamom
- 1 teaspoon salt

Directions:

Put the couscous in the slow cooker. Add salt, ground cardamom, and paprika. Chop the zucchini and add it in the slow cooker as well. Peel the garlic cloves and toss them in the slow cooker. Add beef broth and mix the couscous gently with a wooden spatula. Close the slow cooker lid and cook on HIGH for 4 hours. Chop the green sweet peppers and cut the cherry tomatoes into the halves. Chop halloumi cheese roughly. Toss the prepared ingredients into a big salad bowl. When the couscous is done, stir it carefully and put into the salad bowl. Mix and chill for 5 minutes.

Nutrition: calories 170, fat 9.6, fiber 1, carbs 12.59, protein 9

Quinoa Salad

Prep time: 15 minutes | Cooking time: 7 hours | Servings: 6

Ingredients:

- ½ lemon, juiced
- 1 avocado, pitted
- 1 red onion
- 1 cup white quinoa
- 1 cup water
- 1 teaspoon canola oil
- ½ cup fresh dill
- 1 cup green peas, frozen
- 1 teaspoon garlic powder

Directions:

Put the quinoa in the slow cooker. Add water and green peas. Close the slow cooker lid and cook for 7 hours on LOW. Meanwhile, peel the onion and avocado. Dice the red onion and chop the avocado. Put the diced onion and chopped avocado in the bowl. Chop the fresh dill and add it in the bowl too. When the quinoa is cooked, chill the mixture till it is warm and sprinkle with the canola oil. Transfer the quinoa mixture to the bowl and sprinkle with the lemon juice. Mix the salad gently and serve it immediately.

Nutrition: calories 195, fat 7.7, fiber 6, carbs 26.77, protein 6

Lunch Chicken Wraps

Prep time: 18 minutes | Cooking time: 6 hours | Servings: 6

Ingredients:

- 6 tortillas
- 3 tablespoon Caesar dressing
- 1-pound chicken breast
- ½ cup lettuce
- 1 cup water
- 1 oz. bay leaf
- 1 teaspoon salt
- 1 teaspoon ground pepper
- 1 teaspoon coriander
- 4 oz. Feta cheese

Directions:

Put the chicken breast in the slow cooker. Sprinkle the meat with the bay leaf, salt, ground pepper, and coriander. Add water and cook the chicken breast for 6 hours on LOW. Then remove the cooked chicken from the slow cooker and shred it with a fork. Chop the lettuce roughly. Then chop Feta cheese. Combine the chopped ingredients together and add the shredded chicken breast and Caesar dressing. Mix everything together well. After this, spread the tortillas with the shredded chicken mixture and wrap them.

Nutrition: calories 376, fat 18.5, fiber 3, carbs 29.43, protein 23

Nutritious Lunch Wraps

Prep time: 20 minutes | Cooking time: 4 hours | Servings: 5

Ingredients:

- 7 oz. ground pork
- 5 tortillas
- 1 tablespoon tomato paste
- ½ cup onion, chopped
- ½ cup lettuce
- 1 teaspoon ground black pepper
- 1 teaspoon salt
- 1 teaspoon sour cream
- 5 tablespoons water
- 4 oz. Parmesan, shredded
- 2 tomatoes

Directions:

Combine the ground pork with the tomato paste, ground black pepper, salt, and sour cream. Transfer the meat mixture to the slow cooker and cook on HIGH for 4 hours. Meanwhile, chop the lettuce roughly. Slice the tomatoes. Place the sliced tomatoes in the tortillas and add the chopped lettuce and shredded Parmesan. When the ground pork is cooked, chill to room temperature. Add the ground pork in the tortillas and wrap them.

Nutrition: calories 318, fat 7, fiber 2, carbs 3.76, protein 26

Butternut Squash Soup

Prep time: 10 minutes | Cooking time: 8 hours | Servings: 9

Ingredients:

- 2-pound butternut squash
- 4 teaspoon minced garlic
- ½ cup onion, chopped
- 1 teaspoon salt
- ¼ teaspoon ground nutmeg
- 1 teaspoon ground black pepper
- 8 cups chicken stock
- 1 tablespoon fresh parsley

Directions:

Peel the butternut squash and cut it into the chunks. Toss the butternut squash in the slow cooker. Add chopped onion, minced garlic, and chicken stock. Close the slow cooker lid and cook the soup for 8 hours on LOW. Meanwhile, combine the ground black pepper, ground nutmeg, and salt together. Chop the fresh parsley. When the time is done, remove the soup from the slow cooker and blend it with a blender until you get a creamy soup. Sprinkle the soup with the spice mixture and add chopped parsley. Serve the soup warm.

Nutrition: calories 129, fat 2.7, fiber 2, carbs 20.85, protein 7

Eggplant Bacon Wraps

Prep time: 17 minutes | Cooking time: 5 hours | Servings: 6

Ingredients:

- 10 oz. eggplant, sliced into rounds
- 5 oz. halloumi cheese
- 1 teaspoon minced garlic
- 3 oz. bacon, chopped
- ½ teaspoon ground black pepper
- 1 teaspoon salt
- 1 teaspoon paprika
- 1 tomato

Directions:

Rub the eggplant slices with the ground black pepper, salt, and paprika. Slice halloumi cheese and tomato. Combine the chopped bacon and minced garlic together. Place the sliced eggplants in the slow cooker. Cook the eggplant on HIGH for 1 hour. Chill the eggplant. Place the sliced tomato and cheese on the eggplant slices. Add the chopped bacon mixture and roll up tightly. Secure the eggplants with the toothpicks and return the eggplant wraps back into the slow cooker. Cook the dish on HIGH for 4 hours more. When the dish is done, serve it immediately.

Nutrition: calories 131, fat 9.4, fiber 2, carbs 7.25, protein 6

Mexican Warm Salad

Prep time: 26 minutes | Cooking time: 10 hours | Servings: 10

Ingredients:

- 1 cup black beans
- 1 cup sweet corn, frozen
- 3 tomatoes
- ½ cup fresh dill
- 1 chili pepper
- 7 oz. chicken fillet
- 5 oz. Cheddar cheese
- 4 tablespoons mayonnaise
- 1 teaspoon minced garlic
- 1 cup lettuce
- 5 cups chicken stock
- 1 cucumber

Directions:

Put the chicken fillet, sweet corn, black beans, and chicken stock in the slow cooker. Close the slow cooker lid and cook the mixture on LOW for 10 hours. When the time is done remove the mixture from the slow cooker. Shred the chicken fillet with 2 forks. Chill the mixture until room temperature. Chop the lettuce roughly. Chop the cucumber and tomatoes. Place the lettuce, cucumber, and tomatoes on a large serving plate. After this, shred Cheddar cheese and chop the chili pepper. Add the chili pepper to the serving plate too. After this, add the chicken mixture on the top of the salad. Sprinkle the salad with the mayonnaise, minced garlic, and shredded cheese. Enjoy the salad immediately.

Nutrition: calories 182, fat 7.8, fiber 2, carbs 19.6, protein 9

Hot Chorizo Salad

Prep time: 20 minutes | Cooking time: 4 hours 30 minutes | Servings: 6

Ingredients:

- 8 oz. chorizo
- 1 teaspoon olive oil
- 1 teaspoon cayenne pepper
- 1 teaspoon chili flakes
- 1 teaspoon ground black pepper
- 1 teaspoon onion powder
- 2 garlic cloves
- 3 tomatoes
- 1 cup lettuce
- 1 cup fresh dill
- 1 teaspoon oregano
- 3 tablespoons crushed cashews

Directions:

Chop the chorizo sausages roughly and place them in the slow cooker. Cook the sausages for 4 hours on HIGH. Meanwhile, combine the cayenne pepper, chili flakes, ground black pepper, and onion powder together in a shallow bowl. Chop the tomatoes roughly and add them to the slow cooker after 4 hours. Cook the mixture for 30 minutes more on HIGH. Chop the fresh dill and combine it with oregano. When the chorizo sausage mixture is cooked, place it in a serving bowl. Tear the lettuce and add it in the bowl too. After this, peel the garlic cloves and slice them. Add the sliced garlic cloves in the salad bowl too. Then sprinkle the salad with the spice mixture, olive oil, fresh dill mixture, and crush cashew. Mix the salad carefully.

Nutrition: calories 249, fat 19.8, fiber 2, carbs 7.69, protein 11

Stuffed Eggplants

Prep time: 20 minutes | Cooking time: 8 hours | Servings: 4

Ingredients:

- 4 medium eggplants
- 1 cup rice, half cooked
- ½ cup chicken stock
- 1 teaspoon salt
- 1 teaspoon paprika
- ½ cup fresh cilantro
- 3 tablespoons tomato sauce
- 1 teaspoon olive oil

Directions:

Wash the eggplants carefully and remove the flesh from them. Then combine the rice with the salt, paprika, and tomato sauce. Chop the fresh cilantro and add it to the rice mixture. Then fill the prepared eggplants with the rice mixture. Pour the chicken stock and olive oil in the slow cooker. Add the stuffed eggplants and close the slow cooker lid. Cook the dish on LOW for 8 hours. When the eggplants are done, chill them little and serve immediately.

Nutrition: calories 277, fat 9.1, fiber 24, carbs 51.92, protein 11

Light Lunch Quiche

Prep time: 21 minutes | Cooking time: 4 hours 25 minutes | Servings: 7

Ingredients:

- 7 oz. pie crust
- ¼ cup broccoli
- 1/3 cup sweet peas
- ¼ cup heavy cream
- 2 tablespoons flour
- 3 eggs
- 4 oz. Romano cheese, shredded
- 1 teaspoon cilantro
- 1 teaspoon salt
- ¼ cup spinach
- 1 tomato

Directions:

Cover the inside of the slow cooker bowl with parchment. Put the pie crust inside and flatten it well with your fingertips. Chop the broccoli and combine it with sweet peas. Combine the heavy cream, flour, cilantro, and salt together. Stir the liquid until smooth. Then beat the eggs into the heavy cream liquid and mix it with a hand mixer. When you get a smooth mix, combine it with the broccoli. Chop the spinach and add it to the mix. Chop the tomato and add it to the mix too. Pour the prepared mixture into the pie crust slowly. Close the slow cooker lid and cook the quiche for 4 hours on HIGH. After 4 hours, sprinkle the quiche surface with the shredded cheese and cook the dish for 25 minutes more. Serve the prepared quiche!

Nutrition: calories 287, fat 18.8, fiber 1, carbs 17.1, protein 11

Chicken Open Sandwich

Prep time: 15 minutes | Cooking time: 8 hours | Servings: 4

Ingredients:

- 7 oz. chicken fillet
- 1 teaspoon cayenne pepper
- 5 oz. mashed potato, cooked
- 6 tablespoons chicken gravy
- 4 slices French bread, toasted
- 2 teaspoons mayo
- 1 cup water

Directions:

Put the chicken fillet in the slow cooker and sprinkle it with the cayenne pepper. Add water and chicken gravy. Close the slow cooker lid and cook the chicken for 8 hours on LOW. Then combine the mashed potato with the mayo sauce. Spread toasted French bread with the mashed potato mixture. When the chicken is cooked, cut it into the strips and combine with the remaining gravy from the slow cooker. Place the chicken strips over the mashed potato. Enjoy the open sandwich warm!

Nutrition: calories 314, fat 9.7, fiber 3, carbs 45.01, protein 12

Onion Lunch Muffins

Prep time: 15 minutes | Cooking time: 8 hours | Servings: 7

Ingredients:

- 1 egg
- 5 tablespoons butter, melted
- 1 cup flour
- ½ cup milk
- 1 teaspoon baking soda
- 1 cup onion, chopped
- 1 teaspoon cilantro
- ½ teaspoon sage
- 1 teaspoon apple cider vinegar
- 2 cup water
- 1 tablespoon chives
- 1 teaspoon olive oil

Directions:

Beat the egg in the bowl and add melted butter. Add the flour, baking soda, chopped onion, milk, sage, apple cider vinegar, cilantro, and chives. Knead into a dough. After this, spray a muffin form with the olive oil inside. Fill the ½ part of every muffin form and place them in the glass jars. After this, pour water in the slow cooker vessel. Place the glass jars with muffins in the slow cooker and close the lid. Cook the muffins for 8 hours on LOW. Check if the muffins are cooked with the help of the toothpick and remove them from the slow cooker. Enjoy the dish warm!

Nutrition: calories 180, fat 11, fiber 1, carbs 16.28, protein 4

Tuna in Potatoes

Prep time: 16 minutes | Cooking time: 4 hours | Servings: 8

Ingredients:

- 4 large potatoes
- 8 oz. tuna, canned
- ½ cup cream cheese
- 4 oz. Cheddar cheese
- 1 garlic clove
- 1 teaspoon onion powder
- ½ teaspoon salt
- 1 teaspoon ground black pepper
- 1 teaspoon dried dill

Directions:

Wash the potatoes carefully and cut them into the halves. Wrap the potatoes in the foil and place in the slow cooker. Close the slow cooker lid and cook the potatoes on HIGH for 2 hours. Meanwhile, peel the garlic clove and mince it. Combine the minced garlic clove with the cream cheese, tuna, salt, ground black pepper, onion powder, and dill. Then shred Cheddar cheese and add it to the mixture. Mix it carefully until homogenous. When the time is over – remove the potatoes from the slow cooker and discard the foil only from the flat surface of the potatoes. Then take the fork and mash the flesh of the potato halves gently. Add the tuna mixture in the potato halves and return them back in the slow cooker. Cook the potatoes for 2 hours more on HIGH.

Nutrition: calories 247, fat 5.9, fiber 4, carbs 35.31, protein 14

Banana Lunch Sandwiches

Prep time: 15 minutes | Cooking time: 2 hours | Servings: 4

Ingredients:

- 2 banana
- 8 oz. French toast slices, frozen
- 1 tablespoon peanut butter
- ¼ teaspoon ground cinnamon
- 5 oz. Cheddar cheese, sliced
- ¼ teaspoon turmeric

Directions:

Peel the bananas and slice them. Spread the French toast slices with the peanut butter well. Combine the ground cinnamon with the turmeric and stir the mixture. Sprinkle the French toasts with the spice mixture. Then make the layer of the sliced bananas on the toasts and add the sliced cheese. Cover the toast with the second part of the toast to make the sandwich. Place the banana sandwiches in the slow cooker and cook them on HIGH for 2 hours. Serve the prepared banana sandwiches hot.

Nutrition: calories 248, fat 7.5, fiber 2, carbs 36.74, protein 10

Parmesan Potato with Dill

Prep time: 17 minutes | Cooking time: 4 hours | Servings: 5

Ingredients:

- 1-pound small potato
- ½ cup fresh dill
- 7 oz. Parmesan
- 1 teaspoon rosemary
- 1 teaspoon thyme
- 1 cup water
- ¼ teaspoon chili flakes
- 3 tablespoon cream
- 1 teaspoon salt

Directions:

Peel the potatoes and put them in the slow cooker. Add water, salt, thyme, rosemary, and chili flakes. Close the slow cooker lid and cook the potato for 2 hours on HIGH. Meanwhile, shred Parmesan cheese and chop the fresh dill. When the time is done, sprinkle the potato with the cream and fresh dill. Stir it carefully. Add shredded Parmesan cheese and close the slow cooker lid. Cook the potato on HIGH for 2 hours more. Then open the slow cooker lid and do not stir the potato anymore. Gently transfer the dish to the serving plates.

Nutrition: calories 235, fat 3.9, fiber 2, carbs 32.26, protein 1

Light Taco Soup

Prep time: 24 minutes | Cooking time: 7 hours | Servings: 5

Ingredients:

- 7 oz ground chicken
- ½ teaspoon sesame oil
- 3 cup vegetable stock
- 3 oz. yellow onion
- 1 cup tomato, canned
- 3 tomatoes
- 5 oz. corn kernels
- 1 jalapeno pepper, sliced
- ½ cup white beans, drained
- 3 tablespoon taco seasoning
- ¼ teaspoon salt
- 3 oz. black olives, sliced
- 5 corn tortillas, for serving

Directions:

Peel the onion and dice it. Chop the fresh and canned tomatoes. Place the ground chicken, sesame oil, vegetable stock, diced onion, chopped tomatoes, sliced black olives, sliced jalapeno pepper, and corn in the slow cooker. Add the white beans, taco seasoning, and salt. Stir the soup mixture gently and close the slow cooker lid. Cook the soup for 7 hours on LOW. Meanwhile, cut the corn tortillas into the strips and bake them in the preheated to 365 F oven for 10 minutes. When the soup is cooked, ladle it into the serving bowls and sprinkle with the baked corn tortilla strips.

Nutrition: calories 328, fat 9.6, fiber 10, carbs 45.19, protein 18

Slow Cooker Risotto

Prep time: 20 minutes | Cooking time: 3 hours 30 minutes | Servings: 6

Ingredients:

- 7 oz. Parmigiano-Reggiano
- 2 cup chicken broth
- 1 teaspoon olive oil
- 1 onion, chopped
- ½ cup green peas
- 1 garlic clove, peeled and sliced
- 2 cups long grain rice
- ¼ cup dry wine
- 1 teaspoon salt
- 1 teaspoon ground black pepper
- 1 carrot, chopped
- 1 cup beef broth

Directions:

Spray a skillet with olive oil. Add the chopped onion and carrot and roast the vegetables for 3 minutes on the medium heat. Then put the seared vegetables in the slow cooker. Toss the long grain rice in the remaining oil and saute for 1 minute on the high heat. Add the roasted long grain rice and sliced garlic in the slow cooker. Add green peas, dry wine, salt, ground black pepper, and beef broth. After this, add the chicken broth and stir the mixture gently. Close the slow cooker lid and cook the risotto for 3 hours. Then stir the risotto gently. Shred Parmigiano-Reggiano and sprinkle over the risotto. Close the slow cooker lid and cook the dish for 30 minutes more. Enjoy the prepared risotto immediately!

Nutrition: calories 268, fat 3, fiber 4, carbs 53.34, protein 7

Lemon Orzo

Prep time: 20 minutes | Cooking time: 2 hours 30 minutes | Servings: 5

Ingredients:

- 4 oz. shallot
- 7 oz. orzo
- 2 cup chicken stock
- 1 teaspoon paprika
- 1 teaspoon ground black pepper
- 1 teaspoon salt
- 1 lemon
- ¼ cup cream
- 2 yellow sweet pepper
- 1 cup baby spinach

Directions:

Chop the shallot and place it in the slow cooker. Add the chicken stock and paprika. Sprinkle the mixture with the ground black pepper and salt. Stir it gently and cook on HIGH for 30 minutes. Meanwhile, grate the zest from the lemon and squeeze the juice. Add the lemon zest and juice in the slow cooker and stir it. After this, chop the baby spinach. Add it into the slow cooker. Remove the seeds from the yellow sweet peppers and chop into tiny pieces. Add the chopped peppers to the slow cooker. Add orzo and heavy cream. Stir the mass carefully and close the slow cooker lid. Cook the dish for 2 hours on LOW. Mix the dish gently.

Nutrition: calories 152, fat 4, fiber 3, carbs 24.79, protein 7

Veggie Bean Stew

Prep time: 20 minutes | Cooking time: 7 hours | Servings: 8

Ingredients:

- ½ cup barley
- 1 cup black beans
- ¼ cup red beans
- 2 carrots
- 1 cup onion, chopped
- 1 cup tomato juice
- 2 potatoes
- 1 teaspoon salt
- 1 teaspoon ground black pepper
- 4 cups water
- 4 oz. tofu
- 1 teaspoon garlic powder
- 1 cup fresh cilantro

Directions:

Place barley, black beans, and red beans in the slow cooker vessel. Add chopped onion, tomato juice, salt, ground black pepper, and garlic powder. After this, add water and close the slow cooker lid. Cook the dish for 4 hours on HIGH. Meanwhile, peel the carrots and cut them into the strips. Peel the potatoes and chop. Add the carrot strips and chopped potatoes in the slow cooker after 4 hours of cooking. Chop the fresh cilantro and add it in the slow cooker too. Stir the mix and close the slow cooker lid. Cook the stew for 3 hours more on LOW. Serve the prepared dish immediately or keep it in the fridge, not more than 3 days.

Nutrition: calories 207, fat 3.5, fiber 8, carbs 37.67, protein 8

Carrot Soup with Cardamom

Prep time: 18 minutes | Cooking time: 12 hours | Servings: 9

Ingredients:

- 1-pound carrot
- 1 teaspoon ground cardamom
- ¼ teaspoon nutmeg
- 1 teaspoon salt
- 3 tablespoons fresh parsley
- 1 teaspoon honey
- 1 teaspoon marjoram
- 5 cups chicken stock
- ½ cup yellow onion, chopped
- 1 teaspoon butter

Directions:

Toss the butter in a pan and add chopped onion. Chop the carrot and add it to the pan too. Roast the vegetables for 5 minutes on the low heat. After this, place the roasted vegetables in the slow cooker. Add ground cardamom, nutmeg, salt, marjoram, and chicken stock. Close the slow cooker lid and cook the soup for 12 hours on LOW. Chop the fresh parsley. When the time is over, blend the soup with a hand blender until you get a smooth texture. Then ladle the soup into the serving bowls. Sprinkle the prepared soup with the chopped fresh parsley and honey. Enjoy the soup immediately!

Nutrition: calories 80, fat 2.7, fiber 2, carbs 10.19, protein 4

Cod Chowder

Prep time: 20 minutes | Cooking time: 3 hours | Servings: 6

Ingredients:

- 1 yellow onion
- 10 oz. cod
- 3 oz. bacon, sliced
- 1 teaspoon sage
- 5 oz. potatoes
- 1 carrot, grated
- 5 cups water
- 1 tablespoon almond milk
- 1 teaspoon ground coriander
- 1 teaspoon salt

Directions:

Peel the onion and chop it. Put the chopped onion and grated carrot in the slow cooker bowl. Add the sage, almond milk, ground coriander, and water. After this, chop the cod into the 6 pieces. Add the fish in the slow cooker bowl too. Then chop the sliced bacon and peel the potatoes. Cut the potatoes into the cubes. Add the ingredients in the slow cooker bowl and close the slow cooker lid. Cook the chowder for 3 hours on HIGH. Ladle the prepared cod chowder in the serving bowls. Sprinkle the dish with the chopped parsley if desired.

Nutrition: calories 108, fat 4.5, fiber 2, carbs 8.02, protein 10

Sweet Corn Pilaf

Prep time: 21 minutes | Cooking time: 8 hours | Servings: 5

Ingredients:

- 2 cups rice
- 1 cup sweet corn, frozen
- 6 oz. chicken fillet
- 1 sweet red pepper
- 1 yellow sweet pepper
- ½ cup green peas, frozen
- 1 carrot
- 4 cups chicken stock
- 2 tablespoon chopped almonds
- 1 teaspoon olive oil
- 1 teaspoon salt
- 1 teaspoon ground white pepper

Directions:

Peel the carrot and cut into the small cubes. Combine the carrot cubes with the frozen sweet corn and green peas. After this, place the vegetable mixture in the slow cooker vessel. Add the rice, chicken stock, olive oil, salt, and ground white pepper. After this, cut the chicken fillet into the strips and add the meat to the rice mixture. Chop all the sweet peppers and add them in the slow cooker too. Close the slow cooker lid and cook the pilaf for 8 hours on LOW. When the pilaf is cooked, stir it gently and sprinkle with the almonds. Mix the dish carefully again. Serve it immediately.

Nutrition: calories 390, fat 18.6, fiber 13, carbs 54.7, protein 18

Zucchini Lasagna

Prep time: 26 minutes | Cooking time: 5 hours | Servings: 7

Ingredients:

- 1-pound green zucchini
- 7 tablespoons tomato sauce
- ½ cup fresh parsley
- 1 tablespoon fresh dill
- 1 tablespoon minced garlic
- 7 oz. Parmesan
- 1 onion, chopped
- 4 tablespoons ricotta cheese
- 5 oz. mozzarella
- 2 eggs
- ½ cup baby spinach
- 1 teaspoon olive oil

Directions:

Slice the zucchini. Spray the slow cooker vessel with the olive oil and make a layer of the zucchini slices using 2 or 3 slices. Then combine the tomato sauce, fresh dill, minced garlic, onion, ricotta cheese. Chop the spinach and fresh parsley and add the greens to the mixture. Then shred Cheddar cheese and add in the tomato sauce mixture. Beat the egg in a separate bowl then combine the tomato sauce mixture and whisked egg together and stir. Spread the zucchini layer with the tomato sauce mixture and cover it with the second layer of the zucchini slices. Alternate sauce and zucchini until you are out of both. Spread the last zucchini layer generously and close the slow cooker lid. Cook the dish for 5 hours on HIGH. When the lasagna is cooked , enjoy warm.

Nutrition: calories 233, fat 6.4, fiber 3, carbs 20.74, protein 23

Mediterranean Vegetable Mix

Prep time: 15 minutes | Cooking time: 7 hours | Servings: 8

Ingredients:

- 1 zucchini
- 2 eggplants
- 2 red onion
- 4 potatoes
- 4 oz. asparagus
- 2 tablespoon olive oil
- 1 teaspoon ground black pepper
- 1 teaspoon paprika
- 1 teaspoon salt
- 1 tablespoon Mediterranean seasoning
- 1 teaspoon minced garlic

Directions:

Combine the olive oil, Mediterranean seasoning, salt, paprika, ground black pepper, and minced garlic together. Whisk the mixture well. Wash all the vegetables carefully. Cut the zucchini, eggplants, and potatoes into the medium cubes. Cut the asparagus into 2 parts. Then peel the onions and cut them into 4 parts. Toss all the vegetables in the slow cooker and sprinkle them with the spice mixture. Close the slow cooker lid and cook the vegetable mix for 7 hours on LOW. Serve the prepared vegetable mix hot.

Nutrition: calories 227, fat 3.9, fiber 9, carbs 44.88, protein 6

Spaghetti Cottage Cheese Casserole

Prep time: 21 minutes | Cooking time: 7 hours | Servings: 8

Ingredients:

- 1-pound cottage cheese
- 7 oz. spaghetti, cooked
- 5 eggs
- 1 cup heavy cream
- 5 tablespoons semolina
- 3 tablespoons white sugar
- 1 teaspoon vanilla extract
- 1 teaspoon marjoram
- 1 teaspoon lemon zest
- 1 teaspoon butter

Directions:

Blend the cottage cheese in the blender for 1 minute to fluff. Beat the eggs in the cottage mixture and continue to blend it for 3 minutes more on medium speed. Add the heavy cream, semolina, white sugar, vanilla extract, marjoram, lemon zest, and butter. Blend the mixture on the maximum speed for 1 minute. Then chopped the cooked spaghetti. Place 3 tablespoon of the cottage cheese mixture in the slow cooker to make the bottom layer. After this, make a layer from the chopped cooked spaghetti. Repeat the steps till you use all the chopped spaghetti. Then spread the last layer of the spaghetti with the cottage cheese mixture and close the slow cooker lid. Cook the casserole for 7 hours on LOW. When the casserole is cooked, it will have a light brown color. Serve it warm and

Nutrition: calories 242, fat 13.8, fiber 1, carbs 17.44, protein 12

Meatballs with Coconut Gravy

Prep time: 20 minutes | Cooking time: 7 hours | Servings: 8

Ingredients:

- 3 tablespoons coconut
- 1 tablespoon curry paste
- 1 teaspoon salt
- 1 cup heavy cream
- 1 tablespoon flour
- 1 teaspoon cayenne pepper
- 10 oz. ground pork
- 1 egg
- 1 tablespoon semolina
- ½ cup onion, chopped
- 1 teaspoon kosher salt
- 3 tablespoons bread crumbs
- 1 teaspoon ground black pepper

Directions:

Combine the coconut, curry paste, and salt together. Add heavy cream and flour. Whisk the mixture and pour in the slow cooker. Cook on the LOW for 1 hour. Meanwhile, beat the egg in the big bowl and whisk. Add the cayenne pepper, ground pork, semolina, chopped onion, kosher salt, bread crumbs, and ground black pepper. Mix well and then make the small balls from the meat mixture and place them in the slow cooker. Coat the meatballs with the prepared coconut gravy and close the lid. Cook the dish for 7 hours on LOW. When the meatballs are cooked, serve them only with the coconut gravy.

Nutrition: calories 197, fat 10.1, fiber 1, carbs 12.56, protein 14

Fresh Dal

Prep time: 15 minutes | Cooking time: 5 hours | Servings: 11

Ingredients:

- 1 teaspoon cumin
- 1 oz. mustard seeds
- 10 oz. lentils
- 1 teaspoon fennel seeds
- 7 cups water
- 6 oz. tomato, canned
- 4 oz. onion
- ½ teaspoon fresh ginger, grated
- 1 oz. bay leaf
- 1 teaspoon turmeric
- 1 teaspoon salt
- 2 cups rice

Directions:

Peel the onion. Chop the onion and tomatoes and place them in a slow cooker. Combine the cumin, mustard seeds, and fennel seeds in a shallow bowl. Add the bay leaf and mix. Sprinkle the vegetables in the slow cooker with the spice mixture. Add salt, turmeric, and grated fresh ginger. Add rice and mix. Add the lentils and water. Stir gently. Then close the slow cooker lid and cook Dal for 5 hours on LOW. When the dish is done, stir and transfer to serving plates.

Nutrition: calories 124, fat 5.9, fiber 6, carbs 20.68, protein 6

Side Dishes

Parsley Cauliflower Rice

Prep time: 15 minutes | Cooking time: 4 hours | Servings: 6

Ingredients:

- 2-pounds cauliflower
- 1 cup parsley
- 1 teaspoon salt
- 1 teaspoon cilantro
- ¼ teaspoon red pepper
- 4 cups chicken stock
- ½ teaspoon cumin
- 1 onion
- 1 carrot

Directions:

Wash the cauliflower carefully and separate into the florets. Put the cauliflower florets in the slow cooker. Sprinkle with the salt, cilantro, red pepper, and cumin. Peel the onion and carrot. Grate the carrot and onion and add them in the slow cooker vessel too. After this, add chicken stock and mix gently. Close the slow cooker lid and cook the dish for 2.5 hours on HIGH. After this, take the spatula and mash the vegetable mixture carefully till you get a rice-like consistency. Then chop the parsley and add it to the cauliflower rice mixture. Close the slow cooker lid and cook the dish for 1.5 hours more. When the dish is cooked, mix it well then serve.

Nutrition: calories 111, fat 2.5, fiber 4, carbs 16.57, protein 8

Butter Couscous

Prep time: 10 minutes | Cooking time: 8 hours | Servings: 7

Ingredients:

- 1 teaspoon cilantro
- 1 tablespoon sesame seeds
- ½ teaspoon ground coriander
- ¼ teaspoon ground ginger
- 1 teaspoon salt
- 3 tablespoon butter
- 6 cups beef broth
- 5 cups couscous
- 1 tablespoon dried dill
- 1 teaspoon oregano

Directions:

Combine the cilantro, sesame seeds, ground coriander, ground ginger, salt, dried dill, and oregano together in the shallow bowl. Mix gently. After this, combine the spice mixture with the couscous and stir. Place the couscous in the slow cooker and add the beef broth. Close the slow cooker and cook the dish on LOW for 8 hours. When the couscous is cooked, it will absorb all the liquid. Add the butter and mix it very well. Serve the side dish immediately.

Nutrition: calories 194, fat 6.4, fiber 2, carbs 26.93, protein 7

Butternut Squash Noodles

Prep time: 15 minutes | Cooking time: 8 hours | Servings: 9

Ingredients:

- 1-pound butternut squash
- 10 oz. pasta
- 1 cup cream
- 3 cups water
- 1 tablespoon butter
- 1 teaspoon salt
- 1 teaspoon oregano
- ½ tablespoon parsley
- 1 teaspoon cilantro
- 1 garlic clove
- 1 teaspoon onion powder

Directions:

Put the butternut squash in the microwave oven and cook for 1 minute. Then peel the butternut squash and cut it into width-wise strips. Put the prepared butternut squash in the slow cooker. Add water, salt, oregano, cilantro, parsley, and onion powder. Peel the garlic clove and minced it. Add the minced garlic clove in the slow cooker too. After this, add water and close the slow cooker lid. Cook the butternut squash strips for 7 hours on LOW until the butternut squash is soft. Then add the pasta and cream. Cook the dish for 1 hour on HIGH. Mix up the dish carefully and strain the excess liquid. Serve the side dish.

Nutrition: calories 127, fat 6.7, fiber 3, carbs 16.07, protein 2

Slow Cooker Tomatoes

Prep time: 10 minutes | Cooking time: 2 hours | Servings: 4

Ingredients:

- 1-pound tomatoes
- ½ teaspoon salt
- ½ teaspoon oregano
- 1 teaspoon rosemary
- 2 teaspoons olive oil
- 4 garlic clove
- 1 teaspoon apple cider vinegar

Directions:

Wash the tomatoes and slice them roughly. Line the slow cooker bowl with the parchment and place the sliced tomatoes there. Combine the salt, oregano, rosemary, olive oil, and apple cider vinegar together. Whisk the mixture. After this, peel the garlic cloves and smash them. Sprinkle the tomato slices with the spice mixture and with the smashed garlic and close the slow cooker lid. Cook the tomatoes for 2 hours in HIGH. Chill well then serve.

Nutrition: calories 44, fat 2.5, fiber 1, carbs 4.87, protein 2

Red Beans

Prep time: 16 minutes | Cooking time: 9 hours | Servings: 5

Ingredients:

- 1 cup red beans
- 4 cups water
- 1 white onion
- ½ cup tomato paste
- 1 tablespoon sugar
- 1 teaspoon salt
- 1 teaspoon ground black pepper
- 2 carrots
- 1 peach
- ¼ teaspoon ground ginger
- 2 teaspoon butter

Directions:

Put the red beans in the slow cooker and pour the water on top. Close the lid and cook the beans for 7 hours on LOW. Meanwhile, peel the onion and carrots. Slice the onion and grate the carrot. Combine the tomato paste, sugar, salt, ground black pepper, and ground ginger in the mixing bowl. Whisk it gently. When the time is done, add the sliced onion and grated carrot into the beans. Add the tomato paste mixture and mix it with the help of the wooden spatula. Cook the side dish for 2 hours on HIGH. When the dish is cooked, add the butter and mix it well.

Nutrition: calories 188, fat 2.2, fiber 8, carbs 34.46, protein 10

Quinoa Stuffed Bell Peppers

Prep time: 12 minutes | Cooking time: 3 hours | Servings: 6

Ingredients:

- ½ cup quinoa, cooked
- 6 bell peppers
- ½ teaspoon minced garlic
- ¼ teaspoon red pepper
- ¼ teaspoon ground black pepper
- ½ onion, chopped
- ¼ teaspoon olive oil
- 1 oz. bay leaf
- 4 oz. Cheddar cheese

Directions:

Cut the bell peppers crosswise and remove the seeds. After this, combine the quinoa, minced garlic, red pepper, ground black pepper, and chopped onion together. Mix and fill the bell peppers with the prepared quinoa blend. After this, shred Cheddar cheese and sprinkle the prepared stuffed peppers with the shredded cheese. Put the bay leaf in the slow cooker and add the olive oil. Put the prepared bell peppers in the slow cooker and close the lid. Cook the side dish for 3 hours on HIGH. When the bell peppers are cooked – serve them immediately.

Nutrition: calories 126, fat 3.3, fiber 3, carbs 20.05, protein 6

Lentil Chili

Prep time: 10 minutes | Cooking time: 7 hour | Servings: 8

Ingredients:

- 1 teaspoon garlic clove
- 3 oz. white onion, chopped
- 1 chili pepper
- 4 oz. sweet red pepper
- 5 oz. carrot
- 1 cup diced tomatoes
- 1 teaspoon salt
- 1 teaspoon ground black pepper
- 14 oz. lentil
- 5 cups chicken stock
- 5 tablespoons tomato sauce
- 1 teaspoon chili flakes

Directions:

Put the diced tomatoes, chopped onion, garlic, salt, ground black pepper, lentils, chicken stock, tomato sauce, and chili flakes in the slow cooker bowl. Peel the carrot and discard the seeds from the sweet red pepper. Chop the sweet red pepper and chili pepper. Cut the carrot into strips. After this, add the vegetables in the slow cooker. Mix and close the slow cooker lid. Cook the lentil chili for 7 hours on LOW. When the lentil chili is cooked, let cool slightly. Serve the dish warm!

Nutrition: calories 152, fat 2.9, fiber 3, carbs 25, protein 9

Side Dish Jambalaya

Prep time: 8 hours | Cooking time: 5 hours | Servings: 6

Ingredients:

- 1 cup tomatoes, diced
- 1 cup yellow onion, chopped
- 1 sweet green pepper
- 6 oz. celery, chopped
- 1 cup beef broth
- 1 tablespoon dried dill
- 1 teaspoon oregano
- ½ teaspoon thyme
- 1 oz. Cajun seasoning
- 1 chili pepper
- 1 teaspoon onion powder
- 1 teaspoon salt

Directions:

Put the chopped onion in the slow cooker bowl. Add diced onion, chopped celery, dried dill, beef broth, oregano, thyme, Cajun seasoning, onion powder, and salt. Chop the chili pepper and add it to the slow cooker bowl. Mix gently. Close the slow cooker lid and cook the dish for 5 hours on LOW. When the dish is cooked, cool slightly. Serve the side dish with the seafood.

Nutrition: calories 55, fat 2, fiber 2, carbs 8, protein 2

Dumplings

Prep time: 20 minutes | Cooking time: 6 hours | Servings: 6

Ingredients:

- ¼ teaspoon baking powder
- 1 teaspoon apple cider vinegar
- 1 cup flour
- ¼ cup Greek Yogurt
- 3 tablespoons heavy cream
- 1 teaspoon salt
- 1 egg
- ¼ cup water
- 2 teaspoons butter
- 1 teaspoon milk

Directions:

Beat the egg in the bowl and add baking powder and heavy cream. After this, add Greek yogurt and sifted flour. Then add salt, water, and apple cider vinegar. Knead the dough until soft. Cut the dough into medium pieces and make small logs. Pour milk and add butter in the slow cooker. Preheat the butter on HIGH for 10 minutes. After this, add the prepared dough logs in the slow cooker and close the lid. Cook the dish for 6 hours on LOW. When the dumplings are cooked, mix them gently and serve the dish hot.

Nutrition: calories 139, fat 8, fiber 1, carbs 19, protein 4

Mashed Potato with Garlic
Prep time: 15 minutes | Cooking time: 6 hours | Servings: 14

Ingredients:

- 3-pound potato
- 5 cup water
- 1 teaspoon salt
- 1 teaspoon onion powder
- 4 garlic cloves
- ½ cup milk, hot
- 3 tablespoon butter
- 1 egg
- 2 tablespoon cream cheese

Directions:

Peel the potato and chop it roughly. Put the chopped potato in the slow cooker. Add salt, onion powder, and water. Close the slow cooker lid and cook the potato on HIGH for 6 hours. Meanwhile, peel the garlic cloves and mince them. Combine the minced garlic with the cream cheese and whisk together. When the time is done and the potato is soft, strain it. Transfer the potato to the big bowl and add butter and cream cheese mixture. Blend it carefully with the help of the hand blender. Crack the egg into the mixture and continue to blend it for 1 minute more. Serve the mashed potato hot.

Nutrition: calories 119, fat 4.2, fiber 2, carbs 18, protein 3

Broccoli Hash
Prep time: 20 minutes | Cooking time: 4 hours | Servings: 6

Ingredients:

- 1-pound broccoli
- 5 oz. potato, frozen, chopped
- 7 oz. Cheddar cheese
- 1 yellow onion, diced
- 1 tablespoon chives
- 5 oz. milk
- 1 teaspoon butter
- 1 can onion soup
- 1 teaspoon salt
- 1 teaspoon ground black pepper

Directions:

Cut the broccoli into the florets and then chop the florets. Place the chopped broccoli in the slow cooker. Add the chopped frozen potato and chives. Add the diced onion in the slow cooker along with the chives, milk, can of the onion soup, salt, and ground black pepper. Mix the mass gently with a spatula and close the slow cooker lid. Cook the dish on HIGH for 4 hours. Open the slow cooker lid and smash with a spatula to get a hash like texture. Add butter and stir. Serve the cauliflower hash immediately.

Nutrition: calories 167, fat 6.9, fiber 3, carbs 18.54, protein 10

Aromatic White Rice
Prep time: 10 minutes | Cooking time: 3 hours | Servings: 6

Ingredients:

- 4 cup white rice
- 3 tablespoons butter
- 1 tablespoon salt
- 4 cups water
- 1 teaspoon almond milk
- ¼ teaspoon dried dill

Directions:

Toss the butter in the slow cooker and melt. After this, add the white rice and dried dill and mix. Add the water, salt, and almond milk and close the slow cooker lid. Cook the dish on HIGH for 3 hours. After this, open the slow cooker lid and see if the rice absorbed all the liquid. Cook the side dish for 30 minutes more if desired. Mix the rice gently and serve it.

Nutrition: calories 508, fat 6.5, fiber 4, carbs 100.87, protein 8

Cheesy Brussels Sprouts

Prep time: 10 minutes | Cooking time: 5 hours | Servings: 8

Ingredients:

- 15 oz. Brussel sprouts
- 5 oz. Romano cheese, shredded
- 1 tablespoon balsamic vinegar
- 1 teaspoon sesame oil
- 1 teaspoon ground black pepper
- ¼ teaspoon salt

Directions:

Wash Brussels sprouts carefully and put them in the slow cooker. Sprinkle the vegetables with the balsamic vinegar and sesame oil. After this, add the ground black pepper and salt. Stir the vegetables and close the slow cooker lid. Cook the dish for 4.5 hours on HIGH. When the time is over, open the slow cooker lid and sprinkle tender Brussels Sprouts with the shredded cheese. Close the slow cooker lid and cook the dish for 30 minutes on LOW or until the cheese is melted. Serve the dish immediately or bake it in the oven for 10 minutes more to get the crunchy surface.

Nutrition: calories 100, fat 5.5, fiber 2, carbs 6, protein 8

Fragrant Garlic Cloves

Prep time: 10 minutes | Cooking time: 3 hours | Servings: 4

Ingredients:

- 1-pound garlic cloves, peeled and sliced
- 3 tablespoon olive oil
- 1 teaspoon dried parsley
- ½ teaspoon dried dill
- ¼ teaspoon sugar

Directions:

Line the slow cooker with the foil inside the bowl. Place the sliced garlic cloves in the slow cooker then combine the olive oil, dried parsley, dried dill, and sugar together. Stir the mixture gently. Sprinkle the sliced garlic with the olive oil mixture generously. Close the slow cooker lid and cook the dish on LOW for 3 hours. When the dish is cooked, the garlic will have a tender texture and fragrant aroma. Serve the prepared side dish immediately.

Nutrition: calories 260, fat 10.7, fiber 3, carbs 37.81, protein 7

Turmeric Chickpea

Prep time: 16 minutes | Cooking time: 5 hour | Servings: 6

Ingredients:

- 3 cups chickpea
- 2 tablespoons turmeric
- 1 teaspoon olive oil
- 1 teaspoon salt
- ½ teaspoon coconut oil
- 2 oz. minced garlic
- 4 cups chicken stock
- 1 tablespoon dried basil
- 1 teaspoon oregano
- 1 teaspoon cilantro
- ½ cup spinach, chopped
- 2 tablespoons cream

Directions:

Toss the olive oil and coconut oil in the slow cooker. Add the chickpea and mix. Close the slow cooker lid and cook the dish on HIGH for 1 hour. After this, add the turmeric, salt, minced garlic, chicken stock, dried dill, oregano, and cilantro. Mix it gently and cook the chickpea for 4 hours on HIGH. When the time is done, add the spinach to the slow cooker and mix it. Cook the dish for 1 hour more on HIGH. Stir it gently and add the cream. Serve the turmeric chickpeas immediately.

Nutrition: calories 480, fat 10.2, fiber 13, carbs 74, protein 26

Creamed corn

Prep time: 7 minutes | Cooking time: 4 hours | Servings: 7

Ingredients:
- 10 oz. cream cheese
- 5 oz. butter
- 1-pound sweet corn
- ½ teaspoon salt
- ¼ teaspoon ground cardamom
- 5 oz. milk
- 1 tablespoon green onion, chopped
- 1 teaspoon oregano

Directions:

Place the sweet corn in the slow cooker. Add the salt, ground cardamom, and oregano. After this, pour milk and add the cream cheese and butter. Close the slow cooker lid and cook the dish on HIGH for 4 hours. When the dish is cooked, sprinkle it with the chopped green onions. Stir it gently and serve immediately.

Nutrition: calories 325, fat 29, fiber 1, carbs 14.34, protein 5

Tomato Cabbage Petals

Prep time: 10 minutes | Cooking time: 5 hours | Servings: 11

Ingredients:
- 1 cup tomato juice
- 3 tablespoons sour cream
- 1 cup onion, chopped
- 16 oz. cabbage
- 1 tablespoon salt
- 1 teaspoon sugar
- ½ teaspoon dill
- 1 teaspoon chili pepper

Directions:

Cut the cabbage into the medium petals and place them in the slow cooker. Add the chopped onion, sour cream, and tomato juice. After this, sprinkle the dish with the salt, sugar, dill, and chili pepper. Mix well and close the lid. Cook the cabbage petals on LOW for 5 hours. When the dish is cooked – the cabbage will be very soft. Let the dish chill little and serve it.

Nutrition: calories 26, fat 0.5, fiber 2, carbs 5.31, protein 1

Barbecue Beans

Prep time: 10 minutes | Cooking time: 3.5 hours | Servings: 5

Ingredients:
- 8 oz. bacon
- 3 cups black beans, canned
- 6 oz. ketchup
- 3 tablespoons molasses
- 4 tablespoons brown sugar
- 1 teaspoon mustard
- 1 teaspoon vinegar
- 1 cup water
- 1 onion

Directions:

Chop the bacon then peel and dice the onion. Place the prepared ingredients in the skillet and roast them on the high heat for 1 minute. Stir frequently. Place the black beans and roasted mixture in the skillet. Add the molasses, brown sugar, mustard, vinegar, and water in the slow cooker vessel. Mix gently then add ketchup. Close the slow cooker lid and cook the dish for 3.5 hours on HIGH. When barbecue beans are cooked – stir it carefully and serve immediately.

Nutrition: calories 297, fat 14.5, fiber 7, carbs 37.06, protein 9

Slow Cooker Spinach with Nuts

Prep time: 11 minutes | Cooking time: 2 hours | Servings: 5

Ingredients:

- 6 oz. cream cheese
- 3 cups spinach
- 1 tablespoon sliced
- ¼ cup walnuts

- 1 tablespoon butter
- 4 tablespoon water
- 1 teaspoon salt
- ¼ teaspoon ground white pepper

Directions:

Wash the spinach and chop it. Toss the chopped spinach in the slow cooker and add sliced almonds. Crush the walnuts and add them to the spinach mixture too. Add butter and cream cheese. After this, pour water, sprinkle the mixture with the salt, and ground white pepper. Mix and close the slow cooker lid. Cook the dish on HIGH for 2 hours. When the spinach becomes tender it is cooked! Mix it up and serve immediately.

Nutrition: calories 153, fat 14.8, fiber 1, carbs 2.66, protein 4

Cheese Mushrooms

Prep time: 20 minutes | Cooking time: 8 hours | Servings: 9

Ingredients:

- 18 oz mushrooms
- 1 tablespoon salt
- 6 oz cream cheese
- 5 oz Cheddar cheese, shredded

- ½ cup parsley
- 1 teaspoon butter
- 1 teaspoon thyme
- ½ teaspoon cilantro

Directions:

Toss the butter in the slow cooker and melt it. Sprinkle the melted butter with the thyme and cilantro. After this, chop the parsley and add it to the slow cooker. Stir carefully. Add the cream cheese. Slice the mushrooms and toss them in the slow cooker. Sprinkle the mushrooms with salt and close the slow cooker lid. Cook the dish for 8 hours on LOW. When the dish is cooked, sprinkle it with the shredded cheese and let sit to melt the cheese. Serve and

Nutrition: calories 256, fat 7.8, fiber 7, carbs 45.32, protein 9

Spicy Marinated Sweet Peppers

Prep time: 13 minutes | Cooking time: 6 hours | Servings: 7

Ingredients:

- 3 garlic cloves
- 1-pound sweet pepper
- 1 tablespoon balsamic vinegar
- 3 tablespoons olive oil

- 1/3 cup water
- 1 teaspoon salt
- 1 teaspoon sugar
- ½ teaspoon dried dill

Directions:

Peel the garlic cloves and slice them. Cut the sweet peppers into strips. Place the sweet pepper strips in the slow cooker and add the sliced garlic cloves. Sprinkle the vegetables with the balsamic vinegar, olive oil, water, salt, sugar, and dried dill. Close the slow cooker lid and cook the dish for 6 hours on LOW. When the time is up, chill the peppers well and keep them in the glass jar with the closed lid.

Nutrition: calories 74, fat 6, fiber 1, carbs 5.35, protein 1

Paprika Carrot with Sesame Seeds

Prep time: 16 minutes | Cooking time: 4 hours | Servings: 6

Ingredients:

- 2 tablespoons paprika
- 1 bell pepper
- 14 oz. baby carrot
- 1 teaspoon cilantro
- 2 tablespoons sesame seeds
- 1 tablespoon olive oil
- 1/3 cup water
- 3 tablespoons sugar
- 1 tablespoon cream cheese
- 1 tablespoon butter

Directions:

Wash the baby carrots well and place in the slow cooker. Add cilantro, sesame seeds, olive oil, water, sugar, cream cheese, and butter. Slice the bell pepper and add in the slow cooker too. Add paprika and close the lid. Cook the dish for 4 hours on HIGH. When the baby carrots are cooked, open the slow cooker lid and mix the dish gently. Serve hot!

Nutrition: calories 109, fat 6.9, fiber 3, carbs 11.77, protein 2

Almond Milk Asparagus

Prep time: 12 minutes | Cooking time: 9 hours | Servings: 8

Ingredients:

- 16 oz. asparagus
- 1 teaspoon salt
- 1 cup almond milk
- 1 teaspoon brown sugar
- 1 teaspoon ground black pepper
- 1 teaspoon curry paste
- 1 cup onion, chopped
- 1 tablespoon butter
- 1 teaspoon chili

Directions:

Wash the asparagus and cut it into halves. Place the prepared asparagus in the slow cooker bowl. Combine the almond milk, brown sugar, ground black pepper, curry paste, chopped onion, and butter in the bowl. Add chili and mix carefully. Pour the prepared liquid in the slow cooker and close the lid. Cook the dish on LOW for 9 hours. When the asparagus is tender, the dish is cooked. Transfer the prepared asparagus to serving plates and sprinkle with ½ of the remaining almond milk liquid.

Nutrition: calories 51, fat 2, fiber 2, carbs 7.76, protein 2

Sweet Corn with Jalapeno Rub

Prep time: 10 minutes | Cooking time: 7 hours | Servings: 6

Ingredients:

- 1 tablespoon powdered chili
- 1 jalapeno pepper
- 2-pound corn cobs
- 1 teaspoon salt
- 2 tablespoons butter
- 1 teaspoon cilantro
- 1 tablespoon ketchup
- 2 tablespoons water

Directions:

Chop the jalapeno pepper roughly and place it in the blender. Add the salt, butter, powdered chili, cilantro, and ketchup. Blend the mix well until smooth. After this, rub every corn cob with the blended jalapeno mix generously. Pour the water into the slow cooker and place the rubbed corn cobs inside. Close the slow cooker and cook the corn for 7 hours on LOW. When the dish is cooked, remove the corn and drizzle it with the sauce from the slow cooker. Serve immediately.

Nutrition: calories 189, fat 5.2, fiber 5, carbs 37.13, protein 5

Herbed Sweet Potato
Prep time: 15 minutes | Cooking time: 10 hours | Servings: 6

Ingredients:

- 1 teaspoon thyme
- 1 teaspoon coriander
- 1 teaspoon salt
- ½ teaspoon chili
- 1 teaspoon oregano
- 1 teaspoon ground black pepper
- 1 teaspoon turmeric
- 1 teaspoon paprika
- 1 teaspoon butter
- 1 cup cream cheese
- ½ cup chicken stock
- 1-pound sweet potato

Directions:

Peel the sweet potatoes and chop roughly. Combine the thyme, coriander, salt, chili, oregano, ground black pepper, turmeric, paprika, and cream cheese together in a mixing bowl. Whisk well and add butter. Keep whisking for 1 minute more. Then combine the whisked cream cheese mix with the chopped potatoes in the slow cooker. Add chicken stock and close the slow cooker lid. Cook the sweet potato on LOW for 10 hours. When the dish is cooked, let it chill. Transfer the sweet potato to the serving plates and drizzle with the remaining liquid from the slow cooker.

Nutrition: calories 540, fat 36.9, fiber 7, carbs 46.58, protein 6

Soy Sauce Green Peas
Prep time: 12 minutes | Cooking time: 3 hours | Servings: 8

Ingredients:

- 14 oz. green peas, frozen
- 3 oz. butter
- ½ cup soy sauce
- 1 tablespoon sesame seeds
- ¼ teaspoon nutmeg
- 1 teaspoon paprika
- 1 teaspoon cilantro
- 1 teaspoon ground black pepper

Directions:

Combine the soy sauce, sesame seeds, paprika, cilantro, ground black pepper, and nutmeg together in the bowl. Place the frozen green peas and butter in the slow cooker and close the lid. Cook the green peas on HIGH for 2 hours. Then add the soy sauce spicy mixture and close the slow cooker lid. Cook the dish on LOW for 1 hours more. When the green peas are soft, they are cooked. Put the green peas on a serving plates and sprinkle with the remaining soy sauce gently.

Nutrition: calories 166, fat 12.6, fiber 3, carbs 10.45, protein 4

German Potato Salad
Prep time: 25 minutes | Cooking time: 4 hours | Servings: 7

Ingredients:

- 4 oz. bacon
- 1-pound red potato
- ½ cup onion, chopped
- 3 oz. celery, chopped
- ¼ teaspoon ground white pepper
- 3 oz. sugar
- 1 can onion soup
- ½ cup chicken stock
- 3 tablespoons fresh dill, chopped
- 1 teaspoon salt
- 1 tablespoon potato starch

Directions:

Chop the bacon and toss it in the skillet. Roast the bacon for 1 minute on the medium heat. Stir frequently. Add the chopped onion and celery. Mix and roast it for 2 minutes more then sprinkle the mixture with the ground white pepper and sugar. Peel the red potatoes and slice. Make a layer of the sliced potatoes in the slow cooker bowl and sprinkle it with the roasted bacon mixture. After this make one more layer of sliced potato and cover it with the bacon mixture again. Repeat the same steps till you layer all the ingredients. After this, sprinkle the dish with the fresh dill and salt. Combine the canned onion soup with the potato starch and chicken stock. Mix and pour in the slow cooker. Close the slow cooker lid and cook the dish on HIGH for 4 hours. When the dish is cooked, cool then serve.

Nutrition: calories 311, fat 9, fiber 4, carbs 39.91, protein 19

Slow Cooker Greens

Prep time: 10 minutes | Cooking time: 6 hours | Servings: 6

Ingredients:

- 1 cup spinach
- 1 cup collard greens
- 1 cup fresh parsley
- 1 cup fresh dill
- 2 cups chicken stock
- 1 cup half and half
- 1 onion, chopped
- 1 teaspoon salt
- 1 teaspoon ground black pepper
- 1 oz. bay leaf

Directions:

Wash all the greens carefully. Chop the washed green roughly and place them in the slow cooker. Sprinkle the green with the chicken stock and half and half. Add chopped onion. After this, sprinkle the mixture with the salt, ground black pepper, and add the bay leaf. Stir it well with and close the slow cooker lid. Cook the dish for 6 hours on LOW. When the greens are cooked, they have a tender and delightful taste. Add more salt if desired. Serve the dish warm.

Nutrition: calories 84, fat 2.1, fiber 2, carbs 13.52, protein 4

Tender Turnips

Prep time: 15 minutes | Cooking time: 9 hours | Servings: 9

Ingredients:

- 19 oz. turnip
- 1 teaspoon salt
- 1 yellow onion
- ½ teaspoon ground black pepper
- 4 cups water
- 3 tablespoons butter
- 3 tablespoons milk

Directions:

Peel the turnips and chop them. Place the chopped turnips in the slow cooker bowl. Add the salt and ground black pepper. Peel the yellow onion and grate it. Add the grated onion to the slow cooker. Then add water and close the slow cooker lid. Cook the dish for 9 hours on LOW. When the turnips are cooked, strain them and place in the blender. Add the butter and milk and blend the mixture until you get the creamy texture of the dish. Add more milk if desired. Serve the dish immediately.

Nutrition: calories 64, fat 4.3, fiber 2, carbs 4.52, protein 2

Creamy Artichoke Dip

Prep time: 10 minutes | Cooking time: 11 hours | Servings: 8

Ingredients:

- 11 oz. mozzarella cheese
- 1 cup cream
- 1-pound artichoke, drained
- 3 tablespoons mayo
- 1 teaspoon minced garlic
- 1 teaspoon chili pepper

Directions:

Chop the artichoke into tiny pieces and put it in the slow cooker. Add the cream and mayo. Mix the mixture gently and sprinkle with the chili pepper and minced garlic. Then slice the mozzarella cheese and make a layer of cheese in the slow cooker. Close the slow cooker lid and cook the artichoke dip for 11 hours on LOW. When the dish is cooked, all the ingredients should be tender and the mozzarella cheese melted. Mix carefully with the help of the spoon and serve the dish. Enjoy the artichoke dip only hot!

Nutrition: calories 143, fat 5.9, fiber 4, carbs 9.02, protein 15

Soft Millet with Dill

Prep time: 10 minutes | Cooking time: 5 hours | Servings: 6

Ingredients:

- 2 tablespoons butter
- ½ cup half and half
- 1 teaspoon salt
- ½ cup fresh dill
- 1 teaspoon basil
- 4 cups water
- 4 cups millet
- 1 teaspoon olive oil

Directions:

Put the millet, water, half and half, olive oil, and basil in the slow cooker vessel. Add salt and mix gently. After this, close the slow cooker lid and cook the millet for 5 hours on LOW. When the time is done, add the butter and let it melt then mix. Chop the fresh dill and add it to the millet. Transfer the hot millet to bowls and serve it immediately.

Nutrition: calories 557, fat 10.5, fiber 11, carbs 98.98, protein 15

Glazed Vegetables

Prep time: 18 minutes | Cooking time: 6 hours | Servings: 12

Ingredients:

- 4 large carrots
- 3 red onions
- 1-pound potato
- 3 sweet potatoes
- ½ cup brown sugar
- 1 tablespoon salt
- 1 teaspoon coriander
- 1 teaspoon cilantro
- 2 tablespoons dried dill
- 1 tablespoon sesame oil
- 3 oz. honey

Directions:

Peel the carrots, onions, potatoes, and sweet potato. Chop the vegetables into medium pieces and place them in a large bowl. Sprinkle the vegetables with sugar, salt, coriander, cilantro, dried dill, and sesame oil. Mix well then transfer it to the slow cooker bowl. Sprinkle the vegetables with honey and do not stir it anymore. Close the slow cooker lid and cook the dish on LOW for 6 hours. When the vegetables are cooked, mix them gently with a wooden spatula. Serve the vegetables immediately.

Nutrition: calories 148, fat 1.4, fiber 3, carbs 33, protein 2

Balsamic Beets

Prep time: 20 minutes | Cooking time: 2 hours | Servings: 6

Ingredients:

- 1-pound beets
- 5 oz. orange juice
- 3 oz. balsamic vinegar
- 3 tablespoons almonds
- 6 oz. goat cheese
- 1 teaspoon minced garlic
- 1 teaspoon olive oil

Directions:

Slice the beets roughly and sprinkle with the balsamic vinegar generously. Transfer the beets to the slow cooker and add the orange juice. After this, add the olive oil and close the slow cooker lid. Cook the beets on LOW for 7 hours. Meanwhile, combine the goat cheese and minced garlic together in the bowl. Stir the mixture well. Crush the almonds and add them to the goat cheese mixture. When the time is over, open the slow cooker lid and add the goat cheese mixture. Stir it gently with the help of the spatula and cook for 10 minutes more on HIGH. Then place the prepared dish on the plates and serve.

Nutrition: calories 189, fat 11.3, fiber 2, carbs 12, protein 10

Chili Orange Squash

Prep time: 15 minutes | Cooking time: 5 hours | Servings: 6

Ingredients:

- 1-pound butternut squash
- 1 Poblano pepper
- 1 teaspoon brown sugar
- 1 teaspoon ground cinnamon
- 1 tablespoon salt
- 1 cup heavy cream
- 1 orange
- ¼ teaspoon ground cardamom

Directions:

Slice the orange with peel still on and place it in the slow cooker. Chop the Poblano pepper and cut the butternut squash into the chunks. After this, put the pepper and squash chunks in the bowl. Sprinkle the vegetables with brown sugar, ground cinnamon, salt, and ground cardamom. Mix the vegetables carefully and transfer them to the slow cooker. Add the heavy cream and close the lid. Cook the dish on the LOW for 5 hours. When the time is done and the dish is cooked, transfer to a serving plate with some cooked oranges and remaining heavy cream mix from the slow cooker. Enjoy the dish hot!

Nutrition: calories 105, fat 7.6, fiber 2, carbs 9, protein 2

Slow Cooker Tamale Side Dish

Prep time: 25 minutes | Cooking time: 7 hours | Servings: 5

Ingredients:

- 12 oz. masa harina
- 1 cup chicken stock
- ½ teaspoon salt
- 1 teaspoon onion powder
- 1 onion, chopped
- 5 tablespoons olive oil
- 5 corn husks
- 5 cups water

Directions:

Combine the masa harina with the chicken salt. Sprinkle the mixture with the salt and onion powder. After this, add the olive oil and chopped onion. Knead the dough with your hands. You should get a soft smooth dough. Soak the corn husks in the water for approximately 15 minutes. Fill the corn husks with the prepared masa harina mixture and place the stuffed husks in the slow cooker. Pour the water in the slow cooker and close the lid. Cook the dish on LOW for 7 hours. When the tamales are cooked, remove them from the slow cooker vessel and chill. Dry it from the excess liquid with a paper towel and serve.

Nutrition: calories 214, fat 14.8, fiber 2, carbs 18, protein 3

Easy Corn Pudding

Prep time: 10 minutes | Cooking time: 8 hours | Servings: 8

Ingredients:

- 6 oz. muffin mix
- 12 oz. corn kernels
- 1 cup heavy cream
- 1 teaspoon salt
- 1 teaspoon ground black pepper
- 3 oz. Parmesan cheese
- 1 tablespoon cilantro
- 1 teaspoon ground cumin

Directions:

Combine the muffin mix with the salt, heavy cream, cilantro, ground black pepper, and ground cumin. Mix with a hand mixer. When you get a smooth liquid texture, add the corn kernels and then pour the mixture in the slow cooker. Close the lid and cook the pudding for 8 hours on LOW. When the pudding is cooked, it will have smooth but liquid-like texture. Shred Parmesan cheese and sprinkle the pudding with it. Wait until the cheese is melted and serve as a side dish immediately.

Nutrition: calories 180, fat 9.6, fiber 2, carbs 18.8, protein 6

Tender Red Onions

Prep time: 15 minutes | Cooking time: 6 hours | Servings: 6

Ingredients:

- 17 oz. red onion, sliced
- 1 tablespoon brown sugar
- ½ teaspoon salt
- 1 tablespoon paprika
- 3 tablespoon butter
- ¼ cup cream cheese
- 1 teaspoon lemon juice
- ½ tablespoon lemon zest
- 1 apple

Directions:

Toss the sliced red onions in the slow cooker. Melt the butter and combine it with the salt, paprika, brown sugar, lemon juice, and lemon zest. Whisk the mixture until smooth and pour in the slow cooker. After this, peel the apple and grate it. Add the grated apples to the slow cooker. Mix the onions carefully with a wooden spatula and close the slow cooker lid. Cook the dish for 6 hours on LOW. When the time is done, mix gently with a spatula and transfer it to a serving plate. Enjoy the dish hot!

Nutrition: calories 138, fat 8.9, fiber 3, carbs 14.44, protein 2

Fragrant Applesauce

Prep time: 18 minutes | Cooking time: 6 hours | Servings: 5

Ingredients:

- 1-pound red apples
- 2 oz. cinnamon stick
- 1 teaspoon ground ginger
- ½ teaspoon nutmeg
- 1 teaspoon ground cinnamon
- 4 oz. water
- ½ teaspoon salt
- 1 tablespoon lime juice

Directions:

Peel the red apples and chop them. Put the cinnamon stick in the slow cooker bowl. Add the ground ginger and nutmeg. Add ground cinnamon, salt, water and lime juice. Stir the mixture gently and close the slow cooker lid. Cook the dish for 6 hours on HIGH. When the time is done, discard the cinnamon stick and blend the mixture until you get a smooth puree. Transfer the dish to the serving bowls and serve it or keep in the fridge for not more than 3 days.

Nutrition: calories 86, fat 0.4, fiber 9, carbs 22.93, protein 1

Wild Rice with Berries

Prep time: 12 minutes | Cooking time: 5 hours 30 minutes | Servings: 4

Ingredients:

- 2 cups wild rice
- 4 cups water
- 1 teaspoon salt
- 6 oz cherries, dried
- 1 tablespoon chives
- 1 tablespoon butter
- 2 tablespoons heavy cream

Directions:

Put the wild rice in the slow cooker bowl. Add water, salt, and dried cherries. Mix gently and close the slow cooker lid. Cook the wild rice for 5 hours on HIGH. When the time is over, add butter and heavy cream and stir. Cook the dish for 30 minutes more on LOW. When the wild rice is cooked, transfer the dish to serving plates. Serve the dish with the chicken.

Nutrition: calories 364, fat 6.6, fiber 6, carbs 66.97, protein 12

Sweet Pumpkin Wedges

Prep time: 15 minutes | Cooking time: 6 hours | Servings: 4

Ingredients:

- 15 oz pumpkin
- 1 tablespoon lemon juice
- 1 teaspoon salt
- 1 teaspoon honey
- ½ teaspoon ground cardamom
- 1 teaspoon lime juice

Directions:

Peel the pumpkin and slice it into the wedges. Combine the lemon juice, salt, honey, ground cardamom and lime juice in the bowl. Brush the pumpkin wedges with the spiced liquid and place them in the slow cooker bowl. Sprinkle the pumpkin wedges with the remaining spiced liquid and close the lid. Cook the dish for 6 hours on LOW. When the pumpkin wedges are cooked, chill them for about 15 minutes. Serve the pumpkin wedges warm.

Nutrition: calories 35, fat 0.1, fiber 1, carbs 8.91, protein 1

Scalloped Potatoes

Prep time: 25 minutes | Cooking time: 7 hours | Servings: 12

Ingredients:

- 2-pounds potato
- 1-pound sweet potato
- 1 tablespoon salt
- 1 teaspoon ground black pepper
- 1/3 cup butter, unsalted
- 4 tablespoons flour
- 1 tablespoon minced garlic
- 4 cups milk
- ¼ teaspoon nutmeg
- 4 oz Parmesan
- 5 oz Cheddar cheese

Directions:

Peel and slice the potatoes and sweet potatoes. Combine the ground black pepper and salt together. Cover the slow cooker bowl with parchment paper. Make the layer of sliced potato in the slow cooker bowl. Sprinkle the potatoes with the salt-pepper mixture lightly. Then make the layer of the sliced sweet potato and repeat this procedure till you put all the sliced potatoes in the slow cooker. Melt butter and combine it with the flour. Add minced garlic, nutmeg and milk. Parmesan and Cheddar cheese. Pour the milk liquid in the slow cooker. After this, make the layer of the shredded cheeses and close the slow cooker lid. Cook the dish on the low for 7 hours. When the dish is cooked, let it chill briefly and serve!

Nutrition: calories 422, fat 21.6, fiber 5, carbs 46, protein 11

Mayo Eggplant Cubes

Prep time: 15 minutes | Cooking time: 4 hours | Servings: 8

Ingredients:

- 17 oz eggplants
- 1 tablespoon salt
- 1 teaspoon ground black pepper
- 1 teaspoon cilantro
- 4 cups water
- 7 tablespoons mayo
- 1 teaspoon onion powder
- 1 teaspoon garlic powder
- 1 tablespoon nutmeg
- 3 tablespoon butter

Directions:

Peel the eggplants and rub the vegetables with the salt. After this, chop the eggplant into cubes and place in the slow cooker bowl. Add water and cook the dish on HIGH for 1 hour. After this, strain the eggplant cubes and return them back to the slow cooker bowl. Add ground black pepper, cilantro, mayo, onion powder, garlic powder, nutmeg, and butter. Stir carefully until well blended then close the slow cooker lid. Cook the dish on LOW for 3 hours more. When the eggplant side dish is cooked, chill to room temperature and serve!

Nutrition: calories 67, fat 4.8, fiber 2, carbs 6.09, protein 1

Turmeric Buckwheat

Prep time: 25 minutes | Cooking time: 4 hours | Servings: 6

Ingredients:

- 4 tablespoons milk powder
- 2 tablespoons butter
- 1 carrot
- 4 cup buckwheat

- 4 cups chicken stock
- 1 tablespoon salt
- 1 tablespoon turmeric
- 1 teaspoon paprika

Directions:

Combine the milk powder, buckwheat, chicken stock, salt, paprika, and turmeric in the slow cooker. Then peel the carrot and cut it into the small strips. Place the carrot strips in the buckwheat mixture and close the slow cooker lid. Cook the dish for 4 hours on HIGH. The buckwheat should absorb all the liquid. Open the slow cooker lid and add the butter. Mix it well and close the slow cooker lid. Leave the side dish for 15 minutes more then serve and

Nutrition: calories 238, fat 6.6, fiber 4, carbs 37.85, protein 9

Mashed Sweet Potato

Prep time: 20 minutes | Cooking time: 3 hours | Servings: 6

Ingredients:

- 16 oz sweet potato
- 3 cups chicken stock
- 1 tablespoon salt

- 3 tablespoons margarine
- 2 tablespoons cream cheese

Directions:

Peel the sweet potato and cut them into the medium pieces. After this, place the sweet potatoes in the slow cooker bowl and add chicken stock. Add salt and close the slow cooker lid. Cook the dish for 5 hours on HIGH. After this, strain the sweet potato pieces and place them in the big bowl. Mash the potato well and add the margarine and cream cheese. Mix well then transfer the prepared mashed sweet potato to serving plates. Enjoy the dish warm or preheated.

Nutrition: calories 472, fat 31.9, fiber 6.7, carbs 43.55, protein 3

Cornbread Pudding

Prep time: 18 minutes | Cooking time: 8 hours | Servings: 8

Ingredients:

- 11 oz cornbread mix
- 1 cup corn kernels
- 3 cups heavy cream
- 1 cup sour cream
- 3 eggs
- 1 chili pepper

- 1 teaspoon salt
- 1 teaspoon ground black pepper
- 2 oz pickled jalapeno
- ¼ tablespoon sugar
- 1 teaspoon butter

Directions:

Beat the eggs in the bowl then add the cornbread mix and heavy cream. Add sour cream and salt. Chop the chili pepper and add it to the cornbread mixture. After this, add ground black pepper, sugar, and butter. Chop the pickled jalapeno and add to the dough. Add the corn kernels and stir the mixture well with the help of the spoon. Transfer the cornbread pudding mixture into the slow cooker bowl and flatten the surface. Then close the slow cooker lid and cook the dish on LOW for 8 hours. When the cornbread pudding is cooked, remove it from the slow cooker. Let it cool briefly and serve it.

Nutrition: calories 398, fat 27.9, fiber 2, carbs 29.74, protein 9

Glazed Yams

Prep time: 20 minutes | Cooking time: 4 hours | Servings: 7

Ingredients:

- 2-pound yams
- 5 tablespoons butter
- 5 oz brown sugar
- 4 oz white sugar
- ½ teaspoon salt
- 1 teaspoon vanilla extract
- 2 tablespoons cornstarch

Directions:

Peel the yams and slice them. After this, melt the butter in the microwave oven and sprinkle it with the salt and vanilla extract. Combine the white sugar and brown sugar together. Combine the sugar mixture with the melted butter mixture and stir it carefully. Place the sliced yams in the slow cooker and add the prepared sugar-butter mixture. Stir gently and close the slow cooker lid. Cook the dish on HIGH for 4 hours. After this, transfer the prepared yams to serving plates. Then take the 1/3 cup of the remaining liquid from the slow cooker and heat it in a pot over medium heat. When the liquid starts to boil, add the cornstarch and whisk. When the liquid starts to thicken, remove it from the heat. Sprinkle the prepared yams with the thick liquid and serve.

Nutrition: calories 404, fat 16.4, fiber 6, carbs 63.33, protein 3

Zucchini Pate

Prep time: 19 minutes | Cooking time: 6 hours | Servings: 6

Ingredients:

- 3 medium zucchini
- 2 red onions
- 6 tablespoons tomato paste
- ½ cup fresh dill
- 1 teaspoon salt
- 1 teaspoon butter
- 1 tablespoon brown sugar
- ½ teaspoon ground black pepper
- 1 teaspoon paprika
- ¼ chili pepper

Directions:

Peel the zucchinis and chop them roughly. After this, place the chopped zucchini in the food processor and blend for 3 minutes or until smooth. After this, peel the onions and grate them. Put the blended zucchini in the slow cooker bowl and add the grated onions. Sprinkle the vegetable mixture with the tomato paste, salt, butter, brown sugar, ground black pepper, and paprika. Chop the fresh dill and chili pepper and add them to the zucchini mixture too. Mix the dish gently and close the slow cooker lid. Cook the zucchini pate on LOW for 6 hours. When the zucchini pate is cooked, open the slow cooker lid and stir it gently with the help of the wooden spatula. Let the dish chill till the room temperature and serve it into the plates.

Nutrition: calories 45, fat 0.8, fiber 2, carbs 9.04, protein

Red Cabbage with Onions

Prep time: 15 minutes | Cooking time: 8 hours | Servings:9

Ingredients:

- 17 oz red cabbage, sliced
- 1 cup fresh cilantro, chopped
- 3 red onions, diced
- 1 tablespoon sliced almonds
- 1 cup sour cream
- ½ cup chicken stock
- 1 teaspoon salt
- 1 tablespoon tomato paste
- 1 teaspoon ground black pepper
- 1 teaspoon cumin
- ½ teaspoon thyme
- 2 tablespoons butter
- 1 cup green peas

Directions:

Place the sliced red cabbage in the slow cooker. Sprinkle the cabbage with the chopped fresh cilantro and diced onion. Add the sliced almonds. Combine the chicken stock, sour cream, salt, tomato paste, ground black pepper, cumin, and thyme. Whisk everything together. After this, toss the butter in the slow cooker and add the green peas. Pour the chicken stock mix in the slow cooker bowl and close the lid. Cook on the LOW for 8 hours. When the dish is cooked, stir well. Place the prepared dish on serving plates.

Nutrition: calories 112, fat 5.9, fiber 3, carbs 12.88, protein 4

Broccoli Stuffing

Prep time: 16 minutes | Cooking time: 5 hours | Servings: 6

Ingredients:
- 10 oz broccoli
- 7 oz Cheddar cheese, shredded
- 4 eggs
- ½ cup onion, chopped
- 1 cup heavy cream
- 3 tablespoons mayo sauce
- 3 tablespoons butter
- ½ cup bread crumbs

Directions:

Chop the broccoli roughly and put it in the slow cooker. Add the ½ cup of heavy cream and close the slow cooker. Cook the dish on HIGH for 3 hours. Mash the broccoli with a fork. Crack the eggs into a bowl and whisk. Add the chopped onion, the remaining heavy cream, mayo sauce, and bread crumbs. Mix well and add to the slow cooker. Add the butter and cheese to the slow cooker bowl too. Mix gently and close the lid. Cook the dish for 2 hours on HIGH. When the broccoli stuffing is cooked, mash it gently with a fork and transfer to serving plates.

Nutrition: calories 289, fat 22.9, fiber 2, carbs 9.07, protein 13

Slow Cooker Shallots
Prep time: 15 minutes | Cooking time: 6 minutes | Servings: 7

Ingredients:
- 1 large carrot
- 1-pound shallots, chopped
- 1 cup heavy cream
- 1 tablespoon sugar
- 1 teaspoon salt
- 1 teaspoon ground black pepper
- 1 teaspoon cilantro
- 1 tablespoon butter, unsalted
- 1 tablespoon minced garlic

Directions:

Peel the carrot and cut it into the small strips. Combine the carrot strips and chopped shallot in the slow cooker bowl. Whisk the heavy cream with the sugar and salt in the mixing bowl. Add the ground black pepper, cilantro, butter and minced garlic. Mix well and pour it into the slow cooker. Close the slow cooker lid and cook the dish for 6 hours on LOW. When the time is over, remove the shallot and carrot strips from the heavy cream liquid and place it on serving plates. Sprinkle the prepared shallot dish with the 3 tablespoons of the remaining heavy cream mixture.

Nutrition: calories 133, fat 8.1, fiber 3, carbs 14.5, protein 2

Lemon-Garlic Mushrooms
Prep time: 10 minutes | Cooking time: 8 hours | Servings: 6

Ingredients:
- 2-pounds cremini mushrooms
- 1 lemon
- ½ cup fresh parsley
- 1 teaspoon salt
- 1 teaspoon ground black pepper
- 1/3 cup half and half
- 1 teaspoon thyme
- 1 teaspoon coriander
- 1 teaspoon turmeric
- 3 tablespoons garlic, chopped

Directions:

Cut the cremini mushrooms into 4s and place them in the slow cooker bowl. Combine the half and half with the thyme, coriander, turmeric, and chopped garlic. Add the ground black pepper and salt. Chop the parsley and add it to the half and half mixture. Mix well. Chop the lemon into the tiny pieces and add in the slow cooker. Sprinkle the mushroom mixture with the half and half mixture and close the slow cooker lid. Cook the dish for 8 hours on LOW. When the mushrooms are cooked, remove them from the half and half sauce and serve.

Nutrition: calories 55, fat 0.8, fiber 2, carbs 9.43, protein 6

Paprika Potato Strips
Prep time: 10 minutes | Cooking time: 5 hours | Servings: 8

Ingredients:

- 3-pounds potato
- 2 tomatoes, chopped
- 1 tablespoon paprika
- 1 sweet pepper, chopped
- 1 teaspoon salt
- ½ teaspoon turmeric
- 2 tablespoons sesame oil

Directions:

Peel the potato and cut it into the strips. Sprinkle the potato strips with the paprika, salt, and turmeric and toss. Transfer the potato strips in the slow cooker bowl and sprinkle with the olive oil. Close the slow cooker lid and cook the dish on HIGH for 3 hours. Place the sweet pepper and tomatoes in the blender and blend them well. Open the slow cooker lid and transfer the tomato-pepper mixture there. Mix and close the slow cooker lid. Cook the dish on HIGH for 2 hours more. Serve the paprika potato strips hot.

Nutrition: calories 176, fat 3.8, fiber 5, carbs 32.97, protein 4

Macaroni with Cream Cheese

Prep time: 15 minutes | Cooking time: 3.5 hours | Servings: 6

Ingredients:

- 12 oz elbow macaroni
- 1 cup cream cheese
- 3 tablespoons fresh parsley
- 1 tablespoon fresh dill
- 3 cups chicken stock
- 1 teaspoon salt
- 1 egg
- ¼ teaspoon turmeric

Directions:

Beat the egg then add the chicken stock and cream cheese. Mix for 1 minute more. Chop the fresh parsley and fresh dill and sprinkle into the cream cheese mixture. Stir gently with a spoon. After this, put the elbow macaroni in the slow cooker bowl and add the cream cheese mixture. Stir and close the slow cooker lid. Cook the macaroni for 3.5 hours on HIGH. When the side dish is cooked, stir carefully one more time. Transfer the prepared dish to serving plates. Serve the side dish immediately.

Nutrition: calories 398, fat 15.5, fiber 2, carbs 48.96, protein 15

Baked Potato with Mushrooms

Prep time: 20 minutes | Cooking time: 8 hours | Servings: 6

Ingredients:

- 6 large potatoes
- 3 oz mushrooms, chopped
- 1 onion, chopped
- 1 teaspoon butter
- ½ teaspoon salt
- ½ teaspoon minced garlic
- 1 teaspoon sour cream
- ½ teaspoon turmeric
- 1 teaspoon olive oil

Directions:

Combine the chopped mushrooms and onion together. Add the butter, salt, minced garlic, and sour cream. After this add turmeric and mix well. Then wash the potatoes carefully but do not peel them. Chop the potatoes into the medium cubes and add the mushroom mixture. Mix well. Spray the slow cooker bowl with the olive oil inside and toss the potato mixture there. Close the slow cooker lid and cook the dish for 8 hours on LOW. When the side dish is cooked, transfer it to the serving plates. Serve the dish and

Nutrition: calories 309, fat 1.9, fiber 9, carbs 66.94, protein 8

Jalapeno Side Dish

Prep time: 10 minutes | Cooking time: 6 hours | Servings: 6

Ingredients:

- 12 oz jalapeno pepper
- 2 tablespoons olive oil
- 1 tablespoon balsamic vinegar
- 1 onion, sliced

- 1 garlic clove, sliced
- 1 teaspoon ground coriander
- 4 tablespoons water

Directions:
Wash the jalapeno peppers carefully and cut them crosswise. Discard the seeds from the jalapeno peppers. Place the jalapeno peppers in the slow cooker bowl. Combine the olive oil, balsamic vinegar, ground coriander, and water together. Add the onion and garlic to the liquid vinegar mixture and stir it gently. Then sprinkle the jalapeno peppers with the vinegar mixture generously and close the slow cooker lid. Cook the dish for 6 hours on LOW. When the jalapeno peppers are cooked, transfer them to serving plates and chill gently.

Nutrition: calories 67, fat 4.7, fiber 2, carbs 6.02, protein 1

Slow Cooker Ramen
Prep time: 5 minutes | Cooking time: 25 minutes | Servings: 5

Ingredients:
- 1 tablespoon ramen seasoning
- 10 oz ramen noodles
- 4 cups chicken stock
- 1 teaspoon salt
- 3 tablespoons soy sauce
- 1 teaspoon paprika
- 1 tablespoon butter

Directions:
Pour the chicken stock into the slow cooker. Add salt, ramen seasoning, paprika, and butter. Stir the mixture gently and add the ramen noodles. Close the slow cooker lid and cook the ramen noodles for 20 minutes on HIGH. After this, add the soy sauce and stir the ramen noodles gently. Cook the dish for 5 minutes on HIGH. Then transfer the prepared side dish into serving bowls.

Nutrition: calories 405, fat 19.2, fiber 6, carbs 49.93, protein 15

Refried Beans
Prep time: 15 minutes | Cooking time: 9 hours | Servings: 10

Ingredients:
- 5 oz white onion
- 4 cups black beans
- 1 chili pepper
- 1 oz minced garlic
- 10 cups water
- 1 teaspoon salt
- ½ teaspoon ground black pepper
- ¼ teaspoon cilantro

Directions:
Peel the onion and chop it. Put the chopped onion in the slow cooker bowl. Add the black beans, minced garlic, salt, ground black pepper, and cilantro. After this, chop the chili pepper and add it to the slow cooker. Pour the water into the mixture and stir it. Close the slow cooker lid and cook the beans for 9 hours on LOW. Check if the beans have absorbed the water and add more water if needed. When the beans are cooked, strain them and leave a ¼ cup of the slow cooker remaining liquid. Transfer the beans mixture in the food processor and blend well. Add the remaining liquid and blend the dish until smooth. Serve the side dish!

Nutrition: calories 73, fat 1.5, fiber 4, carbs 12.34, protein 3

Slow Cooker Fennel
Prep time: 10 minutes | Cooking time: 3 hour | Servings: 7

Ingredients:
- 10 oz fennel bulbs
- 2 tablespoons olive oil
- 1 teaspoon ground black pepper
- 1 teaspoon paprika
- 1 teaspoon cilantro
- 1 teaspoon oregano

- 1 teaspoon basil
- 3 tablespoons white wine
- 1 teaspoon salt
- 2 garlic cloves
- 1 teaspoon dried dill

Directions:

Cut the fennel bulbs into the chunks. Combine the olive oil, ground black pepper, paprika, cilantro, oregano, basil, salt, and dried dill together. Peel the garlic cloves and chop them roughly. Add the chopped garlic to the spice mixture. Place the spice mixture in the slow cooker and cook it on HIGH for 30 minutes. After this, add the fennel bulbs chunks and pour in the white wine. Close the slow cooker lid and cook the dish for 3 hours on HIGH. When the fennel is cooked, open the slow cooker lid and stir the dish. Serve it immediately.

Nutrition: calories 53, fat 4.1, fiber 2, carbs 4, protein 1

Butter Artichokes

Prep time: 18 minutes | Cooking time: 6 hours | Servings: 5

Ingredients:

- 13 oz artichoke heat
- 1 teaspoon salt
- 4 cups chicken stock
- 1 teaspoon turmeric
- 1 garlic clove, peeled
- 4 tablespoons butter
- 4 oz Parmesan, shredded

Directions:

Wash the artichoke heart carefully and prepare them for cooking. Place the prepared artichokes in the slow cooker. Sprinkle the artichokes with the turmeric and salt. Add the chicken stock and close the slow cooker lid. Cook the artichoke hearts on LOW for 6 hours. When the artichokes are cooked, transfer them to a serving plate. Put the butter in the middle of every artichoke heart and sprinkle with the shredded cheese. Let the cheese melt. Serve the dish warm.

Nutrition: calories 272, fat 12.8, fiber 4, carbs 24.21, protein 17

Coriander Rainbow Carrots

Prep time: 15 minutes | Cooking time: 7 hours | Servings: 9

Ingredients:

- 3-pound rainbow carrot
- 3 tablespoons sesame oil
- 1 teaspoon coriander
- ¼ cup coriander leaves
- 1 tablespoon sour cream
- ½ teaspoon salt
- ½ teaspoon sugar

Directions:

Peel the rainbow carrots and place them in the slow cooker vessel. Combine the sesame oil and coriander together in the shallow bowl. Add the salt and sugar and stir the mixture. Then put the coriander leaves in the blender and blend well. Then add the blended coriander leaves to the oil mixture. Stir it and sprinkle the rainbow carrots with the oil mixture. Close the slow cooker lid and cook the dish for 6 hours on LOW. Then sprinkle the rainbow carrots with the sour cream and cook for 1 hour more on LOW. When the rainbow carrots are cooked, let them chill slightly. Serve the side dish immediately.

Nutrition: calories 95, fat 5, fiber 5, carbs 13, protein 1

Creamy Parsnips

Prep time: 15 minutes | Cooking time: 7 hours | Servings: 5

Ingredients:

- 1 cup cream
- 2 teaspoons butter
- 1-pound parsnip
- 1 carrot
- 1 yellow onion
- 1 tablespoon chives
- 1 teaspoon salt
- 1 teaspoon ground white pepper
- ½ teaspoon paprika
- 1 tablespoon salt
- ¼ teaspoon sugar

Directions:

Peel the parsnips and carrot. Chop the vegetables into the chunks and put them in the slow cooker bowl. After this, whisk the heavy cream with the butter, salt, ground black pepper, paprika, and sugar. Peel the onion and chop it roughly. Place all the prepared ingredients in the slow cooker bowl and close the lid. Cook the dish for 7 hours on LOW. When the parsnip side dish is cooked, serve it immediately.

Nutrition: calories 190, fat 11.2, fiber 4, carbs 22, protein 3

Sliced Eggplants with Mayo Sauce

Prep time: 10 minutes | Cooking time: 5 hours | Servings: 8

Ingredients:

- 2 tablespoons minced garlic
- 1 chili pepper
- 1 sweet pepper
- 4 tablespoons mayo
- 1 teaspoon olive oil
- 1 teaspoon salt
- ½ teaspoon ground black pepper
- 18 oz eggplants
- 2 tablespoons sour cream

Directions:

Chop the chili pepper and sweet pepper and place them in the food processor. Add the minced garlic, salt, and ground black pepper. Blend the mixture until you get a smooth texture. After this, slice the eggplants and rub them with the smooth chili mixture on both sides. Spray the slow cooker bowl with the olive oil inside and transfer the sliced eggplants there. Combine the sour cream and mayo and mix well. Spread the surface of the sliced eggplants with the mayo mixture carefully and close the slow cooker lid. Cook the dish for 5 hours on HIGH. When the sliced eggplants are cooked, let them chill. When the dish gets to be room temperature, serve it immediately.

Nutrition: calories 40, fat 1.1, fiber 3, carbs 7.5, protein 1

Party Macaroni Side Dish

Prep time: 10 minutes | Cooking time: 3.5 hours | Servings: 6

Ingredients:

- 8 oz macaroni
- 1 cup tomatoes, chopped
- 1 garlic clove, peeled
- 1 teaspoon butter
- 1 cup heavy cream
- 3 cups water
- 1 tablespoon salt
- 6 oz Parmesan, shredded
- 1 tablespoon dried basil

Directions:

Place the macaroni in the slow cooker and add the water. Sprinkle the macaroni with salt and close the slow cooker lid. Cook the dish on HIGH for 3 hours. Meanwhile, place the chopped tomatoes in the blender and blend them well. Combine the blended tomatoes with the cream, shredded cheese, and dried basil. Add butter and mix. When the time is over, strain the liquid from the slow cooker and leave only macaroni inside. Pour the cream in the slow cooker and stir. Close the slow cooker lid and cook the dish on HIGH for 30 minutes more. When the side dish is cooked, stir it gently and transfer to serving plates. Serve the dish immediately.

Nutrition: calories 325, fat 10.1, fiber 2, carbs 41.27, protein 17

Rosemary Hasselback Potatoes

Prep time: 15 minutes | Cooking time: 8 hours | Servings: 7

Ingredients:

- 7 potatoes
- 2 oz butter
- 1 tablespoon olive oil
- 1 tablespoon dried dill
- 1 teaspoon salt
- 1 teaspoon paprika

Directions:

Wash the potato carefully and slice the potatoes, but not all the way through. The potatoes should be thinly sliced all the way across but still held together. After this, combine the olive oil, butter, dried dill, salt, and paprika. Cover the slow cooker bowl with the foil and place the Hasselback potatoes inside. Sprinkle very potato with the olive oil mixture generously. Close the slow cooker lid and cook the potatoes on LOW for 8 hours. When the time is done and the potatoes are soft, serve the side dish immediately.

Nutrition: calories 363, fat 9, fiber8, carbs 65.17, protein 8

Asian-Style Asparagus

Prep time: 20 minutes | Cooking time: 4 hours | Servings: 4

Ingredients:

- 1 tablespoon sesame seeds
- 1 teaspoon miso paste
- ¼ cup soy sauce
- 1 cup fish stock
- 8 oz asparagus
- 1 teaspoon salt
- 1 teaspoon chili flakes
- 1 teaspoon oregano
- 1 cup water

Directions:

Put the asparagus in the slow cooker and add water. Close the slow cooker lid and cook the asparagus on HIGH for 3 hours. Meanwhile, combine the miso paste, sesame seeds, soy sauce, and fish stock in the bowl. Add the salt, chili flakes, and oregano. Whisk the mixture well until the miso paste is dissolved. When the time is done, strain the asparagus and return it to the slow cooker bowl. Add the soy sauce mixture and close the slow cooker lid. Cook the dish on HIGH for 1 hour more. When the asparagus is cooked, transfer it to a serving plates and sprinkle with the hot soy sauce mixture.

Nutrition: calories 85, fat 4.8, fiber 2, carbs 7.28, protein 4

Mac Cups

Prep time: 25 minutes | Cooking time: 8 hours | Servings: 6

Ingredients:

- 6 oz puff pastry
- 1 cup fresh basil
- 7 oz elbow macaroni, cooked
- 1 egg
- ¼ cup heavy cream
- 1 tablespoon flour
- 1 tablespoon cornstarch
- 1 teaspoon salt
- 1 tablespoon turmeric
- 1 teaspoon olive oil

Directions:

Spray the muffin form with the olive oil. Roll the puff pastry and cut it into 6 squares. Then place the puff pastry squares in the muffin forms. Crack the egg into a bowl and whisk it. Add the heavy cream and flour and stir the mixture well. Add cornstarch and salt. Add turmeric and stir the mixture until combined. Chop the fresh basil and add to the macaroni mix. Fill the muffin forms with the macaroni mixture. Cover the slow cooker bowl with the foil and place the muffin forms inside. Close the slow cooker lid and cook the mac cups for 8 hours on LOW. When the side dish is cooked, serve it only hot.

Nutrition: calories 270, fat 15.4, fiber 2, carbs 26.67, protein 6

Baked White Onions
Prep time: 20 minutes | Cooking time: 9 hours | Servings: 5

Ingredients:
- ½ cup bread crumbs
- 5 oz Romano cheese, shredded
- ¼ cup cream cheese
- ¼ cup half and half
- 3 oz butter
- 1 tablespoon salt
- 5 large white onions
- 1 teaspoon ground black pepper
- 1 teaspoon garlic powder

Directions:
Peel the white onions and cut the tops off. Make the crosswise cuts in the onions. You should not cut them totally through. Combine the cream cheese, butter and half and half together. Sprinkle the mixture with salt and ground black pepper. Add garlic powder and mix. Combine the shredded cheese with the bread crumbs. Place the prepared onions in the slow cooker and sprinkle them with the churned half and half liquid. After this, sprinkle every onion with the shredded bread crumb mixture generously and close the slow cooker lid. Cook the dish on LOW for 9 hours. When the onions are soft, the dish is cooked. Serve it immediately.

Nutrition: calories 349, fat 25.3, fiber 3, carbs 19.55, protein 13

Tomato Okra
Prep time: 10 minutes | Cooking time: 7 hours | Servings: 6

Ingredients:
- 2-pound okra, frozen
- 1 cup tomato sauce
- 4 oz water
- 1 onion, chopped
- 1 teaspoon minced garlic
- ¼ tablespoon salt
- 1 teaspoon sugar

Directions:
Place the frozen okra in the slow cooker. Add the tomato sauce and water. After this, sprinkle the mixture with the chopped onion and minced garlic. Add salt and sugar. Mix and close the slow cooker lid. Cook the dish on LOW for 7 hours. When the okra is soft, the dish is cooked. Serve the prepared side dish when it is chilled well.

Nutrition: calories 107, fat 0.4, fiber 8, carbs 22.55, protein 4

Slow Cooker Corn Salad
Prep time: 20 minutes | Cooking time: 5 hours | Servings: 6

Ingredients:
- 1 cup corn kernels
- 5 oz dried tomatoes
- 1 teaspoon salt
- 1 cup heavy cream
- 2 cucumbers
- 1 red onion, diced
- 1 teaspoon ground paprika
- 1 cup fresh parsley
- 1 carrot, grated
- 1 teaspoon olive oil

Directions:
Put the corn kernels in the slow cooker vessel. Cut the dried tomatoes into the strips and add them to the slow cooker too. Add salt, ground paprika, and heavy cream. Add the diced onion in the slow cooker bowl and stir. Close the slow cooker lid and cook the dish on LOW for 5 hours. When the mixture is cooked, transfer to the salad bowl and stir. Chop the cucumbers and fresh parsley. Add the prepared fresh ingredients in the salad bowl and stir it carefully. Serve the salad warm.

Nutrition: calories 123, fat 8.9, fiber 2, carbs 10.4, protein 2

Smashed Red Potatoes

*Prep time: 18 minutes | **Cooking time:** 8 hours | **Servings:** 4*

Ingredients:

- 1-pound red potato
- 2 tablespoons olive oil
- 1 garlic clove
- 1 teaspoon sage
- 4 tablespoons mayo
- 1 teaspoon minced garlic
- 3 tablespoons fresh dill, chopped
- 1 teaspoon paprika

Directions:

Wash the potatoes carefully. Cover the slow cooker bowl with the parchment and place the prepared potatoes in the bowl. Sprinkle the potatoes with the olive oil. Peel the garlic clove and mash it. Add the mashed garlic clove in the slow cooker. Add the sage and close the slow cooker lid. Cook the dish on LOW for 8 hours. Meanwhile, combine the mayo and minced garlic together. Add chopped fresh dill and paprika. When the red potatoes are cooked, remove them from the slow cooker and smash them with a fork. Place the smashed potatoes on serving plates. Sprinkle each smashed potato with the mayo sauce. Serve the potatoes hot.

Nutrition: calories 164, fat 7.8, fiber 4, carbs 22.87, protein 3

Snacks

Banana Bread
Prep time: 15 minutes | Cooking time: 4 hours | Servings: 6

Ingredients:

- 10 oz biscuit mix
- 4 eggs
- 1 teaspoon vanilla extract
- 1 tablespoon sugar

- 12 oz banana, ripe
- 1/3 cup butter
- 1 teaspoon brown sugar

Directions:

Beat the eggs in the mixing bowl. Melt butter and add it into the whisked eggs. Add vanilla extract, sugar, and brown sugar. Peel the bananas and mash them with a fork. Add the mashed bananas into the egg mixture. Mix and add the biscuit mix. Blend until smooth. After this, cover the slow cooker bowl with parchment and pour the batter inside. Close the slow cooker lid and cook the banana bread for 4 hours on HIGH. When the time is over, check if the banana bread is cooked with a toothpick. Remove the bread from the slow cooker and let cool. Slice and

Nutrition: calories 506, fat 20.2, fiber 6, carbs 75.31, protein 11

Energy Bars with Quinoa
Prep time: 15 minutes | Cooking time: 4 hours | Servings: 4

Ingredients:

- 2 tablespoons almond butter
- 1/3 cup chia seeds
- 3 tablespoons almonds
- 6 oz almond milk
- 3 tablespoons brown sugar

- 3 tablespoons dried apples
- 1 egg
- ½ teaspoon cinnamon
- 7 tablespoons quinoa
- 1 tablespoon raisins

Directions:

Beat the egg in a bowl. Add the chia seeds and whisk. After this, crush the almonds and add them to the egg mixture. Add dried apples, cinnamon, quinoa, raisins, brown sugar, almond milk, and almond butter. Cover the slow cooker with the parchment and pour the quinoa batter inside. Close the slow cooker lid and cook the dish for 4 hours on HIGH. When the dish is cooked, remove it from the slow cooker and cut into the bars. Chill the energy bars carefully and serve.

Nutrition: calories 124, fat 6.4, fiber 4, carbs 13.08, protein 5

Pecan Snac
Prep time: 15 minutes | Cooking time: 3 hours | Servings: 7

Ingredients:

- 1 cup pecan
- 3 tablespoons flour
- 1 egg white

- 1 tablespoon sugar
- 1 tablespoon maple syrup

Directions:

Whisk the egg white until you get stiff peaks. After this, add sugar and the maple syrup and whisk well. Then toss the pecans in the whisked egg white mixture and coat them well. Sprinkle the pecans with the flour and transfer in the slow cooker bowl. Cook the snack on HIGH for 3 hours. Stir the pecans every 30 minutes. When the dish is cooked, let it chill well. Serve it.

Nutrition: calories 124, fat 10.2, fiber 1, carbs 7.6, protein 2

Bacon Sausages

Prep time: 15 minutes | Cooking time: 3 hour | Servings: 7

Ingredients:

- 10 oz breakfast sausages
- 6 oz bacon
- 1 teaspoon cayenne pepper
- 1 teaspoon ground black pepper
- 1 teaspoon salt
- 4 tablespoons tomato sauce
- 1 tablespoon chives
- 1 teaspoon onion powder
- 1 teaspoon minced garlic
- 2 tablespoons butter

Directions:

Cut the sausages into 2 parts. Then combine the cayenne pepper, ground black pepper, salt, onion powder, and minced garlic together. Stir the mixture well. Slice the bacon and sprinkle it with the spice mixture. Wrap the sausages in the sliced bacon and brush the prepared bacon sausages in the tomato sauce. Toss the butter in the slow cooker and melt it. Then add the wrapped bacon sausages and sprinkle the dish with the chives. Close the slow cooker lid and cook the snack for 3 hours on HIGH. When the bacon sausages are cooked, let them cool to room temperature.

Nutrition: calories 215, fat 17.9, fiber 1, carbs 5.27, protein 9

Wrapped Sausages

Prep time: 14 minutes | Cooking time: 6 hours | Servings: 8

Ingredients:

- 10 oz sausages
- 6 oz Cheddar cheese, sliced
- 1 tablespoon mayo
- 1 teaspoon ground black pepper
- 1 teaspoon cilantro
- ½ teaspoon turmeric
- 1 teaspoon ground paprika
- ½ teaspoon ground ginger
- 1 teaspoon canola oil

Directions:

Spread the sliced cheese with the mayo sauce. Then combine the ground black pepper, cilantro, turmeric, ground paprika, and ground ginger together. Sprinkle the sausages with the spice mixture and wrap with the sliced cheese. Spray the wrapped sausages with the canola oil and wrap every sausage in the foil then place them in the slow cooker bowl. Close the slow cooker lid and cook the snack for 6 hours on LOW. When the time is done, remove the snack from the slow cooker. Cool for 10 minutes and remove from the foil.

Nutrition: calories 138, fat 9, fiber 1, carbs 6.81, protein 10

Chili Scrolls

Prep time: 20 minutes | Cooking time: 4 hours | Servings: 8

Ingredients:

- 7 oz puff pastry
- 2 chili pepper
- 1 tablespoon tomato sauce
- 1 tablespoon butter
- 1 egg yolk
- 1 teaspoon salt
- 1 teaspoon minced garlic
- 1 tablespoon mayo
- 1 teaspoon olive oil

Directions:

Roll the puff pastry with the rolling pin. Remove the seeds from the chili peppers and chop them into the tiny pieces. Combine the chopped chili peppers with the tomato sauce and salt. Add minced garlic and mayo. Whisk the egg yolk and spread the rolled puff pastry with the chopped chili mixture and roll it up. Cut the dough into pieces (scrolls). Brush every scroll with the whisked egg. Cover the slow cooker bowl with the parchment and place the scrolls there. Close the slow cooker lid and cook the chili scrolls for 4 hours on HIGH. When the dish is cooked, cool slightly then serve!

Nutrition: calories 169, fat 12.1, fiber 1, carbs 13.02, protein 3

Jalapeno Taquitos

Prep time: 25 minutes | Cooking time: 8 hours | Servings: 5

Ingredients:

- 5 corn tortillas
- 4 oz Cheddar cheese, shredded
- 9 oz chicken fillets
- 3 oz cream cheese
- 1 tablespoon cilantro
- 1 cup water
- 1 teaspoon salt
- 1 teaspoon ground black pepper
- 2 jalapeno peppers
- 1 teaspoon onion powder

Directions:

Place the chicken fillets in the slow cooker. Sprinkle the meat with the cream cheese, cilantro, salt, ground black pepper, and onion powder. Chop the jalapeno peppers and add them in the slow cooker bowl. Add water and close the slow cooker lid. Cook the dish for 8 hours on LOW. When the time is done, open the slow cooker lid and shred the chicken well. Place the shredded chicken mixture and shredded cheese in the tortillas and wrap. Place the dish in the preheated 350 F oven and cook for 10 minutes. Remove the dish from the oven and enjoy.

Nutrition: calories 285, fat 14.9, fiber 3, carbs 27.09, protein 12

Spaghetti Fritters

Prep time: 25 minutes | Cooking time: 3 hours | Servings: 10

Ingredients:

- 10 oz pasta, cooked
- ½ cup bread crumbs
- 4 oz Romano cheese
- 4 teaspoons sesame oil
- 1 teaspoon paprika
- 1 teaspoon ground black pepper
- 1 teaspoon salt
- 3 eggs

Directions:

Chop the pasta gently and combine with the bread crumbs. Beat the eggs in the bowl and whisk them well. Then add the whisked eggs to the pasta mixture. After this, add paprika, bread crumbs, ground black pepper, and salt and mix. Then spray your hands with the sesame oil so the dough doesn't stick as you form the small fritters from the dough. Place the uncooked fritters in the slow cooker and close the slow cooker lid. Cook the fritters on HIGH for 2 hours. After this, flip the fritters over and cook the fritters for 1 hour more on HIGH. Remove the fritters from the slow cooker and chill little.

Nutrition: calories 177, fat 10.1, fiber 2, carbs 12.55, protein 9

Corn Fritters

Prep time: 15 minutes | Cooking time: 6 hours | Servings: 8

Ingredients:

- 1 cup sweet corn
- 1 cup flour
- ¼ cup milk
- ½ teaspoon baking soda
- 1 tablespoon lemon juice
- 1 teaspoon salt
- 1 teaspoon ground black pepper
- 1 teaspoon paprika
- 1 teaspoon butter
- 2 oz Parmesan
- 1 egg

Directions:

Beat the egg in the bowl and whisk well. Add milk and baking soda. Add lemon juice, salt, ground black pepper, paprika, and flour. Mix carefully until you get a smooth dough. Add more flour if desired. Then shred Parmesan cheese and add in the dough mixture. Add the sweet corn and mix well. Form small fritters and place them in the slow cooker bowl. Close the slow cooker lid and cook the fritters on LOW for 6 hours. When the corn fritters are cooked, place them on the serving plate.

Nutrition: calories 135, fat 2.6, fiber 1, carbs 21.87, protein 7

Slow Cooker Meatballs with Sesame Seeds

Prep time: 20 minutes | Cooking time: 9 hours | Servings: 9

Ingredients:

- 3 tablespoons milk
- 5 tablespoons panko bread crumbs
- 1 egg
- 3 tablespoons dried parsley
- 1 teaspoon minced garlic
- 1 teaspoon salt
- 14 oz ground pork

- 1 tablespoon sesame seeds
- ½ cup tomato paste
- 1 onion
- 1 tablespoon sugar
- 1 teaspoon cilantro
- 1 teaspoon cayenne pepper

Directions:

Combine the ground pork and beaten egg together. Add the dried parsley, salt, minced garlic, panko bread crumbs, sesame seeds, and milk. Mix the ground pork mixture with your hands. Form the small meatballs and put the meatballs into the freezer. Meanwhile, combine the tomato paste, sugar, cilantro, and cayenne pepper together. Peel the onion and grate it then add the grated onion into the tomato paste mixture and stir it. Place the tomato paste in the slow cooker bowl. Add the frozen meatballs and close the slow cooker lid. Cook the dish for 9 hours on LOW. When the meatballs are cooked, let them cool briefly and serve.

Nutrition: calories 142, fat 5.3, fiber 1, carbs 8.26, protein 16

Slow Cooker Cheese Dip

Prep time: 20 minutes | Cooking time: 2 hours | Servings: 8

Ingredients:

- 2-pound Velveeta cheese
- 7 oz ground beef
- 1 red onion, chopped
- 1 chili pepper
- ½ cup water

- 1 tablespoon taco seasoning
- 1 teaspoon salt
- 1 tablespoon olive oil
- 1 tablespoon dried dill

Directions:

Put the olive oil in the skillet. Add the chopped onion, ground beef, salt, dried dill, and taco seasoning. Chop the chili pepper and add it to the meat mixture too. Close the lid and cook the meat mixture for 10 minutes or until is it totally cooked. Put the meat mixture in the slow cooker. Add water and Velveeta cheese. Stir gently. Close the slow cooker lid and cook the dish on HIGH for 2 hours. When the cheese is melted, stir it gently again. Serve it.

Nutrition: calories 363, fat 21.3, fiber 1, carbs 16.28, protein 26

Cinnamon Pecans

Prep time: 15 minutes | Cooking time: 4 hours | Servings: 7

Ingredients:

- 1 tablespoon ground cinnamon
- 1 cup pecan halves
- 3 tablespoons brown sugar

- ¼ cup dried milk
- 2 tablespoons water
- 1 egg

Directions:

Beat the egg in the bowl. Add brown sugar and mix it well with a hand blender. After this, add ground cinnamon and dried milk. Whisk the mixture and add the pecans. Put the prepared pecan halves in the slow cooker and close the slow cooker lid. Cook the dish on HIGH for 3 hours. Add the water and cook the dish for 1 hour more. Transfer the cooked pecan halves in a paper towel and chill well.

Nutrition: calories 141, fat 11.9, fiber 2, carbs 7.62, protein 3

Snack Chicken Wings

Prep time: 15 minutes | *Cooking time:* 9 hours | *Servings:* 5

Ingredients:

- 1 tablespoon honey
- 1 tablespoon sesame seeds
- 1-pound chicken wings
- 1 teaspoon cayenne pepper
- 1 teaspoon salt
- 1 teaspoon mustard
- 1 tablespoon butter
- 1 teaspoon oregano
- 1 teaspoon cilantro

Directions:

Combine the sesame seeds, cayenne pepper, salt, mustard, butter, oregano, and cilantro. Add honey and whisk the mixture well. After this, combine the honey mixture with the chicken wings and stir it carefully. Place the chicken wings in the slow cooker bowl. Add the remaining honey mixture and close the slow cooker lid. Cook the dish for 9 hours on LOW. When the time is over, remove the chicken wings from the slow cooker. Serve the snack as hot.

Nutrition: calories 160, fat 6.6, fiber 0, carbs 4.05, protein 20

Cocktail Meatballs with Tomato Sauce

Prep time: 20 minutes | *Cooking time:* 10 hours | *Servings:* 5

Ingredients:

- 1 cup tomatoes, canned
- 1 tablespoon garlic clove, sliced
- 1 teaspoon salt
- 1 teaspoon cilantro
- ½ cup fresh basil
- 1 teaspoon onion powder
- 1 teaspoon garlic powder
- 1 tablespoon turmeric
- 1 teaspoon sugar
- 1 egg
- 1 teaspoon ground black pepper
- 10 oz ground pork
- 6 oz ground beef

Directions:

Place the canned tomatoes in the blender and blend them well. Pour the blended tomatoes in the slow cooker bowl. Add the sliced garlic clove, salt, cilantro, and sugar. Chop the basil and add it to the mixture too. Stir it gently and close the slow cooker lid. Cook the sauce on LOW for 5 hours. Meanwhile, combine the onion powder, garlic powder, turmeric, ground black pepper, ground pork, and ground beef together. Beat the egg into the mixture and mix it up well. After this, form the meatballs from the meat mixture. Place the meatballs in the slow cooker with the sauce and close the lid. Cook the dish for 5 hours on HIGH. When the dish is cooked, serve it immediately.

Nutrition: calories 154, fat 7.4, fiber 4, carbs 15.93, protein 8

Hamburger Dip

Prep time: 20 minutes | *Cooking time:* 7 hour | *Servings:* 6

Ingredients:

- 7 oz ground beef
- 6 oz nacho cheese
- 1 cup salsa
- 4 oz refried beans
- 1 teaspoon salt
- 1 teaspoon ground black pepper
- 1 teaspoon paprika
- 1 teaspoon cilantro
- 1 teaspoon oregano
- 1 teaspoon minced garlic
- ¼ cup heavy cream

Directions:

Put the ground beef in a skillet and add heavy cream. Mix and simmer it for 10 minutes on medium heat. After this, transfer the ground beef mixture into the slow cooker. Add salsa, refried beans, nacho cheese, ground black pepper, paprika, cilantro, oregano, and minced garlic. Mix it up gently with the help of the wooden spatula. Close the slow cooker lid and cook the hamburger dip on LOW for 7 hours. When the dip is cooked, mix it carefully.

Nutrition: calories 210, fat 15.6, fiber 2, carbs 10.75, protein 8

Sugar Sausages

Prep time: 10 minutes | Cooking time: 7 hours | Servings: 8

Ingredients:

- 10 oz sausage
- 1 teaspoon ground black pepper
- ½ teaspoon cayenne pepper
- 3 tablespoons brown sugar
- 2 teaspoons water
- 1 teaspoon sage
- 2 tablespoons milk

Directions:

Put the sausages in the slow cooker bowl. Sprinkle with the ground black pepper, cayenne pepper, brown sugar, sage, milk, and water. Close the slow cooker lid and cook the dish on LOW for 7 hours. Stir the sausages every 35 minutes. When the sausages are cooked, place them on a serving plate and sprinkle with the remaining sugar mixture.

Nutrition: calories 120, fat 6.6, fiber 1, carbs 10.45, protein 7

Sugared Pecans

Prep time: 17 minutes | Cooking time: 3 hours | Servings: 10

Ingredients:

- 2 egg whites
- 2 cups pecan halves
- 1 teaspoon vanilla extract
- 1 cup sugar
- 3 tablespoons brown sugar
- 1 teaspoon butter

Directions:

Whisk the egg whites until you get stiff peaks. Add the sugar and vanilla extract. Continue to whisk the mixture for 1 minute more. Toss the pecan halves in the whisked egg white mixture and sprinkle the pecan halves with the brown sugar. Toss the butter in the slow cooker vessel and melt. Add the prepared pecan halves and close the slow cooker lid. Cook the dish on HIGH for 3 hours. Stir the pecans gently during the cooking. Serve the prepared snack chilled.

Nutrition: calories 201, fat 14.64, fiber 2, carbs 17.24, protein 2.54

Snack Party Mix

Prep time: 10 minutes | Cooking time: 2.5 hours | Servings: 8

Ingredients:

- 5 oz rice cereal
- 5 oz corn cereal
- 8 oz wheat cereal
- 5 oz butter
- 2 tablespoons maple sauce
- 1 teaspoon minced garlic
- 1 oz onion powder
- 6 oz pretzel
- 1 teaspoon salt
- 1 tablespoon dried dill

Directions:

Combine the rice cereal, corn cereal, and wheat cereal together in the slow cooker bowl. Melt the butter and combine it with the maple syrup, minced garlic, onion powder, salt, and dried dill. Crush the pretzels roughly and add them in the slow cooker bowl. Then, sprinkle the mixture with the melted butter mixture and close the slow cooker lid. Cook the dish for 2.5 hours on HIGH. Stir the mixture every 20 minutes. Let the prepared dish cool then serve it immediately.

Nutrition: calories 403, fat 15.5, fiber 2, carbs 58.87, protein 7

Boiled Peanuts

Prep time: 10 minutes | Cooking time: 10 hours | Servings: 7

Ingredients:

- 10 oz peanut
- 12 cup water
- 1 tablespoon salt
- 1 tablespoon sriracha

- 1 teaspoon ground black pepper
- 1 teaspoon oregano
- 2 tablespoons onion powder

Directions:

Wash the peanuts carefully and put them in the slow cooker vessel then add water. Combine the salt, sriracha, ground black pepper, oregano, and onion powder together in the shallow bowl. Stir it gently and add the mixture in the slow cooker too. Stir the slow cooker mixture gently and close the lid. Cook the dish for 10 hours on LOW. When the dish is cooked, strain the pecans and chill them well. Serve the snack and

Nutrition: calories 241, fat 20.1, fiber 4, carbs 8.68, protein 11

Kielbasa

Prep time: 15 minutes | Cooking time: 3 hours | Servings: 5

Ingredients:

- 1 onion
- 4 tablespoons tomato sauce
- 1-pound kielbasa
- 1 teaspoon cayenne pepper

- 1 teaspoon paprika
- 1 tablespoon butter
- ¼ teaspoon chili flakes

Directions:

Slice the kielbasa roughly. Sprinkle the sliced kielbasa with the cayenne pepper and paprika. Add chili flakes and mix. After this, peel the onion and grate it. Combine the grated onion with the sliced kielbasa and stir the mixture gently. Then transfer the mixture to the slow cooker and toss butter in as well. Close the slow cooker lid and cook the dish for 3 hours on HIGH. Serve the dish warm.

Nutrition: calories 251, fat 18.5, fiber 2, carbs 8.82, protein 13

Semi-Sweet Meatballs

Prep time: 20 minutes | Cooking time: 7 hours | Servings: 8

Ingredients:

- 2 tablespoons soy sauce
- 1 tablespoon apple cider vinegar
- 1 teaspoon ground black pepper
- 3 tablespoons sugar
- 1 teaspoon cilantro
- ½ cup tomato sauce
- 1 egg

- 2 tablespoons bread crumbs
- 1 teaspoon minced garlic
- 1 teaspoon onion powder
- 1 teaspoon salt
- 1 teaspoon ground white pepper
- 10 oz ground beef
- 3 tablespoons fresh parsley

Directions:

Beat the egg in the bowl. Add the bread crumbs, ground beef, ground black pepper, salt, onion powder, and minced garlic. Mix carefully. Combine the soy sauce, apple cider vinegar, ground white pepper, sugar, tomato sauce, and fresh parsley. Mix and place in the slow cooker bowl. Then form the meatballs from the ground beef mixture and transfer them to the slow cooker. Close the slow cooker lid and cook the dish for 7 hours on LOW. Serve the meatballs with the sauce.

Nutrition: calories 201, fat 13, fiber 2, carbs 12, protein 8

Beer and Chicken Logs

Prep time: 20 minutes | Cooking time: 5 hours | Servings: 7

Ingredients:

- ½ cup beer
- 17 oz ground chicken
- 1 egg
- 2 tablespoons semolina
- 1 tablespoon flour
- 1 teaspoon salt
- 1 teaspoon chili flakes
- 1 cup panko bread crumbs
- 1 tablespoon butter
- 1 teaspoon olive oil

Directions:

Beat the eggs in the bowl. Add the ground chicken, semolina, salt, flour, chili flakes, and butter. Mix well. Make small logs from the ground chicken mixture. Dip the logs in the olive oil then coat the meat logs in the panko bread crumbs carefully. Place the meat logs in the slow cooker. Close the slow cooker lid and cook the dish for 3 hours on HIGH. Pour the beer into the slow cooker and cook the dish for 2 hours more on HIGH. Serve the cooked snack immediately.

Nutrition: calories 200, fat 12.2, fiber 1, carbs 6.96, protein 15

Slow Cooker Taquitos

Prep time: 15 minutes | Cooking time: 8 hours | Servings: 8

Ingredients:

- 8 corn tortillas
- 1 cup fresh dill
- 4 oz Cheddar cheese, shredded
- 8 oz ground beef
- 1 tablespoon onion powder
- 1 chili pepper
- ½ cup tomato sauce
- 1 teaspoon salt
- 1 teaspoon ground black pepper
- 1 teaspoon sugar
- 1 teaspoon minced garlic
- 3 tablespoons heavy cream

Directions:

Put the ground beef in the slow cooker. Add the onion powder, tomato sauce, salt, ground black pepper, sugar, minced garlic, and heavy cream. Chop the fresh dill and add it in the slow cooker too. Chop the chili pepper and add it in the slow cooker too then mix everything well. Close the slow cooker lid and cook the dish on LOW for 8 hours. Sprinkle the tortillas with the shredded cheese. When the ground beef mixture is cooked, add it to the tortillas and wrap them. Serve the snack immediately.

Nutrition: calories 218, fat 12.7, fiber 3, carbs 17.98, protein 8

Snack Hot Dogs

Prep time: 10 minutes | Cooking time: 3.5 hours | Servings: 6

Ingredients:

- 1-pound mini hot dogs
- 7 tablespoons ketchup
- 2 oz sugar
- 1 teaspoon smoke flavoring
- 2 tablespoons Teriyaki sauce
- 1 teaspoon onion powder

Directions:

Slice the mini hot dogs and place them in the slow cooker bowl. Combine the sugar, ketchup, and smoke flavoring together. Add Teriyaki sauce and onion powder. Mix everything well. Sprinkle the sliced hot dogs with the prepared ketchup mixture and close the slow cooker lid. Cook the dish on LOW for 3.5 hours. When the snack is prepared, cool then serve.

Nutrition: calories 312, fat 22.9, fiber 0, carbs 18.16, protein 9

Pita Bites

Prep time: 15 minutes | Cooking time: 9 hours | Servings: 6

Ingredients:

- 9 oz chicken breast
- 1 tablespoon mustard
- 2 tablespoons fresh basil
- 1 teaspoon cayenne pepper
- 1 cup cream
- 1 cup water

- 1 teaspoon salt
- 1 onion, peeled
- 1 teaspoon oregano
- 6 pitas
- 1 tablespoon lemon juice

Directions:

Put the chicken breast in the slow cooker. Add the water and cream. Sprinkle the meat with mustard, salt, oregano, and lemon juice. Chop the peeled onion and add it in the slow cooker as well. Close the slow cooker lid and cook the dish for 9 hours on LOW. When the time is done, strain the chicken breast and shred it with a fork. Chop the fresh basil and combine it with the shredded chicken. Then add the 4 tablespoons of the remaining liquid from the slow cooker and stir it well. Spread the pita bread with the prepared chicken mixture.

Nutrition: calories 237, fat 12.6, fiber 3, carbs 19.21, protein 13

Chocolate nuts

Prep time: 10 minutes | Cooking time: 2 hours 10 minutes | Servings: 4

Ingredients:

- 5 oz dark chocolate
- 5 oz milk chocolate
- 1 cup walnuts halves

- 2 teaspoons tablespoon heavy cream
- ¼ teaspoon vanilla extract

Directions:

Chop the dark chocolate and milk chocolate and place them in the slow cooker. Add heavy cream and vanilla extract. Close the slow cooker lid and cook the chocolate on HIGH for 1 hours or till the mixture is homogenous. Then add the walnuts halves and stir. Cook the dish for 10 minutes on HIGH. Cover the tray with the parchment and transfer the chocolate nuts to the tray. Let the chocolate nuts cool until the chocolate is hard.

Nutrition: calories 521, fat 35.1, fiber 5, carbs 45.16, protein 8

Slow Cooker Fudge

Prep time: 10 minutes | Cooking time: 5 hours | Servings: 7

Ingredients:

- 5 oz condensed milk
- 10 oz chocolate
- ½ teaspoon vanilla extract

- 1 oz butter
- ¼ teaspoon cinnamon

Directions:

Chop the chocolate roughly and place it in the slow cooker bowl. Add the condensed milk and vanilla extract. Add butter and cinnamon. Close the slow cooker lid and cook the mixture on LOW for 5 hours. Stir the chocolate mixture every 30 minutes. Pour the chocolate mixture into a square pan and flatten it well with the help of the spatula. Place the pan in the freezer. Cut the prepared fudge into the squares.

Nutrition: calories 317156, fat 4.4, fiber 1, carbs 27.45, protein 2

Nutella Granola

Prep time: 15 minutes | Cooking time: 3 hours 30 minutes | Servings: 6

Ingredients:

- 2 tablespoons Nutella
- 2 tablespoons honey
- 1 tablespoon raisins
- 1 cup granola
- 5 tablespoons pumpkin puree
- 1 teaspoon cinnamon
- ½ teaspoon ground ginger
- 1 teaspoon ground cardamom
- 3 tablespoons olive oil
- 3 tablespoons sunflower seeds

Directions:

Place the granola in the slow cooker. Add raisins, pumpkin puree, cinnamon, ground ginger, ground cardamom, and sunflower seeds. Mix well and close the slow cooker lid. Cook the mixture on LOW for 3 hours. Meanwhile, combine Nutella, honey, and olive oil together. Mix well. When the time is done, pour the honey mixture into the slow cooker and stir it carefully. After this, close the slow cooker lid and cook the dish for 30 minutes on LOW. Then transfer the granola mixture into the bowl and add the sunflower seeds. Mix it well. Cool the mixture well and separate it into 6 servings.

Nutrition: calories 372, fat 25.1, fiber 3, carbs 32.2, protein 6

Oatmeal-Raisin Bars

Prep time: 20 minutes | Cooking time: 6 hours | Servings: 6

Ingredients:

- 1 cup oatmeal
- 1 tablespoon prunes
- 1 egg
- ¼ cup flour
- 1 tablespoon pumpkin seeds
- 3 tablespoons raisins
- ¼ cup milk
- ¼ teaspoon ground cinnamon
- ¼ teaspoon olive oil

Directions:

Beat the egg in the mixing bowl. Add the milk and ground cinnamon. Stir then crush the pumpkin seeds and combine them with the oatmeal and raisins. Add the eggs and stir again. After this, add flour, prunes, and knead into a smooth dough. After this, spray the slow cooker bowl with the olive oil. Place the prepared dough in the slow cooker bowl and flatten well. Close the lid and cook the dish for 6 hours on LOW. Remove the prepared dish from the slow cooker and cut into the serving bars with the help of the knife. Chill the bars carefully.

Nutrition: calories 92, fat 3.2, fiber 1, carbs 12.7, protein 4

Chicken Nachos

Prep time: 20 minutes | Cooking time: 4 hours | Servings: 10

Ingredients:

- 1 tablespoon taco seasoning
- 16 oz chicken breast, boneless
- 1 teaspoon salt
- 1 teaspoon paprika
- 1 avocado, pitted
- 1 chili pepper
- 1 tablespoon chives
- 6 oz Cheddar cheese, shredded
- 2 tablespoons salsa
- 1 teaspoon minced garlic
- 4 tablespoons tomato sauce
- 1 teaspoon thyme
- 7 oz tortilla chips
- 1 onion

Directions:

Combine the salt, taco seasoning, paprika, and thyme in the shallow bowl. Place the chicken breast in the slow cooker. Sprinkle the chicken with the spice mixture. Add minced garlic, salsa, and tomato sauce. Chop the chili pepper and onion and add the chopped vegetables in the slow cooker bowl and close the lid. Cook the dish on HIGH for 4 hours. Shred the chicken breast with 2 forks. Place the tortilla chip on the serving plate. After this, cover it with the shredded chicken mixture. Sprinkle the dish with the cheese and chives. Peel the avocado and chop it into pieces. Sprinkle the prepared meal with the chopped avocado.

Nutrition: calories 249, fat 11.8, fiber 3, carbs 21.56, protein 14

Meat Balls with Cheese

Prep time: 20 minutes | Cooking time: 9 hours | Servings: 9

Ingredients:

- 10 oz ground pork
- 1 tablespoon minced garlic
- 1 teaspoon ground black pepper
- 1 teaspoon salt
- 1 teaspoon paprika
- 1 teaspoon oregano
- 6 oz Romano cheese
- 1 cup panko bread crumbs
- 1 teaspoon chili flakes
- 1 egg
- 2 teaspoons milk
- 1 teaspoon olive oil

Directions:

Toss the ground pork in a big bowl. Add minced garlic, ground black pepper, salt, paprika, oregano, and chili flakes. Beat the egg into the meat mixture. Add milk and mix with your hands. Cut the hard cheese into the medium cubes. Make balls from the meat mixture and put the cheese cube inside the meatballs. Coat the prepared cheese meatballs with the panko bread crumbs. Spray the slow cooker bowl inside with the olive oil. Place the meatballs in the slow cooker and close the lid. Cook the dish on LOW for 9 hours. When cooked, cool slightly and serve immediately.

Nutrition: calories 167, fat 9.2, fiber 0, carbs 3.92, protein 17

Bean Dip

Prep time: 10 minutes | Cooking time: 6 hours | Servings: 8

Ingredients:

- 10 oz refried beans
- 1 tablespoon pesto sauce
- 1 teaspoon salt
- 7 oz Cheddar cheese, shredded
- 1 teaspoon paprika
- 1 cup salsa
- 4 tablespoons sour cream
- 2-ounce cream cheese
- 1 teaspoon dried dill

Directions:

Combine the pesto sauce and salsa together. Add salt, sour cream, cream cheese, and dried dill. After this, add paprika and whisk the mixture with the help of the hand whisker. Place the salsa mixture in the slow cooker. Add the shredded cheese and refried beans. Close the slow cooker lid and cook the dip on LOW for 6 hours. Stir the dish once during the cooking. When the dip is cooked, blend it gently with a hand blender. Transfer the dish to the bowl and cool. Serve the snack with tortillas.

Nutrition: calories 102, fat 6.3, fiber 1, carbs 7.43, protein 5

Cayenne Pepper Shrimp

Prep time: 15 minutes | Cooking time: 25 minutes | Servings: 5

Ingredients:

- 1 teaspoon sage
- 1 tablespoon piripiri sauce
- 1 teaspoon thyme
- 1 tablespoon cayenne pepper
- 2 tablespoon heavy cream
- 1 teaspoon salt
- ¼ cup butter
- 1-pound shrimp
- ½ cup fresh parsley

Directions:

Combine the butter with the sage, piripiri, thyme, cayenne pepper, heavy cream, and salt. Blend well. Then place the butter mixture in the slow cooker. Close the lid and cook the mixture for 10 minutes on HIGH. Meanwhile, peel the shrimp. Add the peeled shrimp in the slow cooker. Stir the shrimp carefully and close the slow cooker lid. Cook the shrimp for 15 minutes on HIGH. When the seafood is cooked, transfer to the serving plate and sprinkle with the remaining spicy sauce.

Nutrition: calories 199, fat 12.9, fiber 1, carbs 1.28, protein 19

Marsala Mushrooms

Prep time: 15 minutes | Cooking time: 8 hours 20 minutes | Servings: 6

Ingredients:

- 4 oz marsala
- 8 oz button mushrooms
- ½ cup fresh dill
- 2 oz shallot, chopped
- 3 oz chicken stock
- 5 oz cream, whipped
- 1 oz corn starch
- 3 garlic cloves, chopped
- 3 oz Cheddar cheese
- 1 teaspoon salt
- ½ teaspoon paprika

Directions:

Wash the button mushrooms and place in the slow cooker. Combine the chopped shallot, sliced garlic, salt, and paprika together. Stir the mixture. After this, chop the fresh dill. Combine the Marsala and chicken stock in a separate bowl and stir well. Sprinkle the mushrooms with the chopped shallot and sliced garlic. Pour the chicken stock in the slow cooker and close the slow cooker lid. Cook the dish on LOW for 8 hours. Meanwhile, combine the whipped cream and chopped fresh dill together. Grate the cheddar cheese and add it to the heavy cream liquid. Add the corn starch and stir lightly. When the time is done, sprinkle the Marsala button mushrooms with the whipped cream. Close the slow cooker lid and cook it for 20 minutes on HIGH. Serve the dish immediately.

Nutrition: calories 254, fat 10.3, fiber 5, carbs 35.7, protein 9

Rosemary Fingerling Potatoes

Prep time: 16 minutes | Cooking time: 8 hours | Servings: 15

Ingredients:

- 2 lb. fingerling potatoes
- 8 oz bacon
- 1 teaspoon onion powder
- 1 teaspoon chili powder
- 1 teaspoon garlic powder
- 1 teaspoon paprika
- 3 tablespoons butter
- 1 teaspoon dried dill
- 1 tablespoon rosemary

Directions:

Wash the fingerling potatoes carefully. Butter the slow cooker bowl and make a layer of fingerling potatoes there. Combine the onion powder, chili powder, garlic powder, paprika, and dried dill together in a separate bowl. Stir lightly. Sprinkle the layer of fingerling potatoes with the spice mixture. Then slice the bacon and combine it with the rosemary. Cover the fingerling potatoes with the sliced bacon and close the slow cooker lid. Cook the dish on LOW for 8 hours. Serve the snack immediately.

Nutrition: calories 117, fat 6.9, fiber 2, carbs 12.07, protein 3

Chili Pepper Dip

Prep time: 15 minutes | Cooking time: 9 hours | Servings: 8

Ingredients:

- 4 chili pepper
- 7 oz Monterey cheese
- 3 tablespoons cream cheese
- 1 tablespoon onion powder
- 3 tablespoons dried dill
- 3 oz butter
- 1 tablespoon cornstarch
- 1 tablespoon flour
- ¼ teaspoon salt

Directions:

Wash the chili peppers and discard the seeds. Chop the chili peppers and put them in a blender. Add onion powder, dried dill, and salt. Add butter and blend the chili mixture until it is well mixed. Place the mixture in the slow cooker. Add cream cheese, flour, and cornstarch and stir. Add Monterey cheese and close the slow cooker lid. Cook the dip on LOW for 6 hours. Stir it every hour with a spatula. When the dish is cooked, transfer it to a bowl. Serve the dip with the tortillas.

Nutrition: calories 212, fat 18.2, fiber 1, carbs 6.06, protein 8

Snack Chickpeas

Prep time: 15 minutes | Cooking time: 4 hours | Servings: 9

Ingredients:

- 1-pound chickpea, canned, drained
- 4 oz white onion
- 1 tablespoon minced garlic
- 1 tablespoon chili flakes
- ½ teaspoon thyme
- ½ teaspoon ground coriander
- 1 teaspoon salt
- 12 oz chicken stock
- ½ cup fresh dill
- 1 teaspoon butter
- 3 tablespoon bread crumbs

Directions:

Peel the white onion and grate it. Combine the grated onion with the minced garlic, chili flakes, thyme, ground cinnamon, salt, and butter. Put the canned chickpeas in the slow cooker. Add the chicken stock and grated onion mix. Close the slow cooker lid and cook the dish on HIGH for 4 hours. Meanwhile, wash the fresh dill and chop it. When the chickpeas are cooked, strain the excess liquid and place the chickpeas in a big bowl. Sprinkle with the bread crumbs and chopped fresh dill. Stir it carefully then serve the snack.

Nutrition: calories 270, fat 5.3, fiber 7, carbs 44.09, protein 13

Shiitake Mushroom Bites

Prep time: 25 minutes | Cooking time: 5 hours | Servings: 10

Ingredients:

- 7 oz shiitake mushroom
- 2 eggs
- 1 tablespoon cream cheese
- 3 tablespoons panko bread crumbs
- 2 tablespoons flour
- 1 teaspoon minced garlic
- 1 teaspoon salt
- ½ teaspoon chili flakes
- 1 teaspoon olive oil
- 1 teaspoon ground coriander
- ½ teaspoon nutmeg
- 1 tablespoon almond flour
- 1 teaspoon butter

Directions:

Chop the shiitake mushrooms and put them in a skillet. Sprinkle the mushrooms with the salt, minced garlic, chili flakes, olive oil, ground coriander, and nutmeg. Roast the shiitake mushrooms for 5 minutes over medium heat. Beat the eggs in a bowl then add cream cheese, flour and bread crumbs. Add the shiitake mushroom mixture and butter. Knead into a smooth dough. Add more flour if the dough is sticky. Make the medium bites from the shiitake mushroom dough. Transfer the remaining oil from the skillet into the slow cooker bowl. Then put the mushroom bites inside the bowl. Close the lid and cook the shiitake mushroom bites for 3 hours on HIGH. Turn the bites over and cook for 2 hours more on HIGH. Dry the mushroom bites with a paper towel if desired.

Nutrition: calories 65, fat 3.5, fiber 1, carbs 6.01, protein 3

Veggie Potato Cups

Prep time: 15 minutes | Cooking time: 8 hours | Servings: 8

Ingredients:

- 5 tablespoons mashed potato
- 1 carrot, boiled
- 3 tablespoons green peas
- 1 teaspoon paprika
- 3 tablespoons sour cream
- 1 teaspoon minced garlic
- 7 oz puff pastry
- 1 egg yolk
- 4 oz Parmesan, shredded

Directions:

Chop the boiled carrot into the small cubes. Combine the carrot cubes with the mashed potato. Add green peas, paprika, and sour cream. Add minced garlic and mix with a fork. Roll the puff pastry and cut it into the squares. Take the separated muffin form and put the puff pastry squares into the cups. Then whisk the egg yolk and brush every puff pastry square with the yolk. After this, put the mashed potato mixture in the muffin form with a spoon. Place the muffin cups in the slow cooker and cook it for 8 hours on LOW. When the snack cups are cooked, let them cool then serve.

Nutrition: calories 387, fat 11.5, fiber 6, carbs 59.01, protein 13

Chicken Butter Balls

Prep time: 21 minutes | Cooking time: 3.5 hours | Servings: 9

Ingredients:

- 3 oz butter
- 1 tablespoon mayonnaise
- 1 teaspoon cayenne pepper
- 1 teaspoon ground black pepper
- 1 teaspoon salt
- 1 egg
- 2 oz white bread
- 4 tablespoon milk
- 1 teaspoon olive oil
- 1 tablespoon almond flour
- 1 teaspoon dried dill
- 14 oz ground chicken
- ½ teaspoon olive oil

Directions:

Cut the butter into the cubes and freeze. Meanwhile, combine the mayonnaise, cayenne pepper, ground black pepper, salt, dried dill, and ground chicken together. Beat the egg into the mixture. Combine the white bread and milk together and stir the mixture until homogenous. Then add the white bread mix into the ground chicken mixture. Mix carefully with your hands. Spray the slow cooker bowl with the olive oil. Then make the meat balls from the meat mix and press a few frozen butter cubes into each ball. Sprinkle every ball with the almond flour and place them in the slow cooker. Cook the dish on HIGH for 3.5 hours. Chill the snack until room temperature and serve or keep them in the fridge.

Nutrition: calories 181, fat 14.1, fiber 1, carbs 4.02, protein 10

Spicy Nuts

Prep time: 25 minutes | Cooking time: 40 minutes | Servings: 6

Ingredients:

- ½ teaspoon cooking spray
- 1 teaspoon chili flakes
- 1 teaspoon ground cinnamon
- 2 oz butter, melted
- 1 teaspoon salt
- 1 cup peanuts
- 1 cup cashew
- 1 cup walnuts
- 3 tablespoons maple syrup

Directions:

Combine the peanuts, cashew, and walnuts together in a bowl. Stir them gently and put on a tray. Put the tray in the preheated 350 F oven and bake the nuts for 10 minutes. Stir them every 2 minutes while baking. Meanwhile, combine the chili flakes, ground cinnamon, and salt together. Stir the spices gently. When the nuts are cooked, transfer them to a slow cooker. Sprinkle the nuts with the spices and stir well. After this, combine the maple syrup with the melted butter and whisk it. Sprinkle the nuts with the butter liquid and close the lid of the slow cooker. Cook the snack for 20 minutes on HIGH. After this, open the slow cooker lid and stir the nuts well. Close the lid and cook on HIGH for 20 more minutes. When the time is done, transfer the nuts to a snack bowl. Cool and serve it!

Nutrition: calories 693, fat 55.4, fiber 5, carbs 39.16, protein 20

Spinach Cream Cheese Dip

Prep time: 16 minutes | Cooking time: 3 hours 20 minutes | Servings: 8

Ingredients:

- 2 cups cream cheese
- 2 cups fresh spinach
- 1 teaspoon salt
- 1 teaspoon ground black pepper
- 1 teaspoon paprika
- 1 teaspoon ground white pepper
- 7 oz Mozzarella, cut into strips
- 1 onion
- 1 tablespoon Tabasco sauce
- 1 tablespoon butter
- 3 tablespoons milk

Directions:

Wash the fresh spinach carefully and chop it into small pieces. Then combine the cream cheese with the salt, ground black pepper, paprika, ground white pepper, Tabasco sauce, and milk. Whisk the cream cheese by hand. Then peel the onion and grate it. Add the grated onion into the cream cheese mixture. Butter the slow cooker bowl and transfer the whisked cream cheese mixture inside. Close the slow cooker lid and cook it for 20 minutes on HIGH. After 20 minutes, add the chopped spinach and Mozzarella strips. Close the lid and cook the spinach dip for 3 hours on HIGH. Stir the dip every 30 minutes. When the spinach dip is cooked, transfer it to a serving bowl. Enjoy with nachos!

Nutrition: calories 241, fat 18.9, fiber 1, carbs 6.03, protein 13

Mozzarella Tomatoes

Prep time: 10 minutes | Cooking time: 30 minutes | Servings: 8

Ingredients:

- 3 tablespoons fresh basil
- 1 teaspoon chili flakes
- 5 oz Mozzarella
- 4 large tomatoes
- 1 tablespoon olive oil
- 1 teaspoon minced garlic
- ½ teaspoon onion powder
- ½ teaspoon cilantro

Directions:

Slice the large tomatoes roughly. Then slice Mozzarella. Combine chili flakes, olive oil, minced garlic, onion powder, and cilantro together. After this, rub the sliced tomatoes with the chili flakes mixture. Then put 1 slice of Mozzarella over the tomato slice and cover with the second tomato slice. Secure with a toothpick. Transfer the tomato-mozzarella snack into the slow cooker. Close the lid and cook on HIGH for 20 minutes. Tear the fresh basil roughly. Open the slow cooker lid and sprinkle the dish with the fresh basil. Cook it for 10 minutes more on HIGH. Then chill Mozzarella tomatoes well.

Nutrition: calories 59, fat 1.9, fiber 2, carbs 4.59, protein 7

Parsley Dip with Blue Cheese

Prep time: 10 minutes | Cooking time: 7 hours | Servings: 7

Ingredients:

- 1 cup parsley
- 8 oz celery stalk
- 6 oz Blue cheese
- 1 tablespoon apple cider vinegar
- 6 oz cream
- 1 teaspoon minced garlic
- 1 teaspoon paprika
- ¼ teaspoon ground red pepper
- 1 onion

Directions:

Chop the fresh parsley and celery stalk. Then chop blue cheese and add to the parsley and celery. Whip the cream and add it to the cheese mixture. Place in the slow cooker bowl. Sprinkle the parsley mixture with the minced garlic, paprika, ground red pepper, and apple cider vinegar. Peel the onion and grate it. Add the grated onion in the slow cooker and close the lid. Cook on LOW and cook for 7 hours. Mix the dip up with the help of the wooden spoon after 4 hours of the cooking. After the dish is cooked, remove it from the slow cooker and chill lightly. Stir the dip one more time.

Nutrition: calories 151, fat 11.9, fiber 1, carbs 5.14, protein 7

Dill Muffins

Prep time: 20 minutes | Cooking time: 9 hours | Servings: 6

Ingredients:

- 2 egg
- 5 tablespoons butter
- 1 cup fresh dill
- 1 teaspoon baking soda
- 1 tablespoon lemon juice
- 1 teaspoon cilantro
- 1 cup milk
- 2 cups flour
- 1 teaspoon salt
- ¼ teaspoon cooking spray

Directions:

Beat the eggs in the bowl and whisk. Melt the butter and add it in the bowl too. After this, add baking soda and lemon juice. Sprinkle the mixture with the cilantro, milk, salt, and add the flour. Chop the fresh dill and add it to the mix. Whisk the mixture to get a cream-like dough. Then spray the muffin form with the cooking spray. Pour the dough in the muffin forms and put them in the slow cooker. Close the lid and cook muffins for 9 hours on LOW. Chill the muffins and serve.

Nutrition: calories 306, fat 14.6, fiber 1, carbs 34.37, protein 9

Peanut Chicken Strips

Prep time: 15 minutes | Cooking time: 6 hours | Servings: 7

Ingredients:

- 3 tablespoons peanut butter, melted
- 1-pound chicken breast, boneless, skinless
- 1 teaspoon paprika
- 1 teaspoon salt
- 1 teaspoon olive oil
- 2 tablespoons almond flour
- 1 teaspoon cayenne pepper

Directions:

Cut the chicken breast into the thick strips. Then sprinkle the chicken strips with the paprika, salt, and cayenne pepper. Coat the chicken strips in the almond flour. Pour the olive oil into the slow cooker and add the coated chicken strips. Close the slow cooker lid and cook the chicken strips for 4 hours on HIGH. Open the slow cooker lid and stir the chicken strips carefully. Close the lid and cook the snack for 2 hours more on LOW. Chill the chicken strips very well. Serve!

Nutrition: calories 161, fat 9.5, fiber 1, carbs 3.15, protein 16

Pork Cheese Rolls

Prep time: 20 minutes | Cooking time: 7 hours | Servings: 8

Ingredients:

- 3 oz Monterey cheese, sliced
- 6 oz ground pork
- 2 oz onion, chopped
- 1 tablespoon sliced garlic
- 1 teaspoon salt
- 1 teaspoon ground pepper
- 5 oz Cheddar cheese, sliced
- 1 tablespoon pesto sauce
- 8 flour tortilla
- 1 teaspoon olive oil

Directions:

Pour the olive oil in the slow cooker. Add ground pepper, pesto sauce, chopped onion, and ground pork. Close the slow cooker lid and cook the meat on HIGH for 5 hours. When the ground meat is cooked, place it on the flour tortillas. Sprinkle every flour tortilla with the chopped cheese. Roll the flour tortillas and put them in the slow cooker. There should be remaining oil from the ground meat in the slow cooker. Close the lid and cook on HIGH for 2 hours. When the time is done, check if the cheese in the tortillas is melted. Remove the cheese rolls from the slow cooker and cut them into 2 parts. Serve the snack!

Nutrition: calories 270, fat 10.8, fiber 1, carbs 27.52, protein 16

Glazed Turkey Strips

Prep time: 15 minutes | Cooking time: 3.5 hours | Servings: 8

Ingredients:

- 15 oz turkey fillets
- 2 tablespoons honey

- 1 tablespoon maple syrup
- 1 teaspoon cayenne pepper
- 1 tablespoon butter
- 1 teaspoon paprika
- 1 teaspoon oregano
- 1 teaspoon dried dill
- 2 tablespoons mayo

Directions:

Cut the turkey fillet into the strips. Put the turkey strips in the slow cooker. Sprinkle the meat with the cayenne pepper, paprika, oregano, and dried dill. Add the mayo sauce and stir lightly with the help of the wooden spatula. Close the slow cooker lid and cook the strips for 3 hours on HIGH. Meanwhile, combine the maple syrup and honey together in the bowl. Melt the butter and add it to the syrup mixture and stir. When the slow cooker is done, open the lid and stir the meat. Pour the syrup mixture in the slow cooker bowl and close the lid. Glaze the turkey strips on HIGH for 30 minutes. Let cool slightly and serve!

Nutrition: calories 295, fat 25.2, fiber 0, carbs 6.82, protein 10

Spicy Apple Chutney

Prep time: 15 minutes | Cooking time: 9 hours | Servings: 10

Ingredients:

- 1 cup wine vinegar
- 4 oz brown sugar
- 2-pounds apples
- 4 oz onion, chopped
- 1 jalapeno pepper
- 1 teaspoon ground cardamom
- ½ teaspoon ground cinnamon
- 1 teaspoon chili flakes

Directions:

Combine wine vinegar and brown sugar and pour the mixture in the slow cooker bowl. Melt the mixture on HIGH for 1 hour. Meanwhile, chop the apples and then put them in the vinegar mixture. Add the chopped onion. Slice the jalapeno pepper and toss it in the slow cooker as well. Sprinkle the dish with the ground cardamom and ground cinnamon. Add chili flakes and close the slow cooker lid. Cook the chutney for 8 hours on LOW. When the chutney is cooked, mash with a fork. Transfer the chutney to the bowl and let it cool. Serve the dish with chips or on bread.

Nutrition: calories 101, fat 0.2, fiber 3, carbs 25.04, protein

---

Potato Dip with Cheddar Cheese

Prep time: 15 minutes | Cooking time: 5 hours | Servings: 12

Ingredients:

- 1 cup heavy cream
- 1 cup milk
- 2 tablespoons cornstarch
- 5 medium potatoes
- 5 oz Cheddar cheese
- 1 cup fresh cilantro
- 1 teaspoon salt
- 1 teaspoon black pepper
- 1 teaspoon paprika
- ½ teaspoon onion powder
- 1 tablespoon garlic powder
- ¼ teaspoon oregano

Directions:

Peel the potatoes and chop them into the small cubes. Toss the chopped potato in the slow cooker. Pour milk and heavy cream in the slow cooker. Add salt, black pepper, paprika, onion powder, garlic powder, and oregano. Close the slow cooker lid and cook the dish on HIGH for 3 hours. Meanwhile, chop Cheddar cheese and fresh cilantro. Add the cheese and cilantro after the 3 hour cooking time is done. Stir well till the cheese starts to melt. Close the lid and cook the dip on HIGH for 2 hours more. Stir the dip every 30 minutes. Then chill the dip until it is room temperature. Stir frequently. Enjoy the dip with chips.

Nutrition: calories 196, fat 5.6, fiber 4, carbs 31.58, protein 6

Creamy Apple Wedges with Peanuts

Prep time: 15 minutes | Cooking time: 2 hours | Servings: 5

Ingredients:

- 1 tablespoon peanut butter
- 3 tablespoons peanut
- 6 green apples
- ½ teaspoon cinnamon
- 1 tablespoon butter
- 2 teaspoons water
- 1 teaspoon lemon zest
- 1 teaspoon lemon juice

Directions:

Crush the peanuts and combine them with the peanut butter. Add cinnamon and butter to the peanut butter mix. After this, add lemon zest and lemon juice. Cut the green apples into wedges. Brush every apple wedge with the peanut butter mixture. Add the water to the slow cooker bowl then add the prepared apples. Add the remaining peanut butter mixture and close the slow cooker lid. Cook the apple wedges on HIGH for 2 hours. Enjoy the dish cold or hot!

Nutrition: calories 20, fat 6.9, fiber 6, carbs 35.16, protein 4

Egg Muffins

Prep time: 25 minutes | Cooking time: 6 hours | Servings: 8

Ingredients:

- 6 eggs
- ½ cup flour
- 1 teaspoon baking powder
- 1 teaspoon vinegar
- 1 teaspoon salt
- 3 tablespoons almond flour
- 2 tablespoons butter
- 5 oz bacon, chopped, roasted
- ¼ teaspoon cooking spray

Directions:

Crack the eggs into the bowl and whisk. Melt butter and add it in the whisked eggs. After this sift the flour into the egg mixture. Add vinegar, salt, almond flour, chopped bacon, and knead the dough. The dough will be thick but a little sticky. Spray the muffin molds with the cooking spray and pour the dough there. Fill each muffin cup only 1/3 of the way up the sides. After this, place the muffin molds in short glass jars. Transfer the glass jars in the slow cooker and pour ½ cup of water inside the slow cooker bowl. Close the lid and cook the dish for 6 hours on LOW. Serve the muffins warm.

Nutrition: calories 210, fat 15.7, fiber 1, carbs 8.24, protein 10

Carrot Fritters

Prep time: 20 minutes | Cooking time: 4 hours | Servings: 12

Ingredients:

- 2 large carrots
- 4 oz broccoli
- 1 tablespoon cream cheese
- ¼ cup flour
- 1 teaspoon salt
- 1 teaspoon ground black pepper
- 1 teaspoon paprika
- 1 teaspoon butter
- 4 tablespoons fresh cilantro, chopped
- 1 egg
- 3 oz celery stalk

Directions:

Peel the carrots and grate them. Then put the grated carrot in the mixing bowl. Crack the egg into the bowl and add the cream cheese, flour, salt, ground black pepper, paprika, fresh cilantro, and mix it gently. Then grind celery stalk and add to the carrot mixture too. Chop the broccoli and add it to the mixture. Mix into a smooth dough. Butter the slow cooker bowl. Form the fritters from the carrot mass and put them in the slow cooker. Close the lid and cook the dish for 3 hours on HIGH. After this, flip the fritters and cook for 1 hour on HIGH. Serve the snack immediately.

Nutrition: calories 37, fat 1.6, fiber 1, carbs 4.22, protein 2

Garlic Bacon Slices

Prep time: 15 minutes | Cooking time: 4 hours | Servings: 9

Ingredients:

- 10 oz Canadian bacon
- 2 tablespoons garlic powder
- 2 garlic cloves
- 2 tablespoons whipped cream
- 1 teaspoon dried dill
- 1 teaspoon chili flakes
- ½ teaspoon salt

Directions:

Slice the bacon and sprinkle it with the garlic powder. After this, peel the garlic cloves and slice them. Combine the sliced garlic with the whipped cream. Add dried dill and chili flakes. Then add salt and whisk the mixture gently. Sprinkle the sliced bacon with the whipped cream mixture and leave for at least 10 minutes to marinate. Transfer the sliced bacon to the slow cooker. Close the lid and cook the dish on HIGH for 3 hours. Flip the sliced bacon over and remove the excess liquid. Cook the sliced bacon for 1 hour more on HIGH. After this, dry the bacon gently with a paper towel. Serve it!

Nutrition: calories 51, fat 1.6, fiber 0, carbs 2.59, protein 7

Salty Peanut Bombs

Prep time: 15 minutes | Cooking time: 6 hours | Servings: 9

Ingredients:

- 1 cup peanut
- ½ cup flour
- 1 egg
- 1 teaspoon butter
- 1 teaspoon salt
- 1 teaspoon turmeric
- 4 tablespoons milk
- ¼ teaspoon nutmeg

Directions:

Put the peanuts in a blender and blend them well. Combine the blended peanuts with the flour. Crack the egg into the bowl and whisk. Add salt, turmeric, milk, and nutmeg. Stir gently. Combine the flour mixture and egg mixture together. Knead into a smooth dough. Toss the butter in the slow cooker bowl and melt on HIGH for 10 minutes. After this, make small balls from the dough and put them in the slow cooker. Close the lid and cook the bombs on SLOW for 6 hours. Check if the bombs are cooked and remove them from the slow cooker. Put them on paper towel and chill well.

Nutrition: calories 215, fat 12.7, fiber 2, carbs 17.4, protein 10

Crunchy Zucchini Sticks

Prep time: 15 minutes | Cooking time: 2 hours | Servings: 13

Ingredients:

- 9 oz green zucchini
- 4 oz Parmesan, grated
- 1 egg
- 1 teaspoon salt
- 1 teaspoon ground white pepper
- 1 teaspoon olive oil
- 2 tablespoons milk

Directions:

Wash the zucchini and dry it well. Cut the zucchini into thick sticks. Beat the egg in a bowl. Sprinkle the whisked egg with the salt, ground white pepper, and milk. Whisk one more time. Toss the zucchini stick in the whisked egg mixture and coat them well. Pour the olive oil in the slow cooker. Then transfer the zucchini stick in the slow cooker and cook them for 2 hours on HIGH. Then stir the zucchini sticks carefully and sprinkle them with the grated cheese. Close the lid and cook the dish for 2 hours on HIGH. When the zucchini has a crunchy surface, it is dish is cooked. Serve the zucchini sticks warm.

Nutrition: calories 51, fat 1.7, fiber 0, carbs 4.62, protein 5

Pitta Pockets with Sweet Pepper
Prep time: 15 minutes | Cooking time: 4 hours | Servings: 6

Ingredients:

- 6 pita breads
- 2 sweet peppers
- 1 chili pepper
- 1 red onion
- 1 teaspoon salt
- 2 tablespoons vinegar
- 1 tablespoon olive oil
- 1 tablespoon garlic, sliced
- 2 tablespoons pesto

Directions:

Remove the seeds from the sweet peppers and chop them roughly. Put the chopped sweet peppers in a blender. Add chili pepper, salt, vinegar, olive oil, and sliced garlic. Peel the onion and chop. Add the chopped onion to the blender. Pulse the vegetable mixture for 10 seconds. Transfer the mixture in the slow cooker and close the lid. Cook the dish for 4 hours on LOW. Then make pockets in the pita bread and spread the inside with the pesto. When the sweet pepper filling is cooked, fill the pita bread pockets with it. Serve warm!

Nutrition: calories 153, fat 6.1, fiber 3, carbs 22.42, protein 4

Garlic Dip
Prep time: 15 minutes | Cooking time: 6 hours | Servings: 7

Ingredients:

- 10 oz garlic cloves
- 5 oz Parmesan
- 1 cup cream cheese
- 1 teaspoon cayenne pepper
- 1 tablespoon dried dill
- 1 teaspoon turmeric
- ½ teaspoon butter

Directions:

Peel the garlic cloves and place them in the slow cooker. Add cream cheese and cayenne pepper. Shred Parmesan cheese and add it to the slow cooker. Then sprinkle the mixture with the dried dill and turmeric. Add butter and close the lid. Cook the dish on LOW for 6 hours. After this, stir and mash the dip carefully with a wooden spatula. Transfer the prepared garlic dip in the bowl and serve with the corn tortillas.

Nutrition: calories 244, fat 11.5, fiber 1, carbs 23.65, protein 13

Sausage Dip
Prep time: 10 minutes | Cooking time: 5 hours | Servings: 8

Ingredients:

- 8 oz sausage, cooked
- 4 tablespoons sour cream
- 2 tablespoons Tabasco sauce
- ½ cup cream cheese
- 3 tablespoons chives
- 5 oz salsa
- 4 oz Monterey Cheese

Directions:

Chop the sausages and combine with the sour cream. Transfer the mixture to the slow cooker. Add Tabasco sauce and cream cheese. Add chives and salsa. Chop Monterey cheese and add it to the slow cooker. Stir it gently and close the slow cooker lid. Cook the dish on LOW for 5 hours. Stir the dip every 30 minutes. When the sausage dip is cooked, transfer it immediately to a serving bowl. Enjoy the sausage dip with your favorite chips.

Nutrition: calories 184, fat 14.4, fiber 1, carbs 5.11, protein 10

Marinated Chili Peppers

Prep time: 15 minutes | *Cooking time:* 3 hours | *Servings:* 7

Ingredients:

- 2 tablespoons balsamic vinegar
- 10 oz red chili pepper
- 4 garlic cloves
- 1 white onion
- 3 tablespoons water
- 1 teaspoon oregano
- 1 teaspoon ground black pepper
- 4 tablespoons olive oil
- 1 teaspoon ground nutmeg
- ½ teaspoon ground ginger

Directions:

Wash the chili peppers carefully and cut them across. After this, peel the garlic cloves and slice them. Peel the white onion and chop it. Combine the chopped white onion, sliced garlic cloves, water, oregano, ground black pepper, ground nutmeg, and ground ginger together. Add olive oil and whisk the mixture. Make a layer of the chili peppers in the slow cooker. Sprinkle the chili peppers with the olive oil mixture and close the lid. Cook the chili peppers on HIGH for 3 hours. Then let the prepared chili peppers cool. Serve the dish with the white bread toasts.

Nutrition: calories 96, fat 8, fiber 1, carbs 5.87, protein 1

Poultry

Chicken Pita Pockets
Prep time: 14 minutes | Cooking time: 4.5 hours | Servings: 5

Ingredients:

- 4 tablespoons plain yogurt
- 1 teaspoon salt
- 1 teaspoon cilantro
- ½ teaspoon rosemary
- ½ teaspoon tomato paste
- 8 oz chicken fillet, sliced
- 1/3 cup water
- 5 pitas
- 1 sweet pepper
- 1 white onion

Directions:

Pour water in the slow cooker and add the sliced chicken. After this, sprinkle the meat with the salt, cilantro, and rosemary. Close the slow cooker lid and cook the dish on HIGH for 3 hours. Meanwhile, peel the onion and cut it into the medium petals. Then discard the seeds from the sweet pepper and cut it into the strips. When the time is done, open the slow cooker lid and stir the chicken fillet gently. Then add the onion petals and sweet pepper strips over the chicken fillet. Close the slow cooker lid and cook on HIGH for 1.5 hours more. Meanwhile, make the crosswise cut in the pitas. Spread the pitas with the plain yogurt inside. When the time is done, remove the chicken and vegetables from the slow cooker and chill well. Fill the pita bread with the chicken and vegetables and serve it immediately.

Nutrition: calories 222, fat 7.7, fiber 4, carbs 30.94, protein 9

Jerk Chicken Meal
Prep time: 15 minutes | Cooking time: 9 hours | Servings: 6

Ingredients:

- 1 lemon
- 3-pound chicken thighs
- 1 tablespoon taco seasoning
- 1 Habaneros pepper
- 1 tablespoon garlic clove, chopped
- ¼ teaspoon ground cinnamon
- 1 teaspoon ground black pepper
- 7 oz scallions
- 1/3 teaspoon thyme
- 1 oz fresh ginger, grated
- 5 oz pineapple juice
- 2 teaspoons soy sauce
- 1 teaspoon salt
- 1/3 cup chicken stock
- 1 teaspoon butter

Directions:

Peel the lemon and chop it. Chop Habaneros pepper. Place the chopped ingredients in the blender. Add the taco seasoning, chopped garlic clove, ground cinnamon, ground black pepper, scallions, thyme, grated fresh ginger, soy sauce, salt, and butter. Blend the mixture till it is smooth. After this, pour the chicken stock in the slow cooker bowl. Put the chicken thighs in the chicken stock. Cover the chicken thighs with the blended spice mixture. Add the pineapple juice. Close the lid and cook the dish on LOW for 9 hours. When the chicken is cooked, open the slow cooker lid and let it chill. Transfer the dish to the serving plates and sprinkle with the remaining sauce from the slow cooker.

Nutrition: calories 309, fat 7.4, fiber 2, carbs 10.44, protein 48

Chicken Rice with Lemon

Prep time: 20 minutes | Cooking time: 9 hours | Servings: 7

Ingredients:

- 16 oz chicken thighs
- 2 lemon
- 1 cup white rice
- 1 teaspoon salt
- 1 teaspoon turmeric
- 1 teaspoon ground black pepper
- 1 teaspoon cilantro
- 1 teaspoon oregano
- 1 teaspoon chili flakes
- 2 tablespoons butter
- 3 garlic cloves
- 7 oz tomatoes, canned
- 5 oz white onion
- ½ cup green peas, frozen
- 5 oz chicken stock
- 1 oz bay leaf

Directions:

Peel the garlic cloves and slice them. Toss the butter in a saute pan and melt it. Sprinkle the melted butter with the salt, turmeric, ground black pepper, cilantro, oregano, chili flakes, sliced garlic, and bay leaf. Roast the mixture on the high heat for 30 seconds, stirring constantly. After this, place the chicken thighs in the pan and sear the chicken for 4 minutes on the both side. Meanwhile, pour the chicken stock in the slow cooker bowl. Add green peas, canned tomatoes, and white rice. Peel the white onion and slice it. Transfer the chicken thighs in the slow cooker. Put the sliced onion in the remaining butter mixture and roast it for 4 minutes on the medium heat. Put the roasted sliced onion in the slow cooker. Then slice the lemon and layer it in the slow cooker bowl. Close the lid and cook the dish for 9 hours on LOW. When the dish is cooked, chill it gently.

Nutrition: calories 292, fat 10.7, fiber 4, carbs 34.78, protein 16

Poultry Burrito Bowl

Prep time: 20 minutes | Cooking time: 7 hours | Servings: 6

Ingredients:

- 13 oz chicken breast
- 1 cup sweet corn, frozen
- 1 cup chicken stock
- 6 oz tomatoes
- 7 oz wild rice
- 5 oz red kidney beans, canned
- 1 teaspoon salt
- 1 teaspoon turmeric
- 1 teaspoon cilantro
- ½ teaspoon oregano
- 1 teaspoon chili powder
- 1 teaspoon onion powder
- 1 teaspoon garlic powder
- 1 teaspoon butter

Directions:

Put the chicken breast in the slow cooker. Sprinkle it with the salt, turmeric, cilantro, oregano, chili powder, onion powder, and garlic powder. Add chicken stock and close the lid. Cook the chicken for 3 hours on LOW. After this, open the slow cooker lid and add sweet corn, wild rice, red kidney beans, and butter. Slice the tomatoes and add them in the slow cooker as well. Close the lid and cook the mixture for 4 hours on LOW more. Open the slow cooker and remove the chicken breast and put in a serving bowl. Shred the chicken with the fork. Add the remaining juice from the slow cooker into the shredded chicken. Serve it!

Nutrition: calories 315, fat 7.7, fiber 5, carbs 41.22, protein 22

Asian Chicken Bowl

Prep time: 15 minutes | Cooking time: 8 hours | Servings: 7

Ingredients:

- 3 oz orange juice
- 3 tablespoons sriracha
- 1 oz soy sauce
- 1 teaspoon olive oil
- 9 oz zucchini, chopped
- 1-pound chicken breast
- 9 oz cremini mushrooms
- 2 tablespoons fresh parsley
- 1 teaspoon salt
- 1 teaspoon ground ginger

Directions:

Chop the chicken breast roughly and place it in the slow cooker bowl. Sprinkle the chicken breast with the salt, ground ginger, and olive oil. Combine the soy sauce, sriracha, and orange juice. Whisk it. Sprinkle the chicken breast with the soy sauce mixture. Slice the cremini mushrooms and chop the fresh parsley. Add the sliced mushrooms and fresh parsley to the slow cooker bowl. Close the lid and cook the dish on LOW for 8 hours. When the dish is cooked, transfer it to the big serving bowl. Serve the dish immediately.

Nutrition: calories 247, fat 7.8, fiber 5, carbs 30.42, protein 18

Italian Style Chicken

Prep time: 15 minutes | Cooking time: 8 hours | Servings: 7

Ingredients:

- 14 oz chicken breast, boneless
- 1 cup tomatoes
- 4 oz sweet pepper
- 6 oz red onion
- ½ cup fresh celery
- 1 carrot
- 2 oz bay leaf
- 1 teaspoon cilantro
- 1 cup water
- 1 teaspoon ground black pepper
- 1 teaspoon minced garlic
- 1 teaspoon chili flakes
- 1 teaspoon Italian seasoning
- 6 oz Parmesan
- ½ teaspoon coriander

Directions:

Pour water in the slow cooker. Add the chicken breast. Sprinkle the chicken breast with the bay leaf, cilantro, ground black pepper, minced garlic, chili flakes, and coriander. Peel the carrot and chop it. Chop the fresh celery. Cut the sweet potatoes into strips, tomatoes, and red onions. Place the prepared vegetables in the slow cooker. Then add the Italian seasoning. Shred Parmesan cheese and add sprinkle it over the chicken mixture. Close the lid and cook the dish on LOW for 8 hours. When the chicken is cooked, the dish is ready to serve. Transfer the dish to the serving bowl.

Nutrition: calories 240, fat 7.3, fiber 4, carbs 21.92, protein 23

Thai Bowl

Prep time: 15 minutes | Cooking time: 4 hours 15 minutes | Servings: 7

Ingredients:

- 9 oz turkey fillet
- 5 oz coconut milk
- 1 teaspoon salt
- 1 teaspoon turmeric
- 2 tablespoons peanut butter
- 6 oz noodles, cooked
- 6 oz red cabbage, sliced
- 1 jalapeno pepper
- 1 tablespoon oregano
- 1 tablespoon tomato paste
- 1 teaspoon fresh parsley, chopped

Directions:

Chop the turkey fillet roughly and put it in the slow cooker bowl. Combine the coconut milk with salt, turmeric, peanut butter, oregano, tomato paste, and fresh parsley. Mix well. After this, sprinkle the turkey fillet with the coconut milk mixture. Slice the jalapeno pepper and add the sliced jalapeno into the slow cooker and close the lid. Cook the turkey for 4 hours on HIGH. Then add the cooked noodles and stir carefully with a spatula. Cook the dish on HIGH for 15 minutes more. Then transfer the prepared Thai mix into serving bowls.

Nutrition: calories 279, fat 22, fiber 1, carbs 11.6, protein 9

Teriyaki Chicken
Prep time: 15 hours | Cooking time: 9 hours | Servings: 6

Ingredients:
- 5 tablespoons honey
- 10 oz chicken thighs
- 7 tablespoon soy sauce
- 7 oz white onion, chopped
- 2 oz fresh ginger, grated
- 6 oz carrot
- 4 oz zucchini
- 1 teaspoon salt
- 1 tablespoon butter
- ½ cup water
- 1 tablespoon garlic, sliced
- 1 teaspoon corn starch
- 1 teaspoon balsamic vinegar
- 2 tablespoons water

Directions:
Begin by making the teriyaki marinade: combine the soy sauce, grated ginger, chopped white onion, salt, butter, sliced garlic, balsamic vinegar, and water together. Mix the mixture until homogenous. Put the chicken thighs in the slow cooker bowl. Add the prepared marinade and close the lid. Cook the chicken on LOW for 7 hours. Meanwhile, peel the carrot. Chop the carrot and zucchini. Combine the corn starch with the 2 tablespoons of water. Whisk it carefully. When the slow cooker time is complete, open the slow cooker lid and add the prepared chopped vegetables, honey and corn starch liquid. Close the lid and cook on HIGH for 2 hours more. When the time is done, remove the chicken thighs from the slow cooker and sprinkle them with the sauce from the slow cooker generously. Serve hot!

Nutrition: calories 312, fat 11.3, fiber 4, carbs 42.42, protein 13

Stuffed Chicken with Tomatoes
Prep time: 15 minutes | Cooking time: 10 hours | Servings: 8

Ingredients:
- 1 tablespoon honey
- 1 teaspoon turmeric
- 1 teaspoon coriander
- 1 teaspoon paprika
- 1 teaspoon cilantro
- 6 oz dried tomatoes
- 4 tablespoons fresh parsley
- 1 tablespoon mayonnaise
- 1 tablespoon ketchup
- 1 tablespoon butter
- 1 teaspoon salt
- 1 teaspoon ground black pepper
- 3-pounds chicken breast, skinless, boneless

Directions:
Combine honey, turmeric, coriander, paprika, cilantro, salt, ground black pepper, and butter together. After this, combine the mayonnaise and ketchup together and whisk. Make the crosswise cut in the chicken breast. Rub with the melted butter mixture. Then rub with the mayonnaise mixture. Chop the dried tomatoes and fresh parsley. Fill the prepared chicken breast with the chopped dried tomatoes and parsley. Wrap the chicken breast in the foil and put in the slow cooker. Close the lid and cook on LOW for 10 hours. When the chicken is cooked, unwrap from the foil and slice then serve.

Nutrition: calories 330, fat 17.9, fiber 1, carbs 4.54, protein 36

Chicken Liver Pate

Prep time: 20 minutes | Cooking time: 5 hours | Servings: 5

Ingredients:

- 1 carrot
- 3 yellow onions
- ¼ cup fresh dill
- 1-pound chicken liver
- 1 teaspoon salt
- 1 teaspoon paprika
- 1 teaspoon ground white pepper
- 1 cup water
- 4 tablespoons butter

Directions:

Peel the carrot and onions. Chop the vegetables and place in the slow cooker bowl and add the chicken liver. Sprinkle the ingredients with the salt, paprika, ground white pepper, and water. Close the lid and cook the dish on HIGH for 5 hours. When the time has passed, open the slow cooker lid and check if the ingredients are soft. Then strain the ingredients to get rid of the excess liquid and transfer them to the blender. Blend the mixture on high speed for 2 minutes. Add butter and keep blending for 1 minute. Transfer the prepared pate into a bowl. Serve the pate immediately or keep it in the fridge.

Nutrition: calories 300, fat 21.3, fiber 2, carbs 14.41, protein 13

Chicken Soup with Tortillas

Prep time: 15 minutes | Cooking time: 6 hours | Servings: 5

Ingredients:

- 1 cup canned tomatoes
- 1 cup sweet corn
- 11 oz chicken fillet
- 1 teaspoon nutmeg
- 1 teaspoon salt
- 1 teaspoon ground black pepper
- 3 tablespoons garlic clove, sliced
- 4 red sweet peppers
- 2 white onions
- 2 cups chicken stock
- 1 tablespoon fresh parsley, chopped
- 7 oz Parmesan, shredded
- 6 oz corn tortillas

Directions:

Chop the sweet peppers and white onions into small cubes. Put the chicken fillet in the slow cooker. Add nutmeg, salt, ground black pepper, sliced garlic clove, canned tomatoes, chicken stock, fresh parsley, and sweet corn. Close the slow cooker lid and cook the dish for 5 hours on HIGH. Meanwhile, chop the corn tortillas into strips. Preheat a skillet well and put the chopped tortillas there. When the soup mixture is cooked, open the slow cooker lid and shred the chicken fillet. Sprinkle the soup with the shredded cheese and close the lid. Cook the dish on LOW for 1 hour more. Ladle the soup into the serving bowls and sprinkle it with the roasted corn tortillas.

Nutrition: calories 510, fat 13.6, fiber 6, carbs 69.74, protein 30

Ground Turkey Soup

Prep time: 15 minutes | Cooking time: 5 hours | Servings: 6

Ingredients:

- 1 zucchini
- 1 carrot
- 1 red onion
- 1/3 cup white beans, cooked
- 1 tomato
- 1 teaspoon salt
- 1 teaspoon ground cumin
- 1 teaspoon cilantro
- ½ teaspoon paprika
- 10 oz ground turkey
- 1 tablespoon sour cream
- 1 teaspoon butter
- 2 garlic cloves
- 1 cup fresh dill
- 4 cups chicken stock

Directions:

Put the ground turkey in the slow cooker. Add butter and sour cream. Mix and close the slow cooker lid. Cook the dish on HIGH for 2 hours. Meanwhile, peel the carrots, red onion, and garlic cloves. Chop the vegetables into the pieces. Combine the salt, ground cumin, and cilantro together. Chop the fresh dill and tomatoes. When the time is done, add the cooked white beans, spices, and chopped tomatoes in the slow cooker. Add the chopped vegetables and paprika. Add the chicken stock and close the lid. Cook the soup for 3 hours on HIGH. When the soup is cooked, chill then ladle into bowls.

Nutrition: calories 193, fat 6.7, fiber 3, carbs 16.73, protein 17

Chicken Tikka Masala

Prep time: 20 minutes | Cooking time: 5 hours | Servings: 6

Ingredients:

- 2 tablespoons Garam Masala
- 1 teaspoon salt
- 1 teaspoon ground black pepper
- 1 tablespoon ground paprika
- 2 oz fresh ginger
- 1 cup heavy cream
- 2 tablespoons tomato paste
- 1 can tomatoes, diced
- 1 onion
- 1 teaspoon butter
- 1-pound chicken breast, skinless, boneless

Directions:

Combine Garam Masala, salt, ground black pepper, and ground paprika together. Stir the mixture. Peel the fresh ginger and grate. Peel the onion and dice. Dice the chicken breast. Transfer the diced chicken breast to the slow cooker. Add the diced onion and grated ginger along with the mix of spices and diced tomatoes. Add tomato paste and butter. Close the slow cooker lid and cook the chicken on HIGH for 4 hours. When the time is done, stir the chicken carefully with a wooden spatula. Add the heavy cream and cook it on HIGH for 1 hour more. Serve the prepared chicken Tikka Masala immediately.

Nutrition: calories 235, fat 15.4, fiber 2, carbs 7.38, protein 17

Turkey Minestrone

Prep time: 15 minutes | Cooking time: 8 hours | Servings: 8

Ingredients:

- 7 oz chicken thighs
- 1-pound turkey breast
- 7 cup water
- 6 oz diced tomatoes
- 1 teaspoon kosher salt
- 1 teaspoon ground black pepper
- ½ teaspoon paprika
- 1 teaspoon cilantro
- ½ teaspoon ground cumin
- 1 tablespoon garlic clove
- 1 oz bay leaf
- 6 oz pasta, cooked
- 3 oz Swiss chard
- 2 zucchinis
- 1/3 cup red kidney beans, cooked

Directions:

Put the chicken thighs and turkey breast in the slow cooker bowl. Add the water and diced onions. After this, add the kosher salt, ground black pepper, paprika, and cilantro. Then add the ground cumin and garlic cloves. Sprinkle the mixture with the bay leaf and cook on HIGH for 5 hours. When the time is done, remove the poultry from the slow cooker and shred well. Chop the zucchini and Swiss chard. Add the vegetables in the slow cooker. Then add the red kidney beans and shredded chicken and turkey. Close the lid and cook the dish for 3 hours on LOW. After this, add the cooked pasta and stir it carefully. Ladle the soup into the serving bowls and

Nutrition: calories 173, fat 6.6, fiber 3, carbs 10.79, protein 18

Slow Cooker French Chicken

Prep time: 20 minutes | Cooking time: 4 hour | Servings: 6

Ingredients:

- 1 can onion soup
- 1-pound chicken drumsticks
- 7 oz baby carrot
- 4 oz celery stalk
- 1 teaspoon sage
- ¼ teaspoon tarragon
- ½ teaspoon ground coriander
- 1 tablespoon vinegar
- ¼ cup white wine
- ½ teaspoon oregano

Directions:

Put the chicken drumsticks in the slow cooker bowl. Sprinkle with the sage and tarragon. Add the ground coriander and vinegar along with the white wine and oregano. Wash the baby carrots carefully and cut them into the halves. Chop the celery stalk. Add the baby carrot halves and chopped celery stalk in the slow cooker bowl. Add the canned onion soup and close the lid. Cook the dish for 4 hours on HIGH. Serve hot!

Nutrition: calories 182, fat 9.2, fiber 2, carbs 8.79, protein 15

Turkey Chili

Prep time: 15 minutes | Cooking time: 9 hours | Servings: 6

Ingredients:

- 8 oz ground turkey
- 1 cup onions, diced
- 1 can tomatoes, diced
- 8 oz black beans, canned
- 1 teaspoon salt
- 1 teaspoon olive oil
- 1 teaspoon ground black pepper
- ½ teaspoon cilantro
- ¼ cup tomato soup
- 6 oz Cheddar cheese, shredded
- ½ teaspoon sage
- 1 teaspoon garlic powder
- 1 teaspoon oregano

Directions:

Toss the diced onions in a pan and sprinkle with the olive oil. Roast the onions for 2 minutes on the high heat. Put the ground turkey in the slow cooker. Sprinkle with the salt, ground black pepper, cilantro, and sage. Add the black beans, garlic powder and the roasted onions. After this, add the canned tomatoes and oregano. Then add the tomato soup and close the lid. Cook chili for 7 hours on LOW. When the time is done, sprinkle the chili with the shredded cheese and cook it for 2 hours more on LOW. Serve the chili immediately.

Nutrition: calories 153, fat 6.7, fiber 3, carbs 10.96, protein 13

Chicken Cream Soup

Prep time: 15 minutes | Cooking time: 9 hours | Servings: 10

Ingredients:

- 18 oz chicken
- 8 cups water
- 1 tablespoon salt
- ½ cup heavy cream
- 1 teaspoon ground black pepper
- 1 teaspoon turmeric
- 5 oz Monterey cheese
- 1/3 cup fresh dill, chopped
- 2 potatoes, peeled
- 1 teaspoon chili flakes

Directions:

Chop the chicken roughly and put it in the slow cooker. Add water and salt. After this, add the ground black pepper, turmeric and the chili flakes. Chopped peeled potatoes and add them in the slow cooker too. Close the lid and cook the mixture for 9 hours on LOW. Remove the chicken from the slow cooker and shred it. Blend the slow cooker mixture with the help of the hand blender. When you get a smooth soup, it is done. Add Monterey cheese and chopped fresh dill. Return the shredded chicken to the slow cooker and close the lid. Cook the soup for 1 hour on HIGH or until the soup is smooth and the cheese is melted. Serve the soup hot.

Nutrition: calories 207, fat 10.8, fiber 2, carbs 13.96, protein 14

Chicken Paella

Prep time: 20 minutes | Cooking time: 8 hours | Servings: 8

Ingredients:

- 12 oz chicken fillet
- 10 oz chorizo
- 4 garlic clove
- 1 tablespoon salt
- 1 cup white rice
- 1 teaspoon ground paprika
- 1 teaspoon olive oil
- ¼ teaspoon ground cinnamon
- 7 oz tomatoes, diced
- 5 oz wine
- 1 cup green peas
- 2 cups chicken stock
- 7 oz shrimp, peeled

Directions:

Slice the chorizo and chop the chicken fillet. Toss the ingredients in the skillet and sprinkle with the olive oil. Roast the components for 4 minutes on the medium heat. Transfer the chorizo and chicken to the slow cooker. Add white rice, ground paprika, ground cinnamon, wine, green pea, and chicken stock. Peel the garlic cloves and slice them. Add the sliced garlic cloves and sliced tomatoes in the slow cooker and mix. Cook the dish on HIGH for 5 hours. Open the slow cooker lid and add the peeled shrimp. Cook the dish on HIGH for 3 hours more. When the time is done and the dish is cooked, mix it well and transfer to a serving bowl.

Nutrition: calories 429, fat 21.1, fiber 3, carbs 35.65, protein 23

Chicken and Biscuits

Prep time: 20 minutes | Cooking time: 4 hours | Servings: 7

Ingredients:

- 8 oz carrot
- 3 oz celery stalk
- 4 oz white onion
- 8 oz biscuits
- 1 teaspoon salt
- 1 teaspoon ground black pepper
- 1 cup heavy cream
- 6 oz green peas
- 1 teaspoon ground paprika
- 3-pounds chicken thighss
- 1 teaspoon chili flakes
- 1 tablespoon butter
- ½ teaspoon ground ginger

Directions:

Peel the carrot and white onion. Chop the celery stalk. Put the chicken thighs in the slow cooker. Add the prepared vegetables. Sprinkle the mixture with the salt, ground black pepper, ground paprika, green peas, and chili flakes. Add the butter and ground ginger and close the slow cooker lid. Set the slow cooker on HIGH and cook the dish for 4 hours. Cut the biscuits into the halves. When the chicken is cooked, mix gently. Place the biscuit halves on the serving plate and ladle the chicken mixture over the biscuits. Serve it immediately.

Nutrition: calories 458, fat 18.1 fiber 4, carbs 28.41, protein 44

Glazed Chicken Breast

Prep time: 15 minutes | Cooking time: 7 hours | Servings: 6

Ingredients:

- 2 red onions
- ½ cup brown sugar
- 1 tablespoon butter
- 2 teaspoon water
- ¼ cup heavy cream
- 3-pounds chicken breast, skinless, boneless
- 1 teaspoon paprika
- 1 teaspoon ground black pepper
- ½ teaspoon cilantro
- 1 teaspoon chili flakes
- ½ teaspoon curry

Directions:

Peel the onions and slice them. Put the brown sugar and butter in the slow cooker. Add the water and close the lid then cook the mixture for 20 minutes on HIGH or until the sugar is dissolved. Meanwhile, rub the chicken breast with the paprika, ground black pepper, cilantro, chili flakes, and curry. Place the chicken breast in the slow cooker and cook on HIGH for 2 hours. Flip the chicken breast over after 1 hour of cooking. Add the sliced onions. Then add the heavy cream and cook the dish on LOW for 5 hours. When the chicken breast is cooked, remove it from the slow cooker and chop roughly. Place the chopped chicken breast on the serving plates. Sprinkle the poultry with the remaining creamy sweet liquid.

Nutrition: calories 515, fat 24.9, fiber 1, carbs 22.78, protein 48

Balsamic Chicken

Prep time: 15 minutes | Cooking time: 9 hours | Servings:7

Ingredients:

- 8 oz fingerling potatoes
- 5 oz balsamic vinegar
- 1 cup chicken stock
- 3-pounds chicken breast
- 1 teaspoon kosher salt
- ½ teaspoon oregano
- ½ teaspoon ground black pepper
- 1 tablespoon paprika
- 4 red onions
- 1 teaspoon chili flakes
- ½ teaspoon rosemary
- 1 teaspoon brown sugar
- 1 teaspoon mustard

Directions:

Wash the fingerling potatoes carefully and place them in the slow cooker. Peel the red onions and dice them. Sprinkle the red onions over the fingerling potatoes. Combine the chicken stock, balsamic vinegar, oregano, ground black pepper, paprika, chili flakes, rosemary, brown sugar, and mustard in the bowl. Whisk until the sugar is dissolved. Chop the chicken breast roughly and put in with the diced onions. Pour the vinegar balsamic vinegar in the slow cooker vessel and close the lid. Cook the chicken for 9 hours on LOW. After this, let the dish chill and serve.

Nutrition: calories 423, fat 18.7, fiber 2, carbs 17.96, protein 43

Barbecue Chicken Slices

Prep time: 15 minutes | Cooking time: 5 hours | Servings: 6

Ingredients:

- 2 garlic cloves
- ½ cup Barbecue sauce
- 1 tablespoon hot chili sauce
- 1 tablespoon olive oil
- 3 tablespoons lemon juice
- 1 teaspoon lime zest
- 1 teaspoon brown sugar
- 1 teaspoon thyme
- 18 oz chicken breast, boneless, skinless

Directions:

Peel the garlic cloves and mince them. Combine the minced garlic with the hot chili sauce and barbecue sauce. Add lemon juice and lime zest. Along with the brown sugar and thyme. Whisk the sauce mixture with the help of a fork carefully. Then brush the chicken breast with the prepared sauce generously. Place the chicken breast in the slow cooker bowl and add all the remaining sauce in the slow cooker too. Close the lid and cook the chicken breast for 5 hours on HIGH. When the chicken is cooked, transfer it to the plate and slice into the serving pieces. Serve it!

Nutrition: calories 214, fat 10.3, fiber 0, carbs 11.53, protein 18

Honey Chicken

Prep time: 15 minutes | Cooking time: 10 hours | Servings: 6

Ingredients:

- 1 teaspoon ground paprika
- 10 z chicken drumsticks
- 10 oz chicken wings
- 1 teaspoon ground thyme
- 1 teaspoon ground coriander
- 6 oz celery stalk
- 6 tablespoons honey
- 2 tablespoon sugar
- ¼ cup lemon juice
- ½ cup apple juice
- 1 teaspoon ground black pepper
- 1 teaspoon butter

Directions:

Put the ground paprika in a bowl. Add the ground thyme, ground coriander, and ground black pepper. Mix the spices gently. Then add the sugar, lemon juice, and apple juice. Melt the butter and add it to the spice mixture too. Whisk carefully. Chop the celery stalk and place it in the slow cooker bowl. Then add the chicken drumsticks and chicken wings. Pour the spice mixture into the slow cooker vessel. The liquid should cover the meat fully. Add water if needed to cover the chicken. Close the slow cooker lid and cook the chicken on LOW for 8 hours. Open the slow cooker lid and sprinkle with the honey. Cook the chicken on LOW for 2 hours more. Serve the prepared honey chicken immediately.

Nutrition: calories 216, fat 7, fiber 1, carbs 6.1, protein 31

Spicy Peanut Butter Chicken

Prep time: 12 minutes | Cooking time: 4.5 hours | Servings: 7

Ingredients:

- 1 red chili pepper
- ½ cup soy sauce
- 4 tablespoon peanut butter
- 17 oz chicken fillet
- 1 teaspoon fresh rosemary
- 1 teaspoon butter
- 1 teaspoon onion powder
- 1 teaspoon garlic powder
- ½ cup cream
- 1 tablespoon orange juice

Directions:

Place the chicken fillet in the slow cooker vessel. Sprinkle the meat with the soy sauce and peanut butter. Add the fresh rosemary and butter. Sprinkle the meat with the onion powder and garlic powder. Add the orange juice and close the slow cooker lid. Cook the dish on HIGH for 3 hours. Open the slow cooker lid and add a cup of the cream. Close the lid and cook the dish on HIGH for 1.5 hours more. When the time is done, remove the chicken fillet from the slow cooker and transfer it to the serving plates.

Nutrition: calories 306, fat 18.7, fiber 2, carbs 24.57, protein 11

Onion Chicken

Prep time: 10 minutes | Cooking time: 8 hours | Servings: 5

Ingredients:

- 1-pound white onion, sliced
- 1 tablespoon butter
- 1 teaspoon sugar
- ¼ teaspoon salt
- 12 oz chicken wings
- 1 teaspoon ground black pepper
- 1 teaspoon turmeric
- 2 tablespoons balsamic vinegar
- 1 tablespoon soy sauce

Directions:

Rub the chicken wings with the turmeric and ground black pepper. Sprinkle the chicken wings with the balsamic vinegar and soy sauce. Toss the butter in the slow cooker bowl and melt on HIGH for 10 minutes. Add the chicken wings in the slow cooker and close the lid. Cook the chicken wings for 4 hours on HIGH. After this, cover the chicken wings with the sliced onions. Sprinkle the onions with the sugar and salt and close the lid. Cook the dish on LOW for 4 hours. When all the components of the dish are soft, it is done. Serve the onion chicken hot.

Nutrition: calories 261, fat 10.6, fiber 2, carbs 23.92, protein 17

Creamy Chicken

Prep time: 15 minutes | Cooking time: 12 hours | Servings: 4

Ingredients:

- 5 oz bacon, cooked
- 8 oz chicken breast
- 1 garlic clove
- ½ carrot
- 1 cup heavy cream
- 1 egg
- 1 tablespoon paprika
- 1 teaspoon curry
- 3 tablespoons chives
- 3 oz scallions

Directions:

Peel the garlic and carrot. Chop the vegetables. Make the cuts in the chicken breast and fill them with the chopped carrot and garlic clove. Transfer the stuffed chicken breast in the slow cooker. Beat the egg in a bowl and whisk. Add the heavy cream and mix well with a hand mixer. Add the paprika, curry, and scallions. Pour the cream sauce in the slow cooker. Chop the cooked bacon and chives. Add the ingredients into the slow cooker and close the lid. Cook the chicken on LOW for 12 hours. When the chicken is cooked, open the slow cooker lid and shred the chicken with a fork. Transfer the prepared dish to the serving plates/bowls.

Nutrition: calories 362, fat 29.6, fiber 3, carbs 7.17, protein 19

Bourbon Chicken

Prep time: 11 minutes | Cooking time: 5 hours | Servings: 6

Ingredients:

- 4 oz cup bourbon
- 3 tablespoons soy sauce
- 1 tablespoon honey
- 1 teaspoon ketchup
- 3 oz yellow onion, chopped
- 1 teaspoon minced garlic
- 3 lb. chicken breast, skinless, boneless
- 7 oz water
- 1 teaspoon salt

Directions:

Combine the soy sauce and honey together. Add the ketchup, garlic, salt and water. Whisk the mixture until homogenous. Put the chicken breast in the slow cooker. Add the chopped yellow onion and soy sauce mix. Add bourbon and close the lid. Cook the dish on HIGH for 5 hours. When the dish is cooked, transfer it to a serving bowl without any liquid. Shred the chicken breast if desired.

Nutrition: calories 461, fat 24, fiber 0, carbs 6.37, protein 48

Latin Style Chicke

Prep time: 15 minutes | Cooking time: 5 hours | Servings: 6

Ingredients:

- 6 oz sweet pepper
- 1 teaspoon salt
- 1 teaspoon chili flakes
- 21 oz chicken thighs
- 1 onion
- 1 teaspoon garlic powder
- ½ cup salsa verde
- ¼ cup sweet corn, frozen
- 2 cups water
- 1 peach, pitted, chopped
- 1 teaspoon canola oil

Directions:

Cut the sweet pepper into the strips and put it in the slow cooker. Combine the salt and chili flakes together. Peel the onion and cut into petals. After this, combine the spices with the salsa Verde and sweet corn. Put the chicken thighs in the slow cooker. Add the onion petals and garlic powder. Pour the salsa verde sauce in the slow cooker. Add the chopped peach and canola oil in the slow cooker. Pour in the water and close the lid. Cook the chicken on HIGH for 5 hours. Mix the chicken thighs carefully and transfer them to a serving plates. Serve!

Nutrition: calories 182, fat 9.2, fiber 1, carbs 7.35, protein 18

Chicken Pot Pie

Prep time: 20 minutes | Cooking time: 8 hours | Servings: 8

Ingredients:

- 8 oz biscuit dough
- 1 cup sweet corn, frozen
- 1 cup green peas
- 11 oz chicken fillets
- 1 cup white onion, chopped
- 8 oz chicken creamy soup, canned
- 1 carrot
- 1 teaspoon onion powder
- 1 tablespoon ground paprika
- 1 teaspoon cilantro
- ½ teaspoon oregano
- 1 teaspoon turmeric
- 1 tablespoon salt
- 1 teaspoon butter
- 1 cup water

Directions:

Chop the chicken fillets and put in the slow cooker. Sprinkle the chicken with the onion powder, ground paprika, cilantro, oregano, and turmeric. Add salt and green peas. Sprinkle the dish with the sweet corn. Peel the carrot and chop it. Add the chopped carrot and white onion to the slow cooker vessel. Then pour the water and chicken creamy soup in as well. Add butter and close the lid. Cook the dish on HIGH for 5 hours. Stir the mixture carefully. Cover the with the biscuit dough and close the lid. Cook the dish on HIGH for 3 hours more. Serve the prepared chicken pot pie immediately.

Nutrition: calories 283, fat 10.9, fiber 4, carbs 38.42, protein 10

Curry Chicken
Prep time: 15 minutes | Cooking time: 9 hours | Servings: 9

Ingredients:
- 22 oz chicken thighs
- 2 tablespoons curry
- 1 tablespoon curry paste
- 1 cup baby carrot
- 2 red onions
- 1 teaspoon fresh rosemary
- 1 teaspoon ground black pepper
- 1 teaspoon salt
- 3 tablespoons tomato juice
- 1 teaspoon butter
- 1 teaspoon minced garlic
- 2 cups beef stock
- 1 cup water

Directions:
Put the chicken thighs in the slow cooker bowl. Combine the curry and curry paste together in the bowl. Add water and whisk it until the curry paste is dissolved. Wash the baby carrot carefully and toss them in the slow cooker bowl. Add fresh rosemary, ground black pepper, salt, tomato juice, and minced garlic. Then pour the curry mixture and beef stock in the bowl as well. Add butter and close the lid. Cook the curry chicken on LOW for 9 hours. When the chicken is cooked, discard ½ of the prepared liquid. Serve the curry chicken immediately.

Nutrition: calories 130, fat 6.4, fiber 2, carbs 4.98, protein 14

Whole Chicken Stuffed with Soy Beans
Prep time: 15 minutes | Cooking time: 10 hours | Servings: 12

Ingredients:
- 21 oz whole chicken
- 1 chili pepper
- 1 cup soy beans, canned
- 2 red onion
- 1 carrot
- 1 teaspoon onion powder
- 1 teaspoon cilantro
- 1 teaspoon oregano
- 1 teaspoon apple cider vinegar
- 1 teaspoon olive oil
- 1 tablespoon dried basil
- 1 teaspoon paprika
- ¼ teaspoon ground red pepper
- ½ cup fresh dill
- 2 potatoes
- 4 tablespoons tomato sauce

Directions:
Chop the chili pepper roughly and put it in a blender. Add onion powder, cilantro, oregano, apple cider vinegar, olive oil, dried basil, paprika, ground red pepper, tomato sauce, and fresh dill. Pulse the mixture for 2 minutes on medium speed. Then peel the carrot, onions, and potatoes. Chop the vegetables and combine them with the canned soy beans. Brush the whole chicken carefully with the blended spice mixture and inside and outside. Then fill the whole chicken with the soy bean mixture. Put the whole chicken in the slow cooker bowl and close the lid. Cook the poultry on LOW for 10 hours. When the chicken is cooked, transfer it to the big serving plate.

Nutrition: calories 186, fat 4.1, fiber 5, carbs 27.23, protein 11

Fennel Chicken

Prep time: 16 minutes | Cooking time: 9 hours | Servings: 8

Ingredients:

- 8 oz fennel bulb, chopped
- 1 tablespoon kosher salt
- 1 large white onion, peeled and diced
- 1 cup cherry tomatoes, halved
- ½ cup white wine
- 1 teaspoon ground black pepper
- ¼ teaspoon curry powder
- 17 oz chicken drumsticks
- 1 oz fennels seeds
- 1 tablespoon smoked paprika
- 1 cup water
- 1 cup chicken stock

Directions:

Combine the white wine, ground black pepper, curry powder, fennel seeds, and smoked paprika together. Place the chicken drumsticks in the slow cooker bowl and cover with the chopped fennel bulbs and onions. Pour the white wine liquid and add water and chicken stock. Close the slow cooker lid and cook the dish for 9 hours on LOW. Then serve the chicken with the chopped fennel bulbs, onions, and a small amount of the remaining liquid.

Nutrition: calories 143, fat 6.6, fiber 3, carbs 8.15, protein 13

Moscow Chicken

Prep time: 25 minutes | Cooking time: 7 hours | Servings: 5

Ingredients:

- 6 oz Russian dressing
- 17 oz chicken thighs
- 1 tablespoon minced garlic
- 1 teaspoon onion powder
- 1 teaspoon ground black pepper
- 4 oz bacon, sliced
- 1 teaspoon salt
- 1 teaspoon oregano
- ¼ cup water

Directions:

Preheat the skillet well and put the sliced bacon inside. Roast it on high heat for 30 seconds from the both sides. After this, remove the roasted bacon from the skillet and cool. Combine the minced garlic, onion powder, ground black pepper, salt, and oregano in the shallow bowl. Then rub every chicken thigh with the spice mixture. Toss the chicken thighs in the skillet with the remaining fat from the roasted bacon. Sear the chicken on the medium heat on both sides until you get a golden brown color. Place the chicken thighs in the slow cooker and cover with the bacon. Sprinkle the dish with Russian dressing and pour the water in as well. Close the lid and cook the dish on LOW for 7 hours. Serve the cooked dish immediately.

Nutrition: calories 273, fat 18.2, fiber 1, carbs 9.05, protein 20

Chocolate Chicken Mash

Prep time: 15 minutes | Cooking time: 3 hours 10 minutes | Servings: 7

Ingredients:

- 4 oz milk chocolate
- ½ cup heavy cream
- 14 oz ground chicken
- 1 teaspoon salt
- 1 tablespoon tomato sauce
- 1 teaspoon hot chili sauce
- 1 cup water
- 1 tablespoon sesame oil
- 1 teaspoon cumin seeds
- ¼ cup baby carrot

Directions:

Put the ground chicken in the slow cooker bowl. Sprinkle with salt, tomato sauce, hot chili sauce, water, sesame oil, and cumin seeds. Wash the baby carrot carefully and toss the baby carrots in the slow cooker and close the lid. Cook the ground chicken on HIGH for 3 hours. After 1 hour of cooking, stir the ground chicken carefully with a wooden spatula. Meanwhile, chop the milk chocolate roughly and melt in the microwave. Then combine the melted chocolate with the heavy cream and whisk the mixture. When the ground chicken is cooked, open the slow cooker lid and strain the excess liquid carefully. Add the whisked chocolate heavy cream in with the ground chicken and cook it for 10 minutes on HIGH. Serve the prepared dish hot.

Nutrition: calories 219, fat 14.6, fiber 1, carbs 10.56, protein 11

Chicken Adobo
Prep time: 15 minutes | Cooking time: 8 hours | Servings: 6

Ingredients:
- 5 garlic cloves
- 6 white onions
- 1 tablespoon fresh ginger
- 1 oz bay leaf
- 6 medium chicken thighs
- 5 tablespoons soy sauce
- 1 tablespoon apple cider vinegar
- 1 teaspoon white pepper
- ½ teaspoon sugar

Directions:
Peel the garlic cloves and white onions. Mash the garlic cloves and dice the onion. Put the chicken thighs in the slow cooker bowl. Grate the fresh ginger and combine it with the soy sauce, apple cider vinegar, white pepper, and sugar. Then sprinkle the chicken thighs with the grated ginger mixture. Add the diced onions and mashed garlic cloves. After this, add the bay leaf and close the slow cooker lid. Set the slow cooker on HIGH and cook the chicken thighs for 8 hours on LOW. Serve the chicken immediately after cooking.

Nutrition: calories 216, fat 5.6, fiber 4, carbs 18.91, protein 23

Chicken-Dumplings Mix
Prep time: 25 minutes | Cooking time: 6 hours | Servings: 6

Ingredients:
- 8 oz chicken fillets
- 1 tablespoon salt
- 1 cup flour
- 1 onion, chopped
- 1 teaspoon olive oil
- 1 pinch salt
- ¼ cup milk
- 1 egg
- 1 teaspoon ground black pepper
- 1 cup water
- 1 carrot
- 1 teaspoon ground cinnamon
- 1 tablespoon butter

Directions:
Beat the egg in a bowl and whisk. Add a pinch of salt, milk, and flour. Knead into a smooth dough. Add more flour if the dough is sticky. Make the long log from the dough and cut it into the small pieces. Butter the slow cooker bowl carefully. Chop the chicken fillets and toss in the slow cooker bowl. Add the 1 tablespoon of salt, ground black pepper, and ground cinnamon. Add water and close the lid. Cook the meat on HIGH for 3 hours. Meanwhile, peel the carrot and onions. Slice the vegetables. Pour the olive oil in the skillet and add the vegetables. Roast the vegetables for 4 minutes on the medium heat. After this, open the slow cooker lid and add the roasted vegetables. Then add the dough pieces and close the lid. Cook the dish on HIGH for 3 hours. Stir it every 30 minutes. When the dumpling dish is cooked, chill it well and ladle into the bowls. Serve the dish only hot!

Nutrition: calories 221, fat 8.7, fiber 2, carbs 28.83, protein 7

Thyme Whole Chicken

Prep time: 16 minutes | Cooking time: 10 hours | Servings: 6

Ingredients:

- 1 lemon, sliced
- 2 oz fresh thyme leaves, chopped
- 1 tablespoon dried thyme
- 1 teaspoon ground black pepper
- 1 tablespoon salt
- 1 teaspoon cilantro
- 1 tablespoon tomato paste
- 1 cup chicken stock
- 1 teaspoon butter
- 2-pounds whole chicken

Directions:

Combine the sliced lemon with the chopped thyme leaves. Rub the whole chicken with the ground black pepper and salt. Sprinkle the meat with cilantro. Then brush it carefully with the tomato paste. Put the butter inside the whole chicken. Add the sliced lemon mixture and place the chicken in the slow cooker bowl. Add the chicken stock and close the lid. Cook the chicken on LOW for 10 hours. Enjoy the prepared chicken!

Nutrition: calories 345, fat 11.9, fiber 6, carbs 35.28, protein 26

Lime Chicken Drumsticks

Prep time: 10 minutes | Cooking time: 3.5 hours | Servings: 7

Ingredients:

- 3 oz garlic
- 17 oz chicken drumsticks
- 1 lime
- 1 teaspoon lemon zest
- 1 teaspoon kosher salt
- 1 teaspoon coriander
- 1 teaspoon butter

Directions:

Peel the garlic cloves and mash them. Chop the lime into the small pieces and combine with the lemon zest. Add kosher salt and coriander. Add the lime to the spices and mix. Butter the slow cooker carefully and add the chicken drumsticks. Sprinkle the poultry with the lime mixture. Close the lid and cook the chicken on HIGH for 3.5 hours. Serve the chicken drumsticks immediately.

Nutrition: calories 136, fat 7, fiber 0, carbs 4.68, protein 13

Sesame Chicken Wings

Prep time: 25 minutes | Cooking time: 4 hours | Servings: 4

Ingredients:

- 1-pound chicken wings
- ½ cup fresh parsley, chopped
- 1 teaspoon salt
- 1 teaspoon ground black pepper
- ¼ cup milk
- 1 tablespoon sugar
- 5 tablespoons honey
- 2 tablespoons sesame seeds
- ¼ cup chicken stock
- 1 teaspoon soy sauce

Directions:

Combine the salt and ground black pepper together. Then put the chicken wings in the slow cooker bowl. Sprinkle the poultry with the salt-pepper mixture. Add chicken stock and soy sauce to the bowl. After this, sprinkle the chicken wings with the chopped parsley and close the lid. Cook the chicken on HIGH for 4 hours. Meanwhile, preheat the oven to 350 F. Combine the milk, sugar, honey, and sesame seeds together. When the chicken wings are cooked, transfer to a tray and brush with the honey mixture carefully. Put the tray in the oven and cook for 10 minutes. Then remove the tray from the oven and chill.

Nutrition: calories 282, fat 7.5, fiber 1, carbs 27.22, protein 27

African Chicken

Prep time: 10 minutes | Cooking time: 8 hours | Servings: 6

Ingredients:

- 13 oz chicken breast
- 1 teaspoon peanut oil
- 1 teaspoon ground black pepper
- 1 teaspoon oregano
- 1 chili pepper
- 1 carrot
- 1 tablespoon tomato sauce
- 1 cup tomatoes, canned
- 1 tablespoon kosher salt
- ¼ teaspoon ground cardamom
- ½ teaspoon ground anise

Directions:

Brush the chicken breast with the peanut oil and roast it in a skillet over high heat for 1 minute on the each side. Toss the roasted chicken breast in the slow cooker. Sprinkle the chicken with the ground black pepper, oregano, tomato sauce, kosher salt, ground cardamom, and ground anise. Chop the chili pepper and peel and slice the carrot. Add the chopped chili and sliced carrot in the slow cooker. Add the canned tomatoes and close the lid. Cook the chicken on LOW for 8 hours. When the dish is cooked, serve it with the juices from the slow cooker.

Nutrition: calories 131, fat 6.6, fiber 1, carbs 4.14, protein 14

Butter Chicken Wings

Prep time: 20 minutes | Cooking time: 5 hours | Servings: 6

Ingredients:

- 14 oz chicken wings
- 1 teaspoon onion powder
- 1 teaspoon chili flakes
- 1 teaspoon garlic powder
- 1 teaspoon cilantro
- 1 teaspoon olive oil
- 1/3 cup butter
- 1 tablespoon flour
- ¼ cup milk
- 1 teaspoon salt
- 1 tablespoon heavy cream
- 1 egg, beaten

Directions:

Put the chicken wings in the slow cooker and add butter. Sprinkle the meat with the onion powder, chili flakes, garlic powder, cilantro, and olive oil. Add salt and close the lid and cook the chicken wings for 2 hours on HIGH. Meanwhile, combine the beaten egg with the milk and olive oil. Add heavy cream and flour. Mix carefully with a hand mixer. Open the slow cooker lid and pour the cream mixture there. Continue to cook the butter chicken wings for 3 hours more on LOW. When the chicken wings are cooked, transfer them to serving plates and sprinkle with sauce from the slow cooker.

Nutrition: calories 225, fat 16.2, fiber 0, carbs 2.64, protein 17

Soy Sauce Chicken

Prep time: 10 minutes | Cooking time: 15 hours | Servings: 4

Ingredients:

- ½ cup soy sauce
- 1 teaspoon maple syrup
- 1 tablespoon fresh ginger, grated
- 1 teaspoon salt
- 1 lb. chicken breast
- 1 teaspoon ground ginger
- ¼ teaspoon ground cinnamon
- 2 tablespoons red wine

Directions:

Combine the soy sauce, the maple syrup and grated fresh ginger. Add salt, ground ginger, and ground cinnamon. Add the red wine and whisk together. Chop the chicken breast roughly and add it to the soy sauce mixture. Leave it for 10 minutes to marinate. Then, transfer the chopped chicken breast and soy sauce mixture into the slow cooker and close the lid. Cook the dish on LOW for 15 hours. Then remove the chopped chicken from the slow cooker and serve.

Nutrition: calories 259, fat 13.5, fiber 1, carbs 6.71, protein 26

Puerto Ricco Chicken

Prep time: 20 minutes | Cooking time: 8 hours | Servings: 6

Ingredients:

- 8 oz chicken breast
- 7 oz chicken filler
- 6 oz chicken wings
- ½ teaspoon ground cumin
- 1 teaspoon cilantro
- 1 tablespoon fresh thyme leaves
- 1 teaspoon ground coriander
- 1 tablespoon ground celery root
- 2 jalapeno
- 6 tablespoons dry wine
- 3 oz lemon wedges
- 3 red potatoes
- 1 yellow onion
- 1 tablespoon olive oil

Directions:

Put the chicken breast, chicken fillet, and chicken wings in the slow cooker. Sprinkle the poultry with the ground cumin, cilantro, and ground coriander. Then chop the jalapeno pepper roughly. Peel the red tomatoes and onion and chop both. Put the chopped vegetables in the blender. Add ground celery root, fresh thyme leaves, lemon wedges, dry wine, and olive oil. Pulse the mixture until it is smooth. Then sprinkle the prepared chicken mixture with the sauce and close the slow cooker lid. Cook the dish on LOW for 8 hours. After this, stir the dish gently with the help of the spatula and serve it.

Nutrition: calories 310, fat 9.8, fiber 4, carbs 32.42, protein 24

Pomegranate Turkey

Prep time: 25 minutes | Cooking time: 4.5 hours | Servings: 4

Ingredients:

- 1-pound turkey fillet
- ½ cup pomegranate juice
- 2 oz pomegranate juice
- 1 tablespoon soy sauce
- 1 tablespoon potato starch
- 1 teaspoon garlic powder
- ¼ cup onion, grated
- 1 teaspoon butter
- 3 tablespoons brown sugar
- 1 teaspoon salt
- 1 teaspoon ground white pepper

Directions:

Combine the garlic powder, grated onion, salt, and ground white pepper together. Rub the turkey fillet with the spice mixture and chop it roughly. Leave the turkey fillet for 10 minutes to marinate. After this, toss the butter in the slow cooker bowl. Add the turkey and sprinkle it with the pomegranate juice. Close the slow cooker lid and cook it on HIGH for 3 hours. Meanwhile, combine the potato starch and soy sauce together. Add the pomegranate juice and whisk until the potato starch is dissolved. Heat the juice mixture over the medium heat until it is thick. When the time is passed, pour the pomegranate sauce in the slow cooker and stir it carefully. Close the slow cooker lid and cook the dish on HIGH for 1.5 hours more.

Nutrition: calories 676, fat 52.5, fiber 3, carbs 26.15, protein 24

Orange Duck Fillets

Prep time: 20 minutes | *Cooking time:* 8 hours | *Servings:* 4

Ingredients:

- 2 oranges
- 1 tablespoon honey
- 1-pound duck fillet
- 1 teaspoon salt
- ½ teaspoon ground black pepper
- ½ teaspoon cilantro
- 1 teaspoon coriander
- 7 oz celery stalk
- 1 tablespoon chives
- ¼ cup water
- 2 tablespoons butter
- 1 teaspoon cinnamon

Directions:

Slice the duck fillet and sprinkle it with the salt, ground black pepper, cilantro, coriander, and cinnamon. Put the butter in the slow cooker bowl. Add the sliced duck fillet. Then brush the turkey fillets with the honey. Wash the oranges carefully and do not peel them. Slice the oranges and make a layer of the fruit in the slow cooker. Add water as well. Chop the celery stalk and add it in the slow cooker. Add chives and close the slow cooker lid. Cook the meat on LOW for 8 hours. Transfer the prepared duck fillet to the serving plates and serve hot.

Nutrition: calories 353, fat 23.2, fiber 3, carbs 15.68, protein 21

Delightful Chicken Mole

Prep time: 16 minutes | *Cooking time:* 5 hours | *Servings:* 6

Ingredients:

- 3 oz yellow onion
- 4 tablespoons raisins
- 1 tablespoon garlic, sliced
- 1 tablespoon chipotle, chopped
- 1 tablespoon adobo sauce
- 7 tablespoons tomatoes, crushed
- ½ tablespoon white sugar
- 1 tablespoon cocoa powder
- 1 teaspoon salt
- 1 teaspoon ground coriander
- ½ teaspoon turmeric
- 15 oz chicken breast, boneless

Directions:

Peel the yellow onion and grate it. Combine the grated onion with the sliced garlic. Add raisins, chopped chipotle, adobo sauce, and crushed tomatoes. After this, add white sugar, cocoa powder, and salt. Add the ground coriander and turmeric. Mix carefully. Chop the chicken breast and combine it with the prepared sauce mixture. Mix it up and place in the slow cooker. Close the lid and cook the chicken mole for 5 hours on HIGH. Shred the prepared chicken and serve it immediately.

Nutrition: calories 159, fat 8.4, fiber 1, carbs 5.16, protein 16

Chicken-Potato Casserole

Prep time: 20 minutes | *Cooking time:* 10 hours | *Servings:* 6

Ingredients:

- 10 oz ground chicken
- 4 large potatoes
- 2 egg, beaten
- 1 large onion
- 1 teaspoon ground black pepper
- 1 cup heavy cream
- 8 oz Parmesan, shredded
- 1 teaspoon paprika
- 1 teaspoon cilantro
- ½ teaspoon nutmeg
- 1 teaspoon butter
- 1 carrot, grated

Directions:

Brush the slow cooker bowl with the butter. Peel the potato and slice it. Peel the onion and dice. Whisk the eggs and combine with the heavy cream, ground black pepper, paprika, cilantro, and nutmeg together. Put the thin layer of ground chicken in the slow cooker bowl. Then add the layer of the sliced potatoes and cover with the diced onion. Add ½ of the shredded cheese and all the grated carrot. Then repeat the same steps one more time and close the slow cooker lid. Cook the casserole on LOW for 10 hours. When the chicken casserole is done, chill well. Transfer the dish to the serving plates and serve.

Nutrition: calories 534, fat 17.4, fiber 6, carbs 63.33, protein 32

Sweet Curry Chicken Strips

Prep time: 10 minutes | Cooking time: 4 hours | Servings: 6

Ingredients:

- 1 tablespoon curry paste
- 11 oz chicken fillet
- 1 teaspoon salt
- 2 tablespoons maple syrup
- 1 teaspoon olive oil
- 3 tablespoons sour cream
- ½ cup fresh dill
- 1 tablespoon ground paprika

Directions:

Cut the chicken fillet into the strips. Combine the sour cream, maple syrup, olive oil, sour cream, and curry paste together. Add the ground paprika and whisk the mixture until the curry paste is dissolved. Sprinkle the chicken strips with the curry mixture and transfer to a slow cooker bowl. Chop the fresh dill. Close the slow cooker lid and cook the chicken on HIGH for 3 hours. After this, open the slow cooker lid and sprinkle it with the chopped fresh dill. Close the lid and cook the chicken strips for 1 hour more. Serve the prepared chicken strips immediately.

Nutrition: calories 177, fat 9.1, fiber 2, carbs 18.11, protein 6

Incredible Chicken Continental

Prep time: 15 minutes | Cooking time: 9 hours | Servings :5

Ingredients:

- 6 oz dried beef
- 12 oz chicken breast
- 7 oz sour cream
- 1 can onion soup
- 3 tablespoons flour

Directions:

Separate the dried beef into 2 parts. Then line the first part of the dried beef in the slow cooker vessel. Cut the chicken breast into the halves and place them in the slow cooker vessel too. Whisk the sour cream, flour, and canned onion soup together. Then cover the chicken halves with the onion soup. Line the chicken halves with the second part of the dried beef and close the lid. Cook the dish on LOW for 9 hours. When the chicken continental is cooked – serve it immediately.

Nutrition: calories 285, fat 15.1, fiber 1, carbs 12.56, protein 24

Chicken Stew with Pumpkin

Prep time: 20 minutes | Cooking time: 10 hours | Servings: 8

Ingredients:

- 1-pound pumpkin
- 1-pound chicken fillet, chopped
- 2 carrots, chopped
- 1 yellow onion
- 1 cup chicken stock
- ½ cup tomato sauce
- 1 tablespoon minced garlic
- 1 teaspoon ground black pepper
- 3 apples
- 1 cup water
- 1 tablespoon sugar
- ½ teaspoon cinnamon

Directions:

Chop the pumpkin into the medium cubes and sprinkle with the cinnamon and sugar. Put the chopped chicken in the slow cooker. Add the minced garlic, ground black pepper, and tomato sauce. Peel the onion and chop it. Add the chopped onion and carrot in the slow cooker. After this, add the prepared pumpkin cubes. Chop the apples and add them in the slow cooker too. Pour water and close the lid. Cook the stew on LOW for 10 hours. When the stew is cooked, let it sit for at least 15 minutes to cool. Serve it and

Nutrition: calories 560, fat 36.5, fiber 8, carbs 40.01, protein 25

Hawaiian Chicken

Prep time: 15 minutes | Cooking time: 8 hours | Servings: 8

Ingredients:

- 10 oz pineapple
- 14 oz chicken breast
- 5 tablespoons barbecue sauce
- 1 cup bell pepper, chopped
- 1 teaspoon minced garlic
- 4 tablespoons chicken stock
- 1 teaspoon sugar
- 1 teaspoon ground paprika

Directions:

Chop the pineapple into chunks. Chop the chicken breast roughly. Combine the chicken with the pineapple. Then combine the barbecue sauce and chicken stock. Add sugar and ground paprika and stir. Put the chicken mixture in the slow cooker and sprinkle with the barbecue sauce mixture. Add the chopped bell pepper. After this, close the slow cooker lid and cook the chicken for 8 hours on LOW. When the dish is cooked, transfer to a serving plate.

Nutrition: calories 132, fat 4.8, fiber 1, carbs 11.28, protein 11

Apple Chicken Balls

Prep time: 15 minutes | Cooking time: 4 hours | Servings: 7

Ingredients:

- 2 green apple
- 12 oz ground chicken
- 1 teaspoon minced garlic
- 1 teaspoon turmeric
- 1 egg
- 1 tablespoon flour
- 1 teaspoon onion powder
- 1 teaspoon chili flakes
- ½ teaspoon salt
- 1 teaspoon garlic powder
- 1 teaspoon butter
- ½ cup panko bread crumbs

Directions:

Peel the green apples and grate them. Combine the minced garlic, turmeric, flour, onion powder, and chili flakes together. Add the salt, garlic powder, and mix. Beat the egg in the bowl. Add the ground chicken and minced garlic mixture. Then add the grated apple and mix. After this, butter the slow cooker. Make the balls from the ground chicken mixture and coat them into the panko bread crumbs. Put the chicken balls in the slow cooker and close the lid. Cook the chicken balls for 3 hours on HIGH. Then flip the chicken balls over and cook them for 1 hour more on HIGH. Serve the chicken balls immediately.

Nutrition: calories 136, fat 6.1, fiber 2, carbs 10.64, protein 10

Ginger Turkey

Prep time: 17 minutes | Cooking time: 5 hours | Servings: 4

Ingredients:

- 3 oz fresh ginger
- 9 oz turkey fillet
- 1 tablespoon maple syrup
- 1 teaspoon brown sugar
- ¼ cup thyme leaves
- 1 teaspoon thyme
- ½ teaspoon ground celery
- 1 teaspoon salt
- 1 teaspoon sesame oil
- 1 teaspoon ground ginger
- ¼ cup heavy cream

Directions:

Peel the fresh ginger and grate it. Rub the turkey fillet with the grated ginger. Put the thyme leaves, thyme, ground celery, salt, sesame oil, ground ginger, and heavy cream in the blender. Add the brown sugar and maple syrup and pulse the mixture for 2 minutes on the maximum speed. Then transfer the ginger turkey fillet into the slow cooker and pour the heavy cream mixture in as well. Stir it gently. Close the slow cooker lid and cook the dish for 5 hours on HIGH. Serve the prepared turkey immediately.

Nutrition: calories 390, fat 33.6, fiber 1, carbs 8.96, protein 13

Lemon Sauce Pulled Chicken

Prep time: 25 minutes | Cooking time: 7 hours | Servings: 11

Ingredients:

- 23 oz chicken breast, boneless
- 1 lemon
- 1 tablespoon cornstarch
- 1 teaspoon salt
- 1 cup heavy cream
- 1 tablespoons flour
- 1 teaspoon ground black pepper
- 1 teaspoon minced garlic
- 1 tablespoon mustard
- 3 tablespoons lemon juice
- 1 red onion

Directions:

Grate the lemon zest from the lemon and squeeze the juice. Combine the prepared ingredients with the salt, minced garlic, lemon juice, and ground black pepper. Chop the chicken breast and sprinkle with the lemon mixture. Peel the onion and grate it. Add the grated onion to the chicken and leave it for 15 minutes to marinate. Meanwhile, combine the mustard, heavy cream, and flour. Whisk until the mixture is smooth. After this, add the cornstarch and stir it carefully again. Put the mixture on the low heat and simmer it for 10 minutes. Stir it constantly. When you get the thick sauce, it is cooked. Put the chicken in the slow cooker bowl and sprinkle it with the all remaining lemon mixture. Close the slow cooker and cook the dish on HIGH for 3 hours. Add the heavy cream sauce and close the lid. Cook the chicken on LOW for 4 hours more. Shred the prepared chicken and stir the mixture well. Serve the chicken hot.

Nutrition: calories 154, fat 9.6, fiber 0, carbs 3.59, protein 13

Tomato Chicken

Prep time: 15 minutes | Cooking time: 9 hours | Servings: 4

Ingredients:

- 1-pound chicken wings
- 1 cup canned tomatoes, diced
- ½ cup fresh tomatoes
- 1 cup fresh parsley
- 1 teaspoon salt
- 1 teaspoon ground cinnamon
- 1 cup onion
- 1 tablespoon olive oil
- 1 tablespoon red pepper

Directions:

Chop the fresh tomatoes and blend them with a hand blender. Add the fresh parsley and salt into the blended tomato mixture. Sprinkle with the onion and red pepper. Blend the mixture until it is smooth. Put the chicken wings in the slow cooker and add the tomato mix. Close the lid and cook the dish on LOW for 8 hours. Serve the dish with the tomato sauce.

Nutrition: calories 202, fat 7.7, fiber 2, carbs 6.47, protein 26

Slow Cooker Poultry Mix

Prep time: 20 minutes | Cooking time: 8 hours | Servings: 6

Ingredients:

- 3 garlic cloves
- 3 carrots
- 1-pound chicken fillet
- 1-pound duck fillet
- 1 tablespoon smoked paprika
- ¼ cup soy sauce
- 1 tablespoon honey
- 1 teaspoon nutmeg
- 1 teaspoon fresh rosemary
- 1 teaspoon black peas
- 2 cups water

Directions:

Peel the garlic cloves and smash them gently. Then chop the chicken fillet and duck fillet into bite sized pieces. Transfer the prepared poultry pieces in the slow cooker. Add the mashed garlic cloves. Peel the carrots and cut them into 3 parts. Put the carrot in the slow cooker. Add soy sauce, smoked paprika, fresh rosemary, nutmeg, honey, black peas, and water. Close the lid and cook the dish on LOW for 8 hours. Serve hot!

Nutrition: calories 422, fat 24.6, fiber 3, carbs 27.21, protein 23

Parmesan Chicken Fillet

Prep time: 20 minutes | Cooking time: 7 hours | Servings: 4

Ingredients:

- 10 oz chicken fillet
- 6 oz Parmesan, shredded
- 1 tablespoon lemon juice
- 2 tomatoes
- 1 tablespoon butter
- 1 white onion, sliced
- ½ cup bread crumbs
- 3 tablespoons chicken stock
- 1 teaspoon ground black pepper

Directions:

Beat the chicken fillet lightly and sprinkle it with the ground black pepper and lemon juice. Toss the butter in the slow cooker and melt on HIGH for 10 minutes. Make a layer of the chicken fillets. Slice the tomatoes then make a layer of the sliced tomatoes and onion. Combine the bread crumbs and Parmesan cheese together and stir. Cover the sliced onions with the bread crumb mixture and close the slow cooker lid. Cook the dish on LOW for 7 hours. When the chicken is cooked, open the slow cooker and let it cool well. Serve the chicken fillet immediately.

Nutrition: calories 404, fat 15.5, fiber 3, carbs 39.82, protein 27

Tender Chicken Cacciatore

Prep time: 25 minutes | Cooking time: 8 hour | Servings: 7

Ingredients:

- 1 oz olive oil
- 1 cup yellow onion, chopped
- 1-pound chicken thighs
- 1 teaspoon ground black pepper
- 5 oz carrot
- 8 oz tomato passata
- 7 oz mushrooms
- 1 cup green beans, frozen
- 1 cup water
- 1 teaspoon oregano
- 1 teaspoon cilantro

Directions:

Pour the olive oil in the pan and preheat it well. Toss the onion and saute it for 2 minutes. Then add the chicken thighs and roast the mixture for 5 more minutes on the medium heat. After this, transfer the mixture into the slow cooker. Slice the mushrooms and carrot. Add the sliced vegetables in the slow cooker. Then sprinkle it with the tomato passata, green beans, water, oregano, and cilantro. Add the ground black pepper and close the slow cooker lid. Cook the meal on LOW for 8 hours. Serve the prepared chicken Cacciatore immediately.

Nutrition: calories 53, fat 4.1, fiber 2, carbs 4, protein 1

Coca Cola Chicken

Prep time: 25 minutes | Cooking time: 5 hours | Servings: 6

Ingredients:

- 2 cup coca cola
- 1 tablespoon minced garlic
- 1 teaspoon salt
- 1 onion
- 16 oz chicken
- 1 teaspoon ground black pepper
- 1 teaspoon olive oil
- ½ cup fresh dill
- 2 teaspoons oregano

Directions:

Chop the chicken and sprinkle it with coca cola. Leave the chicken for 15 minutes. Meanwhile, combine the salt, minced garlic, ground black pepper, olive oil, and oregano together. Strain ½ of the coca cola from the chicken. Transfer the chicken mixture to the slow cooker. Add the minced garlic mixture. Chop the fresh dill and add it in the slow cooker too. Peel the onion and cut it into 6 parts. Add the onion in the slow cooker. Close the lid and cook the dish on HIGH for 5 hours. Serve the dish immediately.

Nutrition: calories 154, fat 7, fiber 1, carbs 9.56, protein 14

Horseradish Chicken

Prep time: 20 minutes | Cooking time: 11 hours | Servings: 9

Ingredients:

- 3 tablespoons horseradish, grated
- 1 tablespoon mustard
- 1 teaspoon salt
- 1 tablespoon mayonnaise
- 3 tablespoons sour cream
- 1/3 cup beef broth
- 6 oz carrot, grated
- 1 zucchini, sliced
- 1-pound chicken breast
- 1 teaspoon olive oil

Directions:

Put the chicken breast in the slow cooker. Sprinkle it with the grated horseradish, olive oil, and salt. Combine the mayonnaise, sour cream, mustard, grated carrot and sliced zucchini together. Add the mixture in the slow cooker. Pour the beef broth and close the lid. Cook the horseradish chicken on LOW for 11 hours. When the chicken is cooked, stir it carefully with the help of the spatula. Serve it immediately!

Nutrition: calories 203, fat 11.3, fiber 2, carbs 4.67, protein 20

Meat

Beef Shank
Prep time: 20 minutes | Cooking time: 9 hours | Servings: 6

Ingredients:

- 5 garlic cloves
- 2 oz fresh rosemary
- 2 yellow onion
- 2 tablespoons ghee
- 1 teaspoon salt
- 17 oz beef shank

- 1 cup beef stock
- 1 teaspoon thyme
- 2 oz tomato paste
- 1 teaspoon ground black pepper
- 1 teaspoon ground coriander
- 1 teaspoon white pepper

Directions:

Peel the garlic cloves and smash them. Chop the rosemary and yellow onion. Put the ghee in the skillet and add the pork shank. Roast the meat on the medium heat for 10 minutes. Stir frequently. Transfer the beef shank into the slow cooker. Add all the ghee. Add the chopped rosemary and yellow onion. Sprinkle the beef shank with the garlic cloves. Add salt, beef stock, thyme, tomato paste, ground black pepper, ground coriander, and white pepper. Stir the dish gently and close the slow cooker lid. Cook the beef shank on LOW for 9 hours. Stir the meat gently occasionally. Remove the prepared beef shank from the slow cooker and cool slighty. Serve!

Nutrition: calories 151, fat 3.8, fiber 3, carbs 9.49, protein 20

Lamb Tagine
Prep time: 20 minutes | Cooking time: 10 hours | Servings: 6

Ingredients:

- 2-pound lamb
- 2 oz fresh ginger
- 1 tablespoon minced garlic
- 1 teaspoon paprika
- 1 teaspoon turmeric
- 1 teaspoon onion powder
- 1 oz sugar
- 2 cups tomatoes, canned

- 1 tablespoon prune
- 1 tablespoon dried apricot
- 3 oz lemon
- ¼ teaspoon cinnamon
- ½ tablespoon honey
- 2 yellow onion
- 2 cups water

Directions:

Chop the lamb roughly and put it in the slow cooker bowl. Peel the fresh ginger and grate it then add the grated fresh ginger into the slow cooker. Sprinkle the meat with the paprika, minced garlic, turmeric, onion powder, sugar, cinnamon, and honey. Chop the canned tomatoes, prunes, and dried apricots. Add them into the slow cooker as well. Peel the onions and chop them. Add the chopped onions in the slow cooker too. After this, slice the lemon and put it in the chopped onion. Add water and close the lid. Cook the lamb tagine for 10 hours on LOW. When the dish is cooked, let it cool slightly.

Nutrition: calories 462, fat 25.8, fiber 2, carbs 18.26, protein 38

Corned Beef
Prep time: 10 minutes | Cooking time: 6 hours | Servings: 9

Ingredients:

- 6 oz carrot
- 4 oz potato
- 3 oz white pepper

- 5 tablespoons beer
- 21 oz corned beef brisket
- 12 oz water

Directions:

Peel the carrot and cut it into the big strips. Peel the potatoes and cut them into the cubes. Then pour water and beer in the slow cooker. Add white pepper, beef brisket, carrot strips, and potato cubes. Close the lid and cook the corned beef for 6 hours on HIGH. When the time is over, open the slow cooker lid and stir the meat carefully. Serve the corned beef immediately.

Nutrition: calories 175, fat 10.1, fiber 3, carbs 10.33, protein 11

Beer Brats
Prep time: 20 minutes | Cooking time: 2.5 hour | Servings: 6

Ingredients:
- 16 oz smoked bratwurst
- 1 teaspoon olive oil
- 7 oz sweet pepper
- 1 teaspoon minced garlic
- ¼ chili pepper
- 2 cup beer

Directions:

Pour olive oil in the pan and preheat it well. After this, put the smoked bratwurst in the preheated oil and roast them for 1 minute on the each side. When the bratwurst are golden brown, they are cooked. Meanwhile, chop the chili pepper. Remove the seeds from the sweet pepper and cut it into the strips. Put the sweet pepper strips in the slow cooker bowl. Add minced garlic and chili pepper. After this, add the beer. Put the prepared smoked bratwurst over the pepper strips and close the lid. Cook the beer brats for 2.5 hours on HIGH. Then open the lid and stir the mixture with a spoon. Serve the dish!

Nutrition: calories 425, fat 35.5, fiber 1, carbs 9.51, protein 16

Cilantro Meat Bowl

Prep time: 15 minutes | Cooking time: 13 hours | Servings: 10

Ingredients:
- 1 cup cilantro
- 11 oz pork chops
- 8 oz beef brisket
- 1 tablespoon rosemary
- 1 teaspoon ground black pepper
- 1 teaspoon salt
- 1 teaspoon paprika
- 1 cup red onion
- 6 oz sweet yellow pepper, chopped
- 2 tablespoons lemon juice
- 1 teaspoon olive oil
- 1 teaspoon oregano
- 4 oz celery stalk, chopped
- 6 oz salsa
- ½ chili pepper

Directions:

Wash the cilantro carefully and chop it. Chop the pork chops into cubes. Sprinkle the meat with the rosemary. Combine the chopped pork cubes with the beef brisket. Add ground black pepper, salt, paprika, lemon juice, and salsa and marinate it for 10 minutes. Then transfer the meat mixture to the slow cooker. Add the red onion, chili pepper, chopped celery stalk, and sweet yellow pepper. Sprinkle the mixture with the oregano and olive oil. Cover the mixture with the chopped cilantro and close the lid. Cook the meat mixture on LOW for 13 hours. When the meat is cooked, stir it carefully with a wooden spoon. Serve the meat in bowls.

Nutrition: calories 134, fat 7.4, fiber 1, carbs 4.58, protein 12

Sausage Stew

Prep time: 15 minutes | Cooking time: 3.5 hours | Servings: 8

Ingredients:

- 1 cup cream
- 10 oz smoked sausage
- 5 oz onion, chopped
- 1 cup carrot, chopped
- 1 teaspoon salt
- 1 teaspoon paprika
- 1 teaspoon oregano
- 4 bell peppers
- 1 cup potato, chopped
- 1 teaspoon cilantro
- 1 tablespoon dried basil
- 1 teaspoon dried dill
- ½ teaspoon turmeric
- 1 tablespoon kosher salt
- 1 cup water
- 1 tablespoon butter
- ½ cup chicken stock

Directions:

Butter the slow cooker bowl. Then chop the smoked sausages and make the layer of the slices in the slow cooker bowl. Sprinkle the chopped sausages with the salt, paprika, and oregano. After this, layer in the chopped carrot and onion. Slice the bell peppers and add them to the slow cooker too. Add the potato and sprinkle the mixture with the cilantro, dried basil, dried dill, turmeric, kosher salt, and water. Then combine the chicken stock and cream together. Add the cream into the slow cooker. Close the lid and cook the stew for 3.5 hours on HIGH. When the stew is cooked, stir well. Enjoy the stew hot.

Nutrition: calories 205, fat 14.1, fiber 3, carbs 13.7, protein 9

Cuban-Style Beef

Prep time: 14 minutes | Cooking time: 9 hours | Servings: 7

Ingredients:

- 1 teaspoon ground chili pepper
- 3 tablespoons tomato paste
- 1 teaspoon olive oil
- 1/3 cup fresh dill
- 13 oz beef fillet
- 1 onion
- 4 garlic cloves
- 1 teaspoon mayo sauce
- 2 tablespoons water
- 1 teaspoon lemon zest

Directions:

Put the beef fillet in the slow cooker. Combine the tomato paste, olive oil, ground chili pepper mayo sauce, and lemon zest. Coat the beef fillet with the tomato paste mixture. Then chop the fresh dill and peel the garlic cloves. Cut the garlic cloves into 4 parts. After this, put the chopped fresh dill and garlic in the slow cooker. Close the lid and cook it on LOW for 8 hours. Open the slow cooker lid and shred the meat with a fork. Stir the meat well and close the lid. Cook on LOW for 1 hour more. When the meat is cooked, taste it and add salt if desired. Enjoy the dish with the rice.

Nutrition: calories 94, fat 4, fiber 1, carbs 3.5, protein 12

Sausage Gravy

Prep time: 10 minutes | Cooking time: 10 hours | Servings :6

Ingredients:

- 2-pounds sausage
- 8 oz white onion
- 2 tablespoons flour
- 3 cups milk
- 1 teaspoon salt
- ½ teaspoon ground white pepper

Directions:

Chop the sausages and put them in the slow cooker. Add salt and flour and stir the mixture. Close the lid and cook on HIGH for 3 hours. Open the slow cooker lid and stir carefully again. Peel the onion and chop it then add the chopped onion to the slow cooker. Then pour in the milk and stir. Close the lid and cook the sausage gravy on LOW for 5 hours. Stir it after 2 hours of cooking.

Nutrition: calories 529, fat 33.7, fiber 5, carbs 31.5, protein 33

Boeuf Bourguignon

Prep time: 20 minutes | Cooking time: 7 hours | Servings: 7

Ingredients:

- 2 oz bacon, sliced
- 19 oz beef, boneless
- 6 oz red wine
- 12 oz chicken stock
- 4 tablespoons tomato sauce
- 3 tablespoons soy sauce
- 3 tablespoons flour
- 1 tablespoon chopped garlic
- 3 carrots
- 1 cup potato, chopped
- 1 teaspoon salt
- 1 teaspoon cilantro
- 1 tablespoon ground coriander
- 1 teaspoon turmeric
- 2 tablespoons fresh parsley
- 6 oz cremini mushrooms

Directions:

Chop the sliced bacon. Cut the beef into cubes and add them to the slow cooker along with the chopped bacon. Then add the red wine, chicken stock, tomato sauce and soy sauce. Add flour and chopped garlic. Mix well. Then peel the carrots and chop them roughly. Add the chopped carrots and potato in the slow cooker bowl too along with the salt, cilantro, ground coriander, and turmeric. Cut the cremini mushrooms into the halves and add them in the slow cooker. Close the lid and cook the dish on HIGH for 7 hours. When the dish is done, stir it carefully.

Nutrition: calories 294, fat 9, fiber 5, carbs 33.8, protein 22

Bacon Jam

Prep time: 18 minutes | Cooking time: 6 hours | Servings: 9

Ingredients:

- 3-pounds bacon, chopped
- 8 oz white onion, diced
- 5 garlic cloves, peeled, diced
- 5 tablespoons balsamic vinegar
- 3 tablespoons brown sugar
- 2 tablespoons maple syrup
- 2 tablespoons brewed coffee

Directions:

Put the brown sugar in a skillet with the maple syrup and brewed coffee. Cook on the medium heat until the mixture is smooth. Then transfer the chopped bacon, onion and garlic to the slow cooker. Sprinkle with the coffee mixture and stir carefully. Close the lid and cook the jam on HIGH for 6 hours. Stir every hour. Then transfer the prepared bacon jam in the glass jars and chill.

Nutrition: calories 527, fat 46.1, fiber 5, carbs 20.23, protein 17

Ham Soup

Prep time: 16 minutes | Cooking time: 3.5 hours | Servings: 7

Ingredients:

- 15 oz ham, cut in strips
- 6 cups water
- 1 tablespoon kosher salt
- 1 teaspoon ground black pepper
- 8 oz celery, chopped
- 1 egg, boiled
- ¼ cup fresh dill, chopped
- 3 tablespoons chives, chopped
- 1 cup corn
- ½ cup white onion, diced
- 1 tablespoon butter

Directions:

Combine the kosher salt and ground black pepper together in the bowl. Toss the butter in the slow cooker. Add chopped celery, ham strips, kosher salt mixture, chopped dill, and chives. After this, add water and corn. Close the slow cooker lid and cook the soup for 3 hours on HIGH. Peel the boiled egg and chop it then add the chopped egg to the soup and stir. Cook the soup for 30 minutes on HIGH. Ladle the soup into the serving bowls.

Nutrition: calories 217, fat 6.3, fiber 3, carbs 26.14, protein 15

Beef Goulash

Prep time: 11 minutes | Cooking time: 8 hours | Servings: 5

Ingredients:

- 1 cup beef stock
- 1-pound beef fillet
- 2 tablespoons cornstarch
- 1/3 cup tomato paste
- 1 teaspoon salt
- 1 teaspoon brown sugar
- 1 teaspoon ground black pepper
- 4 garlic cloves, peeled
- 3 tablespoons mayo
- ½ cup cream
- 1 tablespoon dried dill

Directions:

Chop the beef fillet and put it in the slow cooker. Add salt, brown sugar, ground black pepper, mayo and cream. Then sprinkle the beef with the dried dill and stir the mixture with a wooden spoon. After this, combine the tomato paste and cornstarch. Put the tomato paste mixture in the pan and preheat it on the medium heat. Stir it carefully till the mixture is thick. Then pour the mixture in the slow cooker and close the lid. Cook the goulash for 6 hours on LOW. Then stir the dish and close the lid again. Cook the meat on HIGH for 2 hours. Serve the goulash immediately.

Nutrition: calories 223, fat 10.6, fiber 1, carbs 11.67, protein 22

Sweet Pork Goulash

Prep time: 10 minutes | Cooking time: 4 hours | Servings: 6

Ingredients:

- 6 oz shallot
- 2 tablespoons honey
- 1 teaspoon sugar
- 1 tablespoon turmeric
- 1 teaspoon paprika
- 1 teaspoon salt
- 1 cup tomato juice
- 3 tablespoons flour
- 1 onion, peeled
- 10 oz pork chunk
- 2 cups chicken stock
- 1 teaspoon mustard seeds

Directions:

Slice the shallot and combine it with the honey, sugar, turmeric, paprika, salt, tomato juice, and flour. Add mustard seeds and chicken stock and whisk the mixture. Then put the pork chunks in the slow cooker. Add the tomato juice mixture. Cut the onion roughly and add it to the slow cooker. Close the lid and cook the dish for 4 hours on HIGH. Ladle the pork goulash into bowls and serve it immediately.**Nutrition:** calories 219, fat 6.7, fiber 3, carbs 19.57, protein 20

Pork Chops with Peppers

Prep time: 15 minutes | Cooking time: 9 hours | Servings: 4

Ingredients:

- 2 jalapenos pepper
- 1 chili pepper
- 2 red sweet peppers
- 1 cup cream
- 1-pound pork chops
- 1 teaspoon garlic powder
- 1 tablespoon lemon juice
- 1 teaspoon cilantro
- 1 teaspoon fresh parsley, chopped

Directions:

Slice the chili pepper, jalapeno pepper, and sweet peppers. Combine the cream with the garlic powder, lemon juice, and cilantro. Add the chopped fresh parsley. Stir the mixture. Put the pork chops in the slow cooker. Cover it with the sliced peppers. Pour in the cream mixture and close the lid. Cook the dish on LOW for 9 hours. Then place the cooked sliced peppers on serving plates to make the "pillow" for the meat. Put the pork chops in the pepper "pillow" and sprinkle with the cream sauce from the slow cooker. Serve it immediately.

Nutrition: calories 370, fat 24.3, fiber 1, carbs 5.96, protein 31

Amazing Swedish Meatballs

Prep time: 18 minutes | Cooking time: 4 hour | Servings: 11

Ingredients:

- 1 cup chicken stock
- 1 tablespoon mayo
- 11 oz ground pork
- 6 oz ground chicken
- 4 oz bread crumbs
- 3 eggs
- 1 teaspoon salt
- 1 teaspoon ground black pepper
- 1 tablespoon butter
- 2 tablespoons flour
- 4 tablespoons heavy cream
- 1 tablespoon fresh parsley, chopped

Directions:

Combine the ground pork and ground chicken together. Add the bread crumbs, salt, ground black pepper, and chopped fresh parsley. Mix well. After this, beat the eggs into the mixture. Then combine the flour with the butter and mix well. Then make meatballs from the meat mixture. Sprinkle the meatballs with the flour-butter mixture and place them in the slow cooker. Add the heavy cream and close the lid. Cook Swedish Meatballs for 4 hours on HIGH. Serve the dish immediately.

Nutrition: calories 181, fat 9.6, fiber 0, carbs 7.9, protein 16

Turmeric Lasagna

Prep time: 20 minutes | Cooking time: hours | Servings: 6

Ingredients:

- 8 oz ground pork
- 7 oz yellow onion, chopped
- 5 tablespoons tomato sauce
- 1 tablespoon basil
- ¼ tablespoon salt
- 12 oz mozzarella cheese, sliced
- 1 cup ricotta cheese
- 11 oz lasagna noodles
- 1 teaspoon paprika
- 1 cup chicken stock

Directions:

Combine the ground pork with the chopped onion, tomato sauce, and basil. Add salt and stir the mixture well. Then put the lasagna noodles in the slow cooker and spread them with the ground pork mixture. Sprinkle the ground pork mixture with a small amount of cheese. Cover the mixture with another lasagna noodle and repeat all the steps again, layering the noodles, cheese and meat. Sprinkle the top of the lasagna with the paprika and then add the chicken stock. Close the slow cooker lid and cook the lasagna on HIGH for 4 hours. Check if the noodles are soft then remove the lasagna from the slow cooker. Serve warm!

Nutrition: calories 36.4, fat 14.4, fiber 4, carbs 18.59, protein 40

Beef Roast

Prep time: 15 minutes | Cooking time: 8 hours | Servings: 8

Ingredients:

- 2 red onions
- 3 tablespoon flour
- 3-pound beef roast
- 3 medium potatoes
- 1 teaspoon garlic, sliced
- 3 cup beef broth
- 1 can onion soup
- 1 teaspoon powdered chili

Directions:

Peel the onions and slice them. Then chop the sliced onions and put them in the slow cooker bowl. Add the onion soup and beef broth. Sprinkle the mixture with the powdered chili and sliced garlic. Then add flour and stir the mixture with a spoon. Add the beef roast. Peel the potatoes and cut them into 6 pieces and add the potatoes in the slow cooker and close the lid. Cook the dish for 8 hours on LOW. Then open the slow cooker lid and stir the dish gently. Serve it!

Nutrition: calories 480, fat 16.4, fiber 4, carbs 33.15, protein 51

Shallot Beef

Prep time: 20 minutes | Cooking time: 7 hours | Servings: 6

Ingredients:

- 1-pound shallot
- 1 tablespoon salt
- 1 tablespoon white sugar
- 1 teaspoon baking soda
- 13 oz beef fillet
- 5 garlic cloves
- 1 tablespoon water
- 1 teaspoon dried dill
- 1 teaspoon dried parsley
- 1 tablespoon oil
- 2 cups beef broth
- ½ teaspoon black peas

Directions:

Peel the shallot and slice it. Combine the sliced shallot with the salt, white sugar, and olive oil. Put the sliced shallot in a saute pan and roast it on the medium heat until the shallot is golden brown. Cut the beef filet into the strips. Sprinkle the beef strips with the dried parsley and dried dill. Put the beef strips in the slow cooker bowl. Peel the garlic cloves and add them in the slow cooker. After this, cover the beef strips with the prepared shallot and add beef broth. Close the slow cooker lid and cook the dish on LOW for 7 hours. When the meat is cooked, stir it gently and transfer to the serving plates.

Nutrition: calories 192, fat 6.1, fiber 3, carbs 20.73, protein 15

Honey Ribs

Prep time: 15 minutes | Cooking time: 7.5 hours | Servings: 4

Ingredients:

- 1 teaspoon nutmeg
- ¼ cup raw honey
- ¼ teaspoon cinnamon
- 1 teaspoon ground black pepper
- ½ teaspoon salt
- 1 tablespoon onion powder
- 1 cup beef stock
- 1-pound beef ribs
- 1 teaspoon butter
- 1 carrot
- 1 onion

Directions:

Put the beef ribs in the slow cooker bowl and sprinkle them with the beef stock and salt. Close the lid and cook the meat for 5 hours on LOW. Meanwhile, peel the carrot and onion and chop roughly. Melt the butter and combine it with the nutmeg, honey, cinnamon, ground black pepper, salt, and onion powder. Open the slow cooker lid and add the chopped vegetables. Then cook the meat for 2 hours more on LOW. Then add the honey mixture and stir carefully. Cook the meat on HIGH for 30 minutes more. Serve immediately.

Nutrition: calories 493, fat 35.2, fiber 2, carbs 26.08, protein 2

Mango Pulled Pork

Prep time: 20 minutes | Cooking time: 7 hours | Servings: 6

Ingredients:

- 1 mango, pitted, peeled chopped
- 2-pounds pork fillet
- 1 teaspoon paprika
- 1 teaspoon ground black pepper
- ½ teaspoon cilantro
- 3 cups water
- 1 teaspoon oregano
- ¼ cup cream
- 1 teaspoon olive oil
- 5 tablespoons tomato paste
- 2 bell pepper, chopped

Directions:

Put the pork fillet in the slow cooker and add water. Close the slow cooker lid and cook the meat on HIGH for 5 hours. Meanwhile, place the chopped mango and bell peppers in the blender. Add paprika, ground black pepper, cilantro, oregano, olive oil, cream, and tomato paste. Blend the mixture until it is smooth. When the pork fillet is cooked, strain the water and shred the meat. Put the shredded meat in the slow cooker. Add the blended mango mixture and stir it. Close the lid and cook the dish for 2 hours on LOW. When the pulled pork is cooked, mix it up with a spoon. Serve it!

Nutrition: calories 485, fat 29.8, fiber 2, carbs 13.73, protein 40

Spicy Pulled Pork for Sandwiches

Prep time: 15 minutes | Cooking time: 9 hours | Servings: 7

Ingredients:

- 1 white onion, peeled and sliced
- 2 oz garlic, peeled and chopped
- 7 oz beef broth
- 1 tablespoon brown sugar
- ½ chili pepper, chopped
- ¼ tablespoon kosher salt
- 1 teaspoon ground coriander
- ¼ teaspoon ground ginger
- 1 tablespoon chili sauce
- 1 teaspoon cayenne pepper
- 1 teaspoon oregano
- 3-pounds pork shoulder
- 1 tablespoon dried dill

Directions:

Combine the brown sugar and beef broth. Stir it until the sugar is dissolved. Combine the kosher salt, ground coriander, ground ginger, cayenne pepper, oregano, and dried dill. Chop the pork shoulder then toss the pork shoulder with the spices and stir. Add the chili sauce. Then transfer the pork shoulder mixture in the slow cooker. Add the sweet beef broth mixture, sliced onion and garlic. Close the lid and cook the pork shoulder on LOW for 9 hours. When the meat is cooked, shred it carefully. Serve the spicy pulled pork with the sandwich bread.

Nutrition: calories 565, fat 34.7, fiber 1, carbs 10.26, protein 50

Parsley Barbecue Meatballs

Prep time: 25 minutes | Cooking time: 4 hours | Servings: 6

Ingredients:

- 4 tablespoons Barbecue sauce
- 4 tablespoons panko bread crumbs
- 1/3 cup fresh parsley
- 1 teaspoon ground white pepper
- 2 tablespoons semolina
- 15 oz ground pork
- 8 oz ground beef
- 1 tablespoon tomato juice
- 1 teaspoon turmeric
- ½ teaspoon nutmeg
- 1 onion, chopped
- 1 teaspoon olive oil

Directions:

Combine the semolina, ground pork, and ground beef. Sprinkle the meat mixture with the turmeric, nutmeg, ground white pepper. Chop the fresh parsley and add into the meat mixture. Pour the olive oil into a pan and add the chopped onion and simmer it until golden brown. Then add the cooked onion to the meat. Form small meatballs and dip them in Barbecue sauce gently. Then coat the meatballs in the panko bread crumbs. Put the uncooked meatballs in the slow cooker and close the lid. Cook the meatballs on HIGH for 2 hours. Then turn the meatballs over and close the slow cooker lid. Cook the meatballs on HIGH for 2 hours more. Enjoy the prepared meatballs hot!

Nutrition: calories 329, fat 17.7, fiber 1, carbs 13.54, protein 29

Cranberry Meatballs

Prep time: 10 minutes | Cooking time: 5 hours | Servings: 8

Ingredients:

- 3 tablespoons yellow onion, diced
- 3 tablespoons butter
- 7 oz bread crumbs
- 6 tablespoons whole milk
- 18 oz minced beef
- 2 large egg
- 17 oz cranberry sauce
- 1 chipotle, chopped

Directions:

Melt butter in the pan and add the diced onion. Simmer the onion for 2 minutes on medium heat, stirring frequently. Combine the minced beef, chopped chipotle, whole milk, and cooked onion. Then beat the eggs into the mixture and stir. Make meatballs from the mixture and sprinkle them with the bread crumbs carefully. Place the meatballs in the slow cooker bowl and cook on HIGH for 3 hours. Flip the meatballs over and add the cranberry sauce. Close the lid and cook the meatballs for 2 hours more on HIGH. Remove the meatballs from the slow cooker and transfer them to the serving plates. Sprinkle the dish with the prepared cranberry sauce from the slow cooker. Serve it!

Nutrition: calories 218, fat 12.7, fiber 3, carbs 17.98, protein 8

Lasagna Soup

Prep time: 15 minutes | Cooking time: 7 hours | Servings :8

Ingredients:

- 6 lasagna noodles
- 1 teaspoon ground black pepper
- 1 teaspoon salt
- ½ cup onion chopped
- 1 teaspoon olive oil
- 1 teaspoon onion powder
- 1-pound ground pork

- 7 oz tomato sauce
- 6 oz canned tomatoes
- 7 cups low sodium chicken stock
- 1 tablespoon garlic, sliced
- 1 teaspoon cilantro
- ¼ cup fresh basil

Directions:

Put the ground pork in the pan. Add onion powder, olive oil, salt, and ground black pepper. Roast the ground pork for 10 minutes. Then put the chopped onion, tomato sauce, canned tomatoes, and prepared ground pork in the slow cooker. Chop the basil and add it in the slow cooker too. Then sprinkle the mixture with the cilantro, sliced garlic, and chicken stock. Close the lid and cook the soup for 7 hours on HIGH. Add the lasagna noodles into the soup 35 minutes before the cooking time ends. Stir the prepared lasagna soup carefully and ladle into serving bowls. Serve it hot. Sprinkle the soup with parmesan cheese if desired.

Nutrition: calories 464, fat 21, fiber 6, carbs 37.19, protein 3

Pork Shepherd Pie

Prep time: 14 minutes | Cooking time: 7 hours | Servings: 8

Ingredients:

- 1-pound pork chunk
- ½ cup green peas
- ½ cup sweet corn
- 1 red onion, chopped
- 1 tablespoon tomato sauce
- 8 oz potato, cooked, mashed
- 3 cups water

- 2 carrots
- ½ cup tomato juice
- 1 tablespoon sour cream
- 1 tablespoon salt
- 1 teaspoon brown sugar
- 1 tablespoon flour

Directions:

Put the pork chunks in the slow cooker. Sprinkle the meat with the tomato sauce, tomato juice, sour cream, salt, and brown sugar. Add flour and stir the mixture well. Add water, sweet corn, and green peas. Close the slow cooker lid and cook the dish for 3 hours on HIGH. Peel the carrot and cut into the small cubes. Add the carrot cubes in the slow cooker and stir the mixture well. Then cover the meat with the mashed potato and close the lid. Cook the dish on LOW for 4 hours. Then transfer the cooked dish to serving plates. Let the shepherd pie chill a little then serve it!

Nutrition: calories 226, fat 6.9, fiber 3, carbs 18.45, protein 22

Cheesy Ground Pork

Prep time: 15 minutes | Cooking time: 6 hours | Servings: 6

Ingredients:

- ¼ teaspoon nutmeg
- ½ teaspoon cilantro
- 1 teaspoon oregano
- ½ teaspoon turmeric
- 1 teaspoon ground black pepper
- 1 tablespoon paprika
- 1 teaspoon olive oil
- 1 cup low sodium chicken stock
- 1 tablespoon sour cream
- 11 oz ground pork
- 8 oz Cheddar cheese, shredded

Directions:

Make the spice mixture by combining the nutmeg, cilantro, oregano, turmeric, ground black pepper, and paprika together in a shallow bowl. Stir the mixture with the help of the fork. Pour the olive oil and low sodium chicken stock in the slow cooker. Add the spice mix and stir. Then add the ground pork mixture and close the lid. Cook the meat on HIGH for 4 hours, stirring the meat mixture every 30 minutes. When the time is done, open the lid and cover the ground pork with the shredded cheese. Close the lid and cook on LOW for 2 hours more. Mix the prepared meal carefully and transfer it to serving plates/bowls.

Nutrition: calories 187, fat 8.5, fiber 1, carbs 6.32, protein 22

Italian Beef Roast with Grapes

Prep time: 15 minutes | Cooking time: 6 hours | Servings: 5

Ingredients:

- 1 cup green grapes
- 13 oz beef chuck roast
- 1 big yellow onion
- 1 cup chicken stock
- 2 tablespoons Italian seasoning
- ½ tablespoon salt
- 1 teaspoon chili pepper
- 2 tablespoons cream

Directions:

Put the green grapes in a blender and add the cream. Pulse the green grapes for 1 minute. Peel the onion and crush it then place it in the slow cooker bowl. Add chicken stock, Italian seasoning, salt, and chili pepper. After this, add the green grape mixture and stir it. Transfer the beef chuck roast in the slow cooker and stir. Close the lid and cook the meat on HIGH for 6 hours. Serve hot!

Nutrition: calories 208, fat 8.1, fiber 1, carbs 12.27, protein 22

Beef Stroganoff

Prep time: 11 minutes | Cooking time: 7 hours | Servings: 8

Ingredients:

- 3-pounds beef sirloin steak
- 7 oz onion, chopped
- 1 teaspoon garlic, sliced
- 6 oz mushroom soup, canned
- 5 oz cremini mushrooms, chopped
- 3 cups rice, cooked
- 1 teaspoon salt
- 1 teaspoon ground black pepper
- 1 cup cream cheese
- 1 cup beef stock
- 4 tablespoons sour cream

Directions:

Chop the meat and put it in the slow cooker. Add the chopped onion and sliced garlic. After this, combine the mushroom soup with the chopped cremini mushrooms. Add salt, ground black pepper, cream cheese, and sour cream. Stir the mixture and add the beef stock. Pour the whisked mixture in the slow cooker and close the lid. Cook the beef stroganoff for 7 hours on LOW. Then put the cooked rice on the plates. Place the prepared beef stroganoff over the rice and serve it hot.

Nutrition: calories 631, fat 37.9, fiber 12, carbs 40.26, protein 47

Stuffed Pork Chops

Prep time: 25 minutes | Cooking time: 8 hours | Servings: 5

Ingredients:

- 16 oz pork chop
- 2 red apples
- 1 teaspoon turmeric
- 1 teaspoon salt
- ½ teaspoon cilantro
- 3 tablespoons mayo
- 1 tablespoon olive oil
- 1 teaspoon dried basil
- 1 garlic clove, sliced
- 3 tablespoons sour cream

Directions:

Beat the pork chops gently. Combine the mayo, cilantro, salt, turmeric, dried basil, and sliced garlic together. Spread the pork chops with the mayo mass carefully. Then cut the red apples into the strips. Combine the red apple strips with the sour cream and stir the mixture. Put the prepared red apple strips in the center of every pork chop. Wrap the pork chops around the apple slices and secure them with the toothpicks. Then place the prepared pork chops in the slow cooker and add olive oil. Close the slow cooker lid and cook the meat for 8 hours on LOW. Transfer the prepared meat from the slow cooker onto the serving plates.

Nutrition: calories 280, fat 13.7, fiber 2, carbs 13.83, protein 24

Pork Strips with Mushrooms

Prep time: 18 minutes | Cooking time: 6 hours | Servings: 6

Ingredients:

- 1 tablespoon flour
- 1 tablespoon cornstarch
- 1 teaspoon salt
- 1 teaspoon ground white pepper
- 8 oz button mushrooms
- 1 onion
- 1-pound pork strips
- 1 cup milk
- ½ tablespoon butter

Directions:

Put butter, milk, salt and ground white pepper into the slow cooker and stir. Cook the milk on LOW for 1 hour. Then add flour and cornstarch and stir it until well blended then cook for 1 hour more. When the mixture is thickened, it is cooked. Peel the onion and grate it. Combine the grated onion with the pork strips. Put the pork strips in the slow cooker and stir well. Close the lid and cook for 6 hours on LOW. Then transfer the prepared pork strips in the big bowl and let it chill well.

Nutrition: calories 512, fat 30.5, fiber 5, carbs 36, protein 27

Slow Cooker French Beef Stew

Prep time: 25 minutes | Cooking time: 10 hours | Servings: 11

Ingredients:

- 1 cup cream, whisked
- 1 tablespoon salt
- 3 cup baby carrot
- 3 eggplant, peeled, cubed
- 1-pound beef fillet chopped
- 2 yellow onion, peeled, diced
- ½ teaspoon onion powder
- 5 oz celery stalk, chopped
- 2 cup low sodium chicken stock
- 1 cup fresh dill, chopped
- 4 oz cremini mushrooms
- 1 oz olive oil

Directions:

Wash the baby carrots and place them in the slow cooker with the eggplant, onion celery and dil. Sprinkle the vegetables with the onion powder and salt. Slice the cremini mushrooms. Preheat a saute pan and pour olive oil inside. Roast the mushrooms for 7 minutes over medium heat. Transfer the roasted mushrooms to the slow cooker. Put the beef fillet in the remaining olive oil and roast on high heat for 1 minute on each side. Put the roasted beef in the slow cooker. Add low sodium chicken stock and whisked cream. Close the lid and cook the dish on LOW for 10 hours. Stir the stew after 8 hours of cooking. Put the prepared stew in bowls and serve it immediately.

Nutrition: calories 207, fat 9.8, fiber 6, carbs 21, protein 13

Country Style Pork

Prep time: 15 minutes | Cooking time: 9 hours | Servings: 6

Ingredients:

- 1 cup tomato sauce
- 3 tablespoons ketchup
- 1 tablespoon sugar
- 2 tablespoons Dijon Mustard
- 1 teaspoon salt
- 1 teaspoon ground black pepper
- 1 teaspoon turmeric
- 1 teaspoon olive oil
- 12 oz pork chunks
- 1 teaspoon onion powder
- 1 teaspoon garlic powder

Directions:

Combine the tomato sauce, ketchup, sugar, Dijon Mustard, salt, and ground black pepper together in the mixing bowl. Whisk the mixture. Sprinkle the pork chunks with the turmeric, onion powder, and garlic powder. Stir it carefully. After this, put the pork in the slow cooker bowl. Add the tomato sauce mix and stir gently with a spatula. Close the slow cooker lid and cook the dish on LOW for 9 hours. When the pork is cooked, stir it carefully. Put the prepared dish in the serving bowls and sprinkle with the hot tomato sauce.

Nutrition: calories 224, fat 7.5, fiber 3, carbs 15.19, protein 22

Beef Ratatouille

Prep time: 20 minutes | Cooking time: 9 hours | Servings: 8

Ingredients:

- 1-pound beef
- 1 cup tomatoes
- 1 cup onion, diced
- 1 cup zucchini
- 1 cup eggplants, chopped
- 1 tablespoon garlic, sliced
- 1 tablespoon salt
- 1 teaspoon ground black pepper
- 1 teaspoon red pepper
- 1 teaspoon basil
- 1 cup fresh cilantro
- 3 tablespoons tomato sauce
- 2 tablespoons olive oil
- ½ cup water

Directions:

Chop the tomatoes and zucchini. Put the prepared vegetables in the slow cooker. Add the chopped eggplants. Chop the beef and put it in a saute pan. Add the diced onion and olive oil. Roast the meat until it is golden brown. Add the tomato paste and roast it for 1 minute more. Then put the meat mixture into the slow cooker. Sprinkle the ratatouille mixture with the salt, sliced garlic, ground black pepper, red pepper, basil, and water. Chop the fresh cilantro and put in the slow cooker. Close the lid and cook the mixture on LOW for 9 hours. Open the slow cooker lid and stir the prepared dish. Add more salt if desired and transfer to serving plates.

Nutrition: calories 128, fat 6.7, fiber 1, carbs 5, protein 13

Pepperoncini Beef

Prep time: 10 minutes | Cooking time: 10 hours | Servings: 6

Ingredients:

- 1-pound beef chuck roast
- 18 oz pepperoncini pepper
- 1 cup chicken stock
- 1 teaspoon salt
- 1 teaspoon ground black pepper
- 1 teaspoon paprika
- 1 onion, diced

Directions:

Pour the chicken stock into the slow cooker. Add the beef chuck roast and sprinkle with the ground black pepper, salt, paprika, and diced onion. Close the lid and cook for 4 hours on HIGH. Meanwhile, slice the pepperoncini peppers and add them into the slow cooker then close the lid. Cook the meat for 6 hours more on LOW. Serve the cooked beef with sandwich buns.

Nutrition: calories 254, fat 10.3, fiber 5, carbs 35.7, protein 9

Curry Lamb

Prep time: 14 minutes | Cooking time: 13 hours | Servings: 6

Ingredients:

- 2 tablespoons curry paste
- 1-pound lamb
- 2 tomatoes
- 3 tablespoons pomegranate sauce or juice
- 1 teaspoon salt
- 1 tablespoon apple cider vinegar
- 1 teaspoon nutmeg
- 1 teaspoon cilantro
- 4 tablespoons beef broth
- 1 cup water
- 1 tablespoon butter
- ¼ cup coriander leaves, chopped

Directions:

Combine the curry paste with the beef broth and stir the paste until it is dissolved. Slice the tomatoes. Butter the slow cooker bowl and make the layer of the tomatoes in the bottom of the bowl. Combine the pomegranate sauce, salt, apple cider vinegar, nutmeg, cilantro, and chopped coriander leaves together. Then chop the lamb roughly and sprinkle with the pomegranate sauce. Mix using your fingertips. Put the meat on top of the sliced tomatoes. Add water and close the lid. Cook the meat on LOW for 13 hours. Serve the cooked lamb with the lime wedges.

Nutrition: calories 235, fat 15.2, fiber 2, carbs 4.76, protein 19

Honey Pulled Pork

Prep time: 10 minutes | Cooking time: 7 hours | Servings: 4

Ingredients:

- 4 teaspoons minced garlic
- 1 teaspoon salt
- 1 teaspoon ground black pepper
- 1 teaspoon cilantro
- ¼ cup honey
- 1-pound pork fillet
- 2 cups water
- 1 teaspoon ground chili pepper

Directions:

Put the pork fillet in the slow cooker. Sprinkle it with the salt, ground black pepper, cilantro, and ground chili pepper. Add the water and close the lid. Cook on HIGH for 5 hours. Then strain the water and shred the pork. Return the pork to the slow cooker and add minced garlic and honey. Stir the shredded meat with a fork. Close the lid and cook on LOW for 2 hours more. Serve it and

Nutrition: calories 376, fat 20.1, fiber 0, carbs 20, protein 29

Delightful Pulled Pork Nachos

Prep time: 25 minutes | Cooking time: 5 hours | Servings: 12

Ingredients:

- 7 oz corn tortilla
- 2 tablespoons mayonnaise
- 3 red onions
- 1 cup tomato, chopped
- ½ cup fresh parsley
- 1 garlic clove, peeled
- 1-pound pork shoulder
- 3 tablespoons mustard
- 1 tablespoon ketchup
- 1 teaspoon cayenne pepper
- 1 teaspoon salt
- 2 teaspoons ground black pepper
- 9 oz Cheddar cheese, shredded
- 1 teaspoon dried mint
- 2 cup water

Directions:

Peel the onions and slice them. Put the 1 tablespoon of onions in the slow cooker. Add the pork shoulder. Sprinkle the meat with the mustard, ketchup, cayenne pepper, salt, ground black pepper, and dried mint. Add the water then close the lid and cook it for 5 hours on HIGH. Remove the pork shoulder from the slow cooker and shred it. Place a corn tortilla in a skillet and add the shredded meat. Then sprinkle it with a small amount of the chopped tomatoes and onions. Cover it with another corn tortillas. Then sprinkle the mixture with a small amount of cheese. Repeat the layers until you use the entire ingredient. Sprinkle the last layer with cheese and mayonnaise. Chop the garlic and fresh parsley and sprinkle on op as well. Put the dish in the oven and cook it at 350 degreed F for 10 minutes.

Nutrition: calories 204, fat 10.1, fiber 2, carbs 14.46, protein 14

Garlic Beef Mash

Prep time: 15 minutes | Cooking time: 12 hours | Servings: 4

Ingredients:

- 1-pound beef
- 1 cup garlic cloves, peeled
- 4 cups beef broth
- 1 tablespoon salt
- 1 teaspoon ground black pepper
- 1 teaspoon paprika
- 1 cup onion, roasted
- 3 oz butter

Directions:

Put the beef in the slow cooker and add the water. Add salt, ground black pepper, paprika, and peeled garlic cloves. Close the slow cooker lid and cook the meat for 12 hours on LOW. Then strain the water and mash the beef with a fork. Add butter and roasted onion and mix well. Place it in a bowl and serve or keep in the fridge for 1 hour to use the mash as a spread.

Nutrition: calories 462, fat 24.3, fiber 2, carbs 36.05, protein 28

Beef Strips in Bread Crumbs

Prep time: 17 minutes | Cooking time: 4 hours | Servings: 6

Ingredients:

- ½ teaspoon onion powder
- 1 teaspoon garlic powder
- 1 cup bread crumbs
- 2 large eggs
- ¼ cup sour cream
- 1 tablespoon salt
- 1 teaspoon turmeric
- 1 teaspoon olive oil
- 10 oz beef fillet
- 1 tablespoon balsamic vinegar

Directions:

Cut the beef fillet into strips and sprinkle them with the onion powder and garlic powder. Add salt, turmeric, and balsamic vinegar. Then beat the egg in a separate bowl. Add sour cream and stir well. Dip the beef strips in the egg mixture, and after this, coat them in the bread crumbs. Spray the inside of the slow cooker bowl with the olive oil. Put the beef strips in the slow cooker and close lid. Cook the dish on HIGH for 4 hours. Stir frequently. Serve the prepared beef strips immediately.

Nutrition: calories 123, fat 6.2, fiber 0, carbs 5.09, protein 12

Pork and Barley Soup

Prep time: 16 minutes | Cooking time: 8 hours | Servings: 9

Ingredients:

- 1 cup barley
- 7 cups water
- 3 oz pickled cucumbers
- 9 oz pork, chopped
- 1 teaspoon paprika
- 1 teaspoon cilantro
- 1 tablespoon ground black pepper
- 1 tomato, chopped
- 1 carrot, peeled
- 1 tablespoon salt
- 1 sweet pepper, chopped
- 1 teaspoon sour cream

Directions:

Chop the pickled cucumbers and carrot then put them in the slow cooker. Add chopped pork, barley, tomatoes and sweet pepper. After this, add the paprika, cilantro, water, ground black pepper, salt, and sour cream. Mix the soup gently and close the lid. Cook the soup on LOW for 8 hours. Ladle the cooked soup in the bowls. Let it chill gently. Serve!

Nutrition: calories 152, fat 3.1, fiber 4, carbs 20.75, protein 11

Hungarian Tender Beef

Prep time: 15 minutes | Cooking time: 10 hours | Servings: 4

Ingredients:

- ½ cup tomato puree
- 1-pound beef
- ½ cup garlic clove
- 1 white onion
- ¼ teaspoon caraway seeds
- 1 teaspoon curry powder
- 1 teaspoon chili flakes
- 3 tablespoons sour cream
- 1 teaspoon cilantro
- ½ teaspoon ground nutmeg
- 3 cups water

Directions:

Rub the beef with the caraway seeds, curry powder, chili flakes, sour cream, cilantro, and ground nutmeg. Make small cuts in the beef. Peel the garlic cloves and cut them into halves. Fill the beef cuts with the garlic halved. Then rub the meat with the tomato puree and put it in the slow cooker. Chop the onion roughly and sprinkle over the meat. Close the lid and cook for 10 hours on LOW. Stir the meat frequently during cooking. Slice the meat into the serving pieces and transfer it to the plates. Serve it!

Nutrition: calories 217, fat 7.9, fiber 2, carbs 12.45, protein 26

Thyme Lamb

Prep time: 25 minutes | Cooking time: 6 hours | Servings: 4

Ingredients:

- 2-pounds lamb leg
- 1 cup fresh thyme leaves
- 1 teaspoon ground thyme
- 1 teaspoon dried rosemary
- 1 cup pomegranate juice
- 1 teaspoon salt
- 1 tablespoon olive oil
- 1 teaspoon ground black pepper
- 2 garlic cloves, peeled

Directions:

Mash the garlic cloves and toss them in a skillet. Add the olive oil and start to roast over medium heat. Meanwhile, chop the thyme leaves. Add the thyme leaves and ground thyme into the smashed garlic. Add salt and ground black pepper. When the spice mixture starts to boil, add the lamb leg and roast it on high heat for 3 minutes on each side. Transfer the lamb leg with remaining olive oil mixture in the slow cooker bowl. Add the pomegranate juice and close the lid. Cook the lamb for 6 hours on HIGH. When the dish is cooked – chill it gently. Serve it.

Nutrition: calories 384, fat 15.7, fiber 2, carbs 12.17, protein 47

Lamb Meatballs

Prep time: 15 minutes | Cooking time: 6 hours | Servings: 8

Ingredients:

- 19 oz minced lamb
- 2 tablespoons minced garlic
- 1 white onion, diced
- 1 egg
- 1 tablespoon flour
- 1 teaspoon olive oil
- 4 tablespoons flour
- 1 teaspoon salt
- 1 teaspoon turmeric
- 1 teaspoon dried basil
- 2 teaspoons paprika

Directions:

Put the minced lamb in a big bowl. Beat the egg into the lamb along with the diced onion. After this, add the minced garlic and flour. Sprinkle the meat with salt, turmeric, dried basil, and paprika. Then make small balls from the lamb mixture and coat them in the flour. Spray the slow cooker bowl with the olive oil. Put the prepared lamb meatballs inside and close the lid. Cook the dish on HIGH for 6 hours. Turn the meatballs to another side after 3 hours of cooking. Then remove the prepared meatballs from the slow cooker and dry them with a paper towels. Serve the lamb meatballs warm.

Nutrition: calories 223, fat 13.3, fiber 1, carbs 6.44, protein 19

Stuffed Lamb with Onions

Prep time: 15 minutes | Cooking time: 6 hours | Servings: 9

Ingredients:
- 3-pounds lamb fillet
- 5 medium onions
- 3 garlic cloves
- 1 carrot
- 1 tablespoon ground black pepper
- 1 tablespoon olive oil
- ¼ cup sour cream
- 1 tablespoon salt
- 1 teaspoon rosemary

Directions:

Peel the onions and slice them. Then peel the garlic cloves and mince them. Combine the sliced onions with the minced garlic. Make a "pocket" in the lamb fillet and fill it with the onion mixture. Peel the carrot and chop it then stuff it into the lamb as well. After this, secure the lamb fillet with toothpicks. Rub the lamb fillet with the ground black pepper, olive oil, sour cream salt, and rosemary. Wrap the prepared meat in the foil and put in the slow cooker. Cook the meat on HIGH for 6 hours. Then remove the meat from the slow cooker and discard the foil. Serve it!

Nutrition: calories 440, fat 27.7, fiber 1, carbs 8, protein 38

Lamb Shoulder

Prep time: 30 minutes | Cooking time: 10 hours | Servings: 5

Ingredients:
- 12 oz lamb shoulder
- 1 tablespoon fresh rosemary
- 1 cup beer
- 1 teaspoon cilantro
- 1 tablespoon chili pepper
- 1 tablespoon cayenne pepper
- 1 cup water
- 1 garlic clove, peeled
- 1 teaspoon onion powder
- 1 tablespoon marjoram

Directions:

Put the lamb shoulder in a bowl and pour the beer over the lamb. Leave the meat for 20 minutes. Meanwhile, combine the fresh rosemary, cilantro, chili pepper, cayenne pepper, onion powder, and marjoram together. Put the mixture in the slow cooker and add water. Close the lid and cook the liquid on LOW for 1 hour. Peel the garlic clove and put it in the slow cooker liquid after 30 minutes of cooking. Then remove the lamb shoulder from the beer and transfer it to the slow cooker. Close the lid and cook the lamb for 10 hours on LOW. When the time is done, the lamb meat should be very tender. Enjoy the dish!

Nutrition: calories 210, fat 13.4, fiber 1, carbs 5.38, protein 17

Lamb Stew

Prep time: 20 minutes | Cooking time: 5 hours | Servings: 10

Ingredients:

- 1 cup corn kernels
- 4 oz fresh celery root
- 1 tablespoon ground ginger
- 10 oz lamb cubes
- 1 teaspoon onion powder
- 1 teaspoon garlic powder
- 1 tablespoon tomato sauce
- ½ cup tomato puree

- 1 teaspoon olive oil
- 2 tablespoons flour
- 1 eggplant
- 1 carrot, peeled, grated
- 1 teaspoon cayenne pepper
- 2 cup water
- 5 medium potatoes

Directions:

Put the lamb in the slow cooker. Sprinkle the meat with the onion powder, garlic powder, and cayenne pepper. Peel the potatoes and chop them. Add the potatoes into the slow cooker. After this, combine the tomato sauce and tomato puree together. Add the flour and stir. Chop the eggplants and add them into the slow cooker. Grate the fresh celery root. Add the celery root into the slow cooker along with the corn kernels, water, tomato mixture and carrot. Add the grated carrot in the slow cooker and close the lid. Cook the stew on HIGH for 5 hours. Then open the slow cooker lid and stir the mixture with a spatula. Transfer the lamb stew in the bowls.

Nutrition: calories 265, fat 5.9, fiber 7, carbs 42.39, protein 12

Lamb Casserole

Prep time: 16 minutes | Cooking time: 9 hours | Servings: 6

Ingredients:

- 1 cup rice
- 4 cups water
- 13 oz lamb fillet
- 1 tablespoon ground paprika
- 1 onion
- 9 oz Cheddar cheese, shredded

- 3 carrots, chopped
- 1 tablespoon olive oil
- 1 teaspoon salt
- 1 teaspoon ground cinnamon
- 1 tablespoon turmeric
- 5 sweet potatoes

Directions:

Combine the rice with the olive oil and turmeric and mix. Transfer the rice in the slow cooker. Make a layer of the chopped carrot in the slow cooker bowl. Then peel the onion and slice. Make the layer of the sliced onion in the bowl as well. Then chop the lamb fillet and add it into the slow cooker. Sprinkle the meat with the ground paprika, salt and ground cinnamon. Slice the sweet potatoes and cover the meat with the vegetables. Add water and sprinkle the casserole with the cheese. Close the slow cooker and cook the dish on LOW for 9 hours. Then transfer the casserole to the bowls carefully. Serve!

Nutrition: calories 436, fat 20.8, fiber 10, carbs 42.77, protein 26

Garlic Lamb

Prep time: 10 minutes | Cooking time: 10 hours | Servings: 7

Ingredients:

- 2 oz fresh rosemary
- ½ cup fresh cilantro
- ¼ cup coriander leaves
- 2-pounds lamb fillet
- 1 teaspoon salt
- 1 teaspoon black peas
- 1 teaspoon chili flakes
- 1 cup garlic
- 1 teaspoon garlic powder
- 6 cups water

Directions:

Wash the fresh rosemary, cilantro, and coriander leaves carefully and chop them roughly. Then line the slow cooker bowl with the chopped greens and put the lamb fillet inside as well. Sprinkle the lamb fillet with the salt, black peas, chili flakes, and garlic powder. Peel the garlic and mince it. Rub the lamb fillet with the minced garlic and add water. Close the slow cooker lid and cook the lamb for 10 hours on LOW. Strain the liquid from the lamb and transfer the lamb fillet to a plate. Slice it and serve. The lamb fillet will be very aromatic and soft.

Nutrition: calories 375, fat 22.4, fiber 2, carbs 8.71, protein 33

Rosemary Lamb

Prep time: 20 minutes | Cooking time: 7 hours | Servings: 8

Ingredients:

- 4 tablespoons dried rosemary
- 1 cup tomatillos
- 1 tablespoon minced garlic
- 2 oz fresh rosemary
- 1 onion, grated
- 18 oz lamb leg
- 1 teaspoon salt
- 1 cup cream
- ½ teaspoon ground black pepper

Directions:

Chop the tomatillos roughly and put them in the blender. Add the minced garlic, dried rosemary, fresh rosemary, salt, pepper and grated onion. Pulse the mixture until it is smooth. Then pour the cream into the blender and pulse it for 30 seconds. Put the lamb leg in the slow cooker and sprinkle it with the tomatillo-rosemary mixture. Close the lid and cook it for 7 hours on LOW. Serve the cooled lamb immediately.

Nutrition: calories 168, fat 9.8, fiber 2, carbs 5.61, protein 14

Lamb and Apricot Tagine

Prep time: 10 minutes | Cooking time: 5 hours | Servings: 7

Ingredients:

- 2-pounds lamb fillet
- ½ cup dried apricots
- 3 tablespoon cashew
- 1 jalapeno pepper
- 2 cups red wine
- 1 tablespoon sugar
- 1 teaspoon salt
- 1 teaspoon ground white pepper
- 1 cup water

Directions:

Cut the lamb fillets into the bite-sized cubes and put them in the slow cooker. Sprinkle the meat with the cashew, salt, and ground white pepper. Chop the jalapeno pepper and dried apricots. Add all the ingredients into the slow cooker. Then add sugar, red wine, and water. Close the lid and cook the lamb tagine for 5 hours on HIGH. Stir the lamb once per cooking. Stir the cooked dish again. Serve it.

Nutrition: calories 416, fat 25.5, fiber 1, carbs 9.96, protein 33

Greek Style Lamb with Olives
Prep time: 11 minutes | Cooking time: 7 hours | Servings: 5

Ingredients:

- 1 cup Greek yogurt
- 4 oz black olives
- 8 oz lamb
- 1 tablespoon ground black pepper
- 1 chili, chopped
- 1 teaspoon powdered chili
- 1 tablespoon balsamic vinegar
- 1 teaspoon oregano
- ½ cup chicken stock
- 1 tablespoon lemon zest

Directions:

Slice the black olives. Put Greek yogurt in the slow cooker and add the sliced black olives and lamb. Sprinkle the mix with the ground black pepper, powdered chili, balsamic vinegar, oregano, and lemon zest. Add chicken stock and chopped chili. Close the lid and cook the lamb for 4 hours on LOW. Then open the lid and stir, shredding the meat with a fork. Close the lid and cook the lamb for 3 hours more on LOW. Serve the prepared meat with all the juice from the slow cooker.

Nutrition: calories 190, fat 10.4, fiber 2, carbs 8.3, protein 16

Succulents Lamb
Prep time: 10 minutes | Cooking time: 9 hours | Servings: 4

Ingredients:

- 3 tablespoons mustard
- 5 tablespoons olive oil
- 3 tablespoons fresh rosemary
- 1 teaspoon ground coriander
- 1 teaspoon dried mint
- 1 teaspoon salt
- 1 teaspoon paprika
- 4 tablespoons maple syrup
- 1-pound lamb fillet
- 2 tablespoon water

Directions:

Combine the mustard and olive oil together. Add the fresh rosemary, ground coriander, dried mint, salt, and paprika. Rub the lamb fillet with the mustard mixture and put it in the slow cooker bowl. Add the water and maple syrup and close the slow cooker lid. Cook the lamb on LOW for 9 hours. When the lamb is cooked, sprinkle with the remaining liquid from the slow cooker. Transfer the meat to a plate and slice. Put the lamb slices on plates and serve!

Nutrition: calories 502, fat 36.5, fiber 1, carbs 14.73, protein 28

Moroccan Lamb
Prep time: 25 minutes | Cooking time: 13 hours | Servings: 8

Ingredients:

- 2-pound lamb shoulder
- 1 teaspoon cumin seeds
- 1 teaspoon ground cumin
- 1 teaspoon ground coriander
- 1 teaspoon celery root
- 1 teaspoon salt
- 1 teaspoon chili flakes
- 4 tablespoons tomato paste
- 3 tablespoons raisins
- 1 tablespoon dried apricots
- 5 cup water
- 1 cup onion, chopped

Directions:

Combine the cumin seeds, ground cumin, ground coriander, celery root, salt, and chili flakes in a shallow bowl. After this, rub the lamb shoulder with the spice mixture and then brush with the tomato paste. Leave the meat for 10 minutes to marinate. Put the chopped onion in the slow cooker with the water. Then put the marinated meat in the slow cooker as well and close the lid. Cook the dish on LOW for 13 hours. Remove the meat from the liquid and serve it.

Nutrition: calories 195, fat 9.6, fiber 1, carbs 4.5, protein 23

Lemon Lamb Fillet

Prep time: 20 minutes | Cooking time: 5 hours | Servings: 4

Ingredients:

- 1 lemon, chopped
- 3 tablespoons lemon juice
- 1 tablespoon lemon zest
- 1 tablespoon minced garlic
- 1 teaspoon paprika
- 1 teaspoon dried rosemary
- 1 cup chicken stock
- 3 tablespoons olive oil
- 1/3 cup fresh dill, chopped
- 1 teaspoon salt
- 1-pound lamb fillet

Directions:

Combine the chopped lemon, lemon zest, and minced garlic together. Slice the lamb fillet and rub it with the lemon mixture. After this, pour the chicken stock in the slow cooker. Add the dried rosemary and dill. Sprinkle the lamb meat with the olive oil and put it in the slow cooker. Cook the meat on HIGH for 5 hours. You can add the tablespoon of sugar to the meat at the end of cooking if desired. Serve the meat hot!

Nutrition: calories 413, fat 30.1, fiber 0, carbs 5.1, protein 30

Indian Pork

Prep time: 14 minutes | Cooking time: 5 hours | Servings: 8

Ingredients:

- 21 oz pork steak, tenderized
- 2 tablespoon curry
- 1 teaspoon harissa
- 1 tablespoon garam masala
- 1 teaspoon chili flakes
- ½ cup cream
- 1 teaspoon ground black pepper
- 1 teaspoon salt
- 1 teaspoon sugar
- 1 cup cashew, crushed
- 1 teaspoon ground nutmeg

Directions:

Rub the pork steaks with the curry, harissa, garam masala, and chili flakes. Sprinkle the meat with the salt and sugar. Then combine the cream with the ground black pepper and ground nutmeg. Whisk the cream mix and pour it into the slow cooker. Add the pork steaks and close the lid. Cook the dish on HIGH for 5 hours. Then transfer the prepared steaks to plates and sprinkle them with the heavy cream mixture. Serve it!

Nutrition: calories 434, fat 33.4, fiber 2, carbs 12.27, protein 23

Lamb Meatballs

Prep time: 21 minutes | Cooking time: 5 hours | Servings: 6

Ingredients:

- 1 red onion
- 1 tablespoon semolina
- 2 tablespoons dried parsley
- 1 teaspoon chili flakes
- 1 teaspoon ground black pepper
- 1 teaspoon oregano
- 1-pound minced lamb
- 2 tablespoons minced garlic
- 1 teaspoon onion powder
- 1 tablespoon butter
- 1 egg

Directions:

Peel the red onion and grate it. Combine the grated onion with the minced lamb. Add the dried parsley, chili flakes, semolina, and ground black pepper. After this, add the oregano, minced garlic, and onion powder. Add the egg and blend it in using your hands. Then make large balls from the minced lamb mixture. Melt the butter and rub the slow cooker bowl with it. Put the lamb balls in the slow cooker and close the lid. Cook the lamb meatballs for 3 hours on HIGH. Then flip the meatballs over and cook them for 2 hours more on LOW.

Nutrition: calories 256, fat 16.4, fiber 1, carbs 5.53, protein 21

Lime Zest Pork

Prep time: 20 minutes | *Cooking time:* 11 hours | *Servings:* 6

Ingredients:

- 5 tablespoons lime zest
- 2-pounds pork shoulder
- 3 garlic cloves, sliced
- 2 tablespoons butter
- 1 teaspoon paprika
- 1 teaspoon chili flakes
- 1 teaspoon ground black pepper
- 1 tablespoon salt
- 3 teaspoons pesto

Directions:

Combine the sliced garlic, lime zest, paprika, chili flakes, butter, ground black pepper, salt, and pesto together. After this, brush the pork shoulder with the lime zest mixture well and wrap it in the foil. Put the meat in the slow cooker and close the lid. Cook the dish on LOW for 11 hours. Then remove the meat from the slow cooker and discard the foil. Get rid of the lemon zest and chop the pork shoulder roughly to serve.

Nutrition: calories 153, fat 6.1, fiber 3, carbs 22.42, protein 4

Lamb Leg in Red Wine

Prep time: 19 minutes | *Cooking time:* 11 hours | *Servings:* 7

Ingredients:

- 2-pounds lamb leg
- 2 cups dry red wine
- 1 cup water
- 1 teaspoon anise
- 1 teaspoon black peas
- 1 tablespoon fresh rosemary
- 1 tablespoon cumin seeds
- 1 carrot
- 1 white onion
- ½ teaspoon ground cinnamon
- 1 tablespoon fresh ginger, grated
- 1 teaspoon olive oil

Directions:

Spray the inside of the slow cooker bowl with the olive oil and put the lamb leg inside. Sprinkle the lamb leg with the ground cinnamon, grated fresh ginger, and cumin seeds. Add the fresh rosemary and close the lid. Cook the lamb leg on HIGH for 3 hours. Meanwhile, combine the dry red wine, water, anise, and black peas together. Stir the mixture. Peel the carrot and white onion. Chop them and add to the red wine mixture. When the time is over, open the slow cooker lid and add the red wine liquid. Close the lid and cook the meat on LOW for 8 hours more. Remove the prepared lamb leg from the slow cooker and chill it a little. Serve it and

Nutrition: calories 208, fat 7.8, fiber 1, carbs 3.41, protein 27

Mongolian Beef

Prep time: 10 minutes | Cooking time: 9 hours | Servings: 6

Ingredients:

- 2-pounds pork steak
- 3 tablespoons chives, chopped
- 5 tablespoons cornstarch
- 2 oz olive oil
- 2 tablespoons brown sugar
- ¼ cup water
- ¼ cup soy sauce
- 8 oz carrot, grated

Directions:

Cut the pork steak into the strips. Sprinkle the pork strips with the cornstarch and stir the mixture well. After this, put the pork strips in the slow cooker. Sprinkle the meat with the olive oil and brown sugar. Add the grated carrot. Then pour the water and soy sauce inside and close the lid. Cook the meat on HIGH for 2 hours. Then open the lid and stir the meat carefully. Close the lid and cook the meat on LOW for 7 hours more or until the meat is tender. Transfer the cooked meat to a serving bowl and sprinkle it with the chopped chives. Serve Mongolian pork immediately.

Nutrition: calories 557, fat 38.2, fiber 1, carbs 11.9, protein 39

Mexican Lamb

Prep time: 20 minutes | Cooking time: 8 hours | Servings: 4

Ingredients:

- 1 chili pepper
- 1 jalapeno pepper
- 1 cup sweet corn
- 1 cup chicken stock
- 14 oz lamb fillet
- 1 teaspoon salt
- 1 teaspoon ground black pepper
- 1 tablespoon ground paprika
- 1 teaspoon grated ginger
- 1 cup tomato juice
- 1 tablespoon white sugar

Directions:

Remove the seeds from the chili and jalapeno peppers and chop them roughly. Put the peppers in the blender. Add the grated ginger and ground paprika. Pulse the mixture for 30 seconds. Place the lamb fillet in the slow cooker bowl. Sprinkle the meat with the pepper mixture. Add salt, ground black pepper, tomato juice, and white sugar. Then add the chicken stock and sweet corn. Close the slow cooker lid and cook the dish on LOW for 8 hours. When the meat is cooked, stir it carefully and shred the lamb gently. Transfer the lamb to serving bowls/plates and

Nutrition: calories 348, fat 18.3, fiber 3, carbs 19.26, protein 28

Fish

Slow Cooker Salmon

Prep time: 15 minutes | Cooking time: 6 hours | Servings: 2

Ingredients:

- 8 oz salmon fillet
- 1 cup fish stock
- ¼ lemon
- 3 oz shallot, diced

- ½ teaspoon salt
- ½ teaspoon ground black pepper
- ½ teaspoon ground white pepper
- ¼ teaspoon fresh rosemary

Directions:

Slice the lemon into the wedges. Combine the diced shallot with the lemon wedges. Then pour the fish stock in the slow cooker. Add the lemon wedges and diced shallot and cook the liquid for 30 minutes on HIGH. Meanwhile, rub the salmon fillet with the salt, ground black pepper, ground white pepper, and fresh rosemary. When the slow cooker time is done, place the salmon fillet in the slow cooker and close the lid. Cook the salmon on LOW for 6 hours. Remove the prepared salmon from the slow cooker and transfer it to serving plates. Strain the fish stock to retain the lemon wedges and diced shallot. Garnish the fish with the lemon wedges and diced shallot. Serve it immediately.

Nutrition: calories 233, fat 9.2, fiber 2, carbs 9.71, protein 28

Cod Fillets

Prep time: 11 minutes | Cooking time: 3 hours | Servings: 5

Ingredients:

- 2 medium tomatoes, sliced
- 1 teaspoon minced garlic
- 1 teaspoon onion powder
- 1 tablespoon ground coriander
- 1 teaspoon cilantro

- 1 teaspoon olive oil
- ½ tablespoon kosher salt
- 2-pounds cod fillet
- 2 tablespoons mayo

Directions:

Combine the minced garlic, onion powder, ground coriander, cilantro, and kosher salt together. Stir the spices and add the mayo. Cut the cod fillets into the serving pieces. Rub every cod fillet with the mayo mixture from the each side with the help of your hands. Then make the layer from the sliced tomatoes in the slow cooker bowl. Put the cod fillets there and close the lid. Cook the cod fillet for 3 hours on HIGH. When the dish is cooked, transfer the cod fillet in the serving plates and cover them with the cooked tomato slices.

Nutrition: calories 147, fat 1.8, fiber 1, carbs 2.97, protein 28

Tilapia in Sour Cream

Prep time: 15 minutes | Cooking time: 2 hours | Servings: 8

Ingredients:

- 4-pounds tilapia fillet
- 1 garlic clove
- 1 tablespoon lemon juice
- 1 teaspoon lime zest

- 1 tablespoon onion powder
- 1 teaspoon ground black pepper
- ½ cup sour cream
- 2 teaspoons fish sauce

Directions:

Peel the garlic and mince it. Combine the lemon juice, lime zest, minced garlic, onion powder, ground black pepper, and sour cream in the mixing bowl. Then add the fish sauce and whisk it for 30 seconds more. Place parchment in the slow cooker. Put the tilapia fillet on the parchment. Pour the sour cream mixture over the tilapia and wrap it gently in the remaining parchment. Close the lid and cook the fish on LOW for 2 hours. Transfer the cooked fish to serving plates and sprinkle it with the hot sour cream sauce. Serve!

Nutrition: calories 244, fat 5.4, fiber 0, carbs 2.6, protein 46

Scallops with Cherry Sauce
Prep time: 25 minutes | Cooking time: 2.5 hours | Servings: 4

Ingredients:

- 1-pound scallops
- 1 teaspoon salt
- 1 teaspoon ground white pepper
- ½ teaspoon olive oil
- 2 tablespoons lemon juice
- 1 cup cherry, pitted
- 1 tablespoon cornstarch
- 3 tablespoons sugar
- ½ teaspoon ground ginger
- 1 tablespoon flour

Directions:

Sprinkle the scallops with the salt, ground white pepper, and lemon juice. Spray the slow cooker bowl with the olive oil and put the scallops inside the bowl. Close the lid and cook the seafood for 30 minutes on HIGH. Meanwhile, put the cherries in a blender and blend them until smooth. Then transfer the blended cherries into a sauce pan, add sugar and bring to a boil. Combine the cornstarch and flour together then add the dry ingredients into the slow cooker bowl and mix with a hand blender. Stir the sauce until it starts to thicken. Add the ground ginger and stir it carefully. When the time is over, open the slow cooker lid and sprinkle the scallops with the cherry sauce. Stir gently and cook the dish on LOW for 2 minutes more. Serve the dish immediately.

Nutrition: calories 150, fat 1.3, fiber 1, carbs 20.11, protein 15

Fish Stew
Prep time: 20 minutes | Cooking time: 7 hours | Servings: 8

Ingredients:

- 1 cup fresh parsley
- 2 oz fresh ginger
- 1 teaspoon salt
- 2 sweet peppers, chopped
- 2 cups baby potatoes
- 7 cups water
- 1 cup baby carrot
- 1 teaspoon thyme
- 1 teaspoon ground black pepper
- 1 teaspoon oregano
- 1 teaspoon cilantro
- 1 teaspoon paprika
- 1 teaspoon nutmeg
- 1 teaspoon butter
- 2-pounds tuna, chopped
- 2 white onions

Directions:

Chop the fresh parsley and peel the fresh ginger. Grate the fresh ginger. Wash the baby potatoes and baby carrot carefully and cut the vegetables into the halves. Peel the onions and slice them. After this, transfer all the vegetables from the list above into the slow cooker. Add the chopped fish. Sprinkle the mixture with the salt, grated ginger, thyme, ground black pepper, oregano, cilantro, paprika, nutmeg, and butter. Add water and close the slow cooker lid. Cook the stew on LOW for 7 hours. When the stew is cooked, let it rest for 20 minutes. Serve!

Nutrition: calories 168, fat 2, fiber 2, carbs 14.83, protein 24

Seafood Stew

Prep time: 15 minutes | Cooking time: 3 hours | Servings: 14

Ingredients:

- 1-pound crab meat
- 9 oz squid
- 7 oz tilapia
- 6 cups water
- ½ cup tomato juice
- 1 teaspoon cayenne pepper
- 1 teaspoon ground black pepper
- ½ teaspoon oregano
- 5 medium potatoes
- 2 carrots
- 1 apple
- 1 tablespoon lemon zest
- 1 teaspoon sugar
- 1 tablespoon salt
- 1 teaspoon ground coriander
- 2 tablespoons sour cream
- 1 tablespoon minced garlic

Directions:

Chop the crab meat, squid, and tilapia roughly. Place the seafood in the slow cooker. Add water and tomato juice. Sprinkle the seafood with the cayenne pepper, ground black pepper, oregano, lemon zest, sugar, ground coriander, sour cream, and minced garlic. Slice the apple and add it into the slow cooker too. After this, chop the potatoes and carrot into cubes and add in the slow cooker. Close the lid and cook the stew on HIGH for 3 hours. When all the components of the stew are cooked, transfer it to bowls and serve.

Nutrition: calories 178, fat 1.2, fiber 4, carbs 27.5, protein 15

Fish Chowder

Prep time: 20 minutes | Cooking time: 3 hours | Servings: 6

Ingredients:

- 14 oz haddock
- 6 oz bacon, chopped
- 1 cup milk
- 1 cup yellow onion, diced
- 1 cup potato, chopped
- 10 oz water
- 1 teaspoon ground thyme
- 1 tablespoon salt
- ½ teaspoon ground black pepper

Directions:

Put the chopped bacon in a skillet and roast it for 2 minutes over high heat. When the bacon is crunchy, transfer it to the slow cooker. Chop the haddock roughly and put it in the slow cooker too. Add the diced onion, chopped potato, water, ground thyme, salt, and ground black pepper. Add water and milk and close the lid. Cook the chowder for 3 hours on HIGH. Stir the chowder with a wooden spoon during the cooking process. Serve!

Nutrition: calories 229, fat 11.9, fiber 2, carbs 9.63, protein 22

Asparagus Tilapia

Prep time: 10 hours | Cooking time: 6 hours | Servings: 6

Ingredients:

- 2 tablespoons cream
- 1 teaspoon salt
- 1-pound asparagus
- 3-pounds tilapia
- 1 teaspoon onion powder
- 1 lemon
- 1 teaspoon lemon juice

Directions:

Put the foil in the slow cooker bowl. Sprinkle the tilapia with the salt and lemon juice and transfer it to the slow cooker. Slice the lemon and cover the tilapia with the slices. Chop the asparagus and toss it with the cream and onion powder. Cover the fish with the chopped asparagus and wrap the foil around the fish. Close the lid and cook the dish for 6 hours on LOW. When the fish is cooked, transfer it to a serving plate. Open the foil to get the fish and serve.

Nutrition: calories 246, fat 4.9, fiber 2, carbs 4.04, protein 47

Delightful Shrimp Scampi

Prep time: 15 minutes | Cooking time: 2 hours | Servings: 6

Ingredients:

- 18 oz shrimps
- ½ cup lemon juice
- 2 tablespoons butter
- 3 tablespoons fresh parsley, chopped
- 2 cups water
- 1 tablespoon fresh dill, chopped
- 1 teaspoon salt
- ½ teaspoon ground black pepper
- 1 teaspoon minced garlic

Directions:

Peel the shrimp and put them in the slow cooker bowl. Sprinkle the shrimps with the chopped fresh dill and fresh parsley. Then add the salt, ground black pepper, and minced garlic. Add lemon juice and stir mixture gently. Pour in the water, add the butter and close the slow cooker lid. Cook the shrimp scampi on LOW for 2 hours. Serve the shrimps scampi with spaghetti.

Nutrition: calories 130, fat 5.2, fiber 0, carbs 2.64, protein 18

Jamaican Fish Stew

Prep time: 15 minutes | Cooking time: 3 hours 45 minutes | Servings: 4

Ingredients:

- ¼ cup butter
- 6 oz yellow onion
- 1 teaspoon minced garlic
- 1 red sweet pepper
- 1 cup tomatoes, chopped
- 5 oz coconut milk
- 1-pound cod fillet
- 1 teaspoon salt
- ½ teaspoon ground black pepper
- 1 tablespoon garlic sauce

Directions:

Toss the butter into the slow cooker bowl. Add the minced garlic, chopped tomatoes, salt, ground black pepper, and garlic sauce. Slice the sweet red pepper and add it to the slow cooker. Add the coconut milk. Dice the yellow onion and add it in the slow cooker too. Close the lid and cook for 3 hours on HIGH or until the vegetables are soft. Chop the cod fillet roughly. Add the chopped cod after 3 hours of cooking and cook the stew for 45 minutes more on HIGH. Then stir the dish gently to not damage the fish and serve.

Nutrition: calories 336, fat 25.4, fiber 2, carbs 8.9, protein 19

Ginger Trout

Prep time: 20 minutes | Cooking time: 2 hours | Servings: 3

Ingredients:

- 1 tablespoon ground ginger
- 1 teaspoon fresh ginger, grated
- 1 teaspoon onion powder
- 1 teaspoon cilantro
- 1 tablespoon cream
- 1-pound trout fillet
- 2 tablespoons fish sauce
- 1 teaspoon oregano
- 2 tablespoons butter
- 1 tablespoon water

Directions:

Rub the trout fillet with the ground ginger, oregano, cilantro, and onion powder. Leave the fish for 10 minutes to let it soak up the spices. Meanwhile, combine the grated fresh ginger, cream, fish sauce, butter, and water in a separate bowl. Cover the slow cooker bowl with the parchment. Then transfer the marinated trout on top of the parchment in the bowl. Brush it with the mixed sauce generously and pour all the remaining sauce into the slow cooker bowl. Close the slow cooker lid and cook the fish for 2 hours on HIGH. Then transfer the fish to the plates gently to not smash it.

Nutrition: calories 316, fat 18.7, fiber 1, carbs 3, protein 33

Clams in Almond Milk Sauce
Prep time: 10 minutes | Cooking time: 3 hours | Servings: 5

Ingredients:
- 1 cup almond milk
- ¼ cup tomato juice
- 1 teaspoon lemon zest
- ¼ teaspoon ground nutmeg
- ¼ teaspoon turmeric
- ½ cup clam juice
- 1-pound clams
- 1 teaspoon kosher salt
- 1 teaspoon ground black pepper
- 1 teaspoon cornstarch
- 2 oz minced garlic

Directions:
Combine the almond milk with the cornstarch and stir it until smooth. Then pour the mixture into the slow cooker. Add the tomato juice, lemon zest, ground nutmeg, turmeric, calm juice, kosher salt, ground black pepper, and minced garlic. Mix and close the lid. Cook the sauce on HIGH for 1 hour. Stir it every 20 minutes. When the sauce gets little bit thick, it is cooked. Add the clams and stir. Close the lid and cook it on LOW for 2 more hours. Then transfer the prepared clams in the bowls and sprinkle them with the sauce generously.

Nutrition: calories 105, fat 1, fiber 1, carbs 23, protein 2

Mango Milkfish
Prep time: 21 minutes | Cooking time: 1 hour 25 minutes | Servings: 4

Ingredients:
- 1 mango, pitted
- 3 tablespoon tomato puree
- 1 teaspoon cilantro
- 1 tablespoon kosher salt
- 1 bay leaf
- 1 tablespoon brown sugar
- ½ teaspoon white pepper
- 1-pound milkfish or flounder
- 1 cup fish stock
- ¼ teaspoon rosemary
- 1 teaspoon turmeric

Directions:
Peel the mango and chop it. Put the chopped mango in the blender and blend until you get a smooth puree. Add the tomato puree and brown sugar and blend for 10 seconds. Pour the mango mixture into the slow cooker bowl. Add cilantro, kosher salt, bay leaf, white pepper, rosemary, turmeric, and fish stock. Mix and close the slow cooker lid. Cook the mango sauce for 1 hour on LOW. Then cut the milkfish into the serving sizes, put the milkfish in the slow cooker and coat it with the mango sauce. Close the lid and cook it for 25 minutes on HIGH. Serve the prepared milkfish immediately.

Nutrition: calories 254, fat 8.5, fiber 2, carbs 19.26, protein 26

Garlic Mussels
Prep time: 10 minutes | Cooking time: 1 hour 50 minutes | Servings: 4

Ingredients:
- 16 oz mussels
- ½ cup garlic, peeled
- ½ cup coconut milk
- 1 tablespoon kosher salt
- 1 teaspoon chili flakes
- 1 teaspoon garlic powder
- ½ teaspoon onion powder
- ½ lemon
- 1 tablespoon orange zest
- ½ teaspoon rosemary

Directions:
Mince the peeled garlic and combine it with the coconut milk. Add the kosher salt, chili flakes, garlic powder, onion powder, orange zest, and rosemary. Whisk and pour in the slow cooker. Squeeze the lemon juice into the slow cooker and close the lid. Cook the liquid for 1 hour on HIGH. After this, add the mussels and close the lid. Cook the mussels for 50 minute more on HIGH or until they are opened. Transfer the prepared mussels into serving bowl and sprinkle with the remaining sauce.

Nutrition: calories 201, fat 9.9, fiber 1, carbs 13, protein 16

Balsamic Catfish

Prep time: 25 minutes | Cooking time: 45 minutes | Servings: 4

Ingredients:

- 2 tablespoons balsamic vinegar
- 1 tablespoon white sugar
- ¼ teaspoon salt
- ½ teaspoon ground cinnamon
- 1 teaspoon cilantro
- 1 teaspoon fish sauce
- 1 teaspoon olive oil
- 10 oz catfish

Directions:

Pour olive oil in a skillet and preheat it until the oil starts to sizzle. Then put the catfish in the oil and fry for 1 minute on high heat on each side. Put the fried catfish in the slow cooker and sprinkle with the remaining olive oil from the skillet. Combine the balsamic vinegar, white sugar, salt, ground cinnamon, cilantro, and fish sauce. Mix the liquid well. Pour the balsamic vinegar mixture in the slow cooker and close the lid. Cook the catfish on HIGH for 45 minutes. Serve the catfish hot.

Nutrition: calories 87, fat 3.3, fiber 0, carbs 2, protein 12

Chili Salmon Cubes

Prep time: 10 minutes | Cooking time: 3 hours 20 minutes | Servings: 6

Ingredients:

- 1 teaspoon chili paste
- 1 red chili
- 4 tablespoons tomato paste
- 1 teaspoon cilantro
- 1 tablespoon salt
- 17 oz salmon fillet
- 1 tablespoon lemon juice
- 1 tablespoon butter
- 1 teaspoon oregano
- ½ teaspoon ground thyme
- 1/ teaspoon ground coriander
- 1 cup fish stock
- 1 teaspoon cayenne pepper
- 2 tablespoons sour cream

Directions:

Chop the chili pepper and combine it with the chili paste. Add the tomato paste, cilantro, salt, lemon juice, oregano, ground thyme, ground coriander, and cayenne pepper. Whisk the spice mixture carefully. After this, brush the salmon fillet with the spice mixture. Cut the salmon fillet into the cubes and put them in the slow cooker. Add the remaining spice mixture. Then add butter, fish stock, and close the lid. Cook the fish on the LOW for 3 hours. Strain the fish stock and cook the salmon cubes on HIGH for 20 minutes more. Sprinkle the cooked fish cubes with the sour cream.

Nutrition: calories 167, fat 8.6, fiber 1, carbs 4, protein 18

Tomato Shrimp

Prep time: 20 minutes | Cooking time: 1 hour | Servings: 3

Ingredients:

- 1 can tomatoes, crushed
- 9 oz shrimp
- 1 onion
- 1 teaspoon minced garlic
- 1 teaspoon ground coriander
- ½ cup tomato juice
- ½ cup water
- 1 tablespoon brown sugar
- 1 teaspoon ground black pepper
- ½ teaspoon salt
- ¼ teaspoon powdered chili pepper
- 2 tablespoons butter
- ½ teaspoon sage

Directions:

Peel the shrimps and put them in the slow cooker. Sprinkle the shrimp with the minced garlic, ground coriander, brown sugar, ground black pepper, salt, powdered chili pepper, and sage. Then add butter and close the lid. Cook the shrimp on LOW for 20 minutes. Meanwhile, peel the onion and dice it. After 20 minutes, add the diced onion, tomato juice, and water. Close the lid and cook the shrimps for 40 minutes on HIGH. Then stir the shrimp carefully and serve them.

Nutrition: calories 225, fat 9.2, fiber 3, carbs 17.36, protein 19

Tuna Salpicao

Prep time: 10 minutes | Cooking time: 1 hour | Servings: 4

Ingredients:

- 1 teaspoon black peas
- 1 chili pepper
- 2 oz olive oil
- 1-pound tuna fillet

- 1 teaspoon salt
- 2 oz garlic cloves
- ½ teaspoon sage

Directions:

Pour the olive oil and black peas in the slow cooker bowl and add salt. Chop the chili pepper and peel the garlic cloves. Slice the garlic. Add the chopped chili pepper and sliced garlic cloves. Add sage and stir the oil mixture. Close the slow cooker lid and cook it on LOW for 40 minutes. Chop the tuna into cubes and add into the slow cooker. Cook the meat for 20 minutes on HIGH. Then remove the tuna from the slow cooker and transfer it to the plates. Sprinkle it with the oil fragrant mixture. Serve it!

Nutrition: calories 249, fat 15.4, fiber 1, carbs 5.88, protein 23

Miso Trout

Prep time: 15 minutes | Cooking time: 2 hours 20 minutes | Servings: 5

Ingredients:

- 2-pounds trout
- 2 tablespoons miso paste
- 1 teaspoon fresh ginger, grated
- ¼ teaspoon nutmeg

- 1 tablespoon sesame seeds
- 4 cups fish stock
- 1 teaspoon salt
- 3 tablespoons chives

Directions:

Pour the fish stock into the slow cooker. Add the miso paste and stir it with a wooden spoon until the miso paste is dissolved. After this, add the nutmeg, grated fresh ginger, sesame seeds, salt, and close the lid. Cook the liquid on LOW for 2 hours. Then, add the tuna and sprinkle it with the chives. Close the slow cooker lid and cook the dish for 20 minutes more. Serve the prepared miso trout with the cooking liquid.

Nutrition: calories 324, fat 15, fiber 1, carbs 2, protein 43

Asian Style Catfish

Prep time: 25 minutes | Cooking time: 1 hour 10 minutes | Servings: 5

Ingredients:

- 1 tablespoon fish sauce
- 1 teaspoon coconut flakes
- 1 teaspoon salt
- 1 tablespoon palm sugar
- 1 tablespoon rice vinegar
- 12 oz catfish, chopped

- ½ teaspoon ground black pepper
- 1 tablespoon butter
- 1 teaspoon garlic powder
- ¼ cup fish stock
- ¼ teaspoon ground celery

Directions:

Put the butter in a skillet and melt. Put the chopped catfish in the melted butter and roast on the medium heat for 5 minutes. Meanwhile, pour the fish sauce, coconut flakes, salt, palm sugar, rice vinegar, ground black pepper, garlic powder, and fish stock in the slow cooker bowl. Add the ground celery and close the lid. Cook the liquid on HIGH for 1 hour. After this, add the catfish and cook it on LOW for 10 minutes more. Serve the prepared dish immediately.

Nutrition: calories 100, fat 4.4, fiber 0, carbs 3, protein 12

Soy Sauce Calamari

Prep time: 10 minutes | Cooking time: 1.5 hours | Servings: 2

Ingredients:

- 7 oz calamari
- ½ cup soy sauce
- 1 teaspoon nutmeg
- 1 teaspoon cilantro
- 1 teaspoon ground black pepper
- ½ teaspoon onion powder
- 2 garlic cloves
- 1 carrot, grated
- 1 teaspoon salt
- 1 tablespoon Dijon mustard
- 1 teaspoon olive oil
- ¼ cup chicken stock

Directions:

Slice the calamari into rings. Combine the nutmeg, cilantro, ground black pepper, onion powder, salt, Dijon mustard, and olive oil in the bowl. Whisk it carefully until you get a smooth sauce. Combine the mustard sauce with the calamari rings and mix them up well with your hands. Pour the chicken stock into the slow cooker and add the calamari rings. Add the grated carrot. Close the lid and cook the dish on HIGH for 1 hour. Then open the slow cooker lid and pour the soy sauce in. Cook the calamari on LOW for 30 minutes more. When the calamari dish is cooked, stir carefully and serve.

Nutrition: calories 436, fat 17.7, fiber 3, carbs 31, protein 37

Ginger Squid

Prep time: 15 minutes | Cooking time: 1 hour | Servings: 4

Ingredients:

- 1-pound squid, peeled
- 3 oz fresh ginger
- 2 tablespoons honey
- 1 tablespoon fish stock
- 1 teaspoon salt
- 1 tablespoon ground coriander
- ½ teaspoon ground thyme
- 1 teaspoon cilantro
- 3 tablespoons mayo
- 1 teaspoon curry paste
- 1 teaspoon ground ginger

Directions:

Make the ginger sauce by grating the fresh ginger and combining it with the honey, fish stock, salt, ground coriander, ground thyme, cilantro, mayo, curry paste, and ground ginger. Whisk the mixture with a fork. Then rub the peeled squid with the ginger sauce. Put the squid in the slow cooker and sprinkle it with the remaining ginger sauce. You can add a little bit water if desired. Close the lid and cook the squid on LOW for 1 hour. Transfer the prepared squid to plates. Serve it with your favorite sauce.

Nutrition: calories 161, fat 1.9, fiber 1, carbs 17, protein 19

Parsley Seabass

Prep time: 15 minutes | Cooking time: 4 hours | Servings: 8

Ingredients:

- 1 cup parsley, chopped
- 1 tablespoon dried parsley
- 1 yellow sweet pepper
- 1 cup carrot, grated
- 3-pound seabass, peeled
- 1 tablespoon minced garlic
- ¼ cup lemon juice
- 1 teaspoon ground coriander
- 1 tablespoon fresh thyme leaves
- 1 onion, peeled and diced
- 2 tomatoes, sliced
- 1 cup cream
- ½ cup fish stock
- 1 tablespoon bread crumbs

Directions:

Sprinkle the seabass with the lemon juice and put it in the slow cooker. Sprinkle the fish with the dried parsley, grated carrot, minced garlic, ground coriander, fresh thyme leaves, cream, and fish stock. Close the lid and cook the seabass for 1 hour on HIGH. When the time is done, open the slow cooker lid and cover the seabass with the sliced tomatoes. Then add the diced onion and cover it all with the chopped parsley. Close the lid and cook the fish on LOW for 3 hours more. When the seabass is done, discard all the greena and leave only tomatoes. The fish will have tender parsley smell. Sprinkle the fish with the bread crumbs.

Nutrition: calories 270, fat 9.8, fiber 2, carbs 11, protein 34

Salmon in Coconut Milk

Prep time: 16 minutes | Cooking time: 4 hours | Servings: 3

Ingredients:

- 1 oz butter, unsalted
- 1 tablespoon kosher salt
- 2 cups coconut milk
- 1 tablespoon coconut flakes
- 1 teaspoon ground black pepper
- 1 teaspoon lime zest
- 2 teaspoons paprika
- 1 garlic clove, peeled
- 1 teaspoon oregano
- 12 oz salmon fillet

Directions:

Melt the butter in the slow cooker on HIGH for 10 minutes. Then add the kosher salt, coconut milk, ground black pepper, lime zest, paprika, peeled garlic clove, and oregano. Then put the salmon fillet in the coconut milk liquid and close the lid. Cook the fish on LOW for 4 hours. When the salmon is cooked, remove it from the slow cooker and transfer to the plates. Sprinkle the salmon with the coconut flakes. Shred the salmon to combine it with the coconut flakes and serve it!

Nutrition: calories 631, fat 54.7, fiber 5, carbs 13, protein 28

Seabass Cutlets

Prep time: 25 minutes | Cooking time: 2 hours | Servings: 8

Ingredients:

- 15 oz minced seabass
- 1 teaspoon salt
- 1 egg, beaten
- 1 tablespoon ground coriander
- 2 teaspoons soy sauce
- 1 tablespoon minced garlic
- ½ cup flour
- 3 tablespoons fresh dill, chopped
- 1 tablespoon olive oil

Directions:

Combine the minced seabass with the beaten egg and salt. Add the ground coriander, soy sauce, minced garlic, and fresh dill. Mix until smooth. Form cutlets from the seabass mixture and dip them in the flour. Pour the olive oil in a skillet and heat it well. Then put the prepared cutlets and cook them on the high heat for 1 minute on each side. Transfer the roasted cutlets in the slow cooker and add ½ cup of water. Close the lid and cook them on HIGH for 2 hours more. Serve the cutlets immediately.

Nutrition: calories 212, fat 14.6, fiber 1, carbs 9.12, protein 11

Fish Sticks

Prep time: 20 minutes | Cooking time: 2.5 hours | Servings: 5

Ingredients:

- 1-pound cod fillet
- 1 teaspoon salt
- 1 teaspoon ground black pepper
- 1 cup panko bread crumbs
- 1 teaspoon thyme
- ½ teaspoon olive oil
- 4 tablespoons milk
- 2 large eggs, beaten

Directions:

Cut the cod fillet into big strips. Then sprinkle the cod strips with the salt, ground black pepper and thyme and stir them carefully. Whisk the eggs with the milk. Then put the bread crumbs in a separate bowl. Spray the slow cooker with the olive oil inside. Then dip the fish strips in the whisked egg mixture. After this, coat them in the bread crumbs. Put the prepared fish sticks in the slow cooker. Close the lid and cook them on LOW for 2.5 hours. Serve the fish sticks warm.

Nutrition: calories 118, fat 3.3, fiber 0, carbs 5, protein 16

Turmeric Shrimp Soup

Prep time: 20 minutes | Cooking time: 3 hours 20 minutes | Servings: 8

Ingredients:

- 8 oz shrimp
- 6 oz celery stalk
- 3 medium potatoes
- ¼ cup fresh dill, chopped
- ¼ teaspoon black peas
- ½ cup corn kernels
- 1 teaspoon salt
- ½ teaspoon ground thyme
- 1 onion
- 6 cups fish stock
- 1 teaspoon olive oil
- 1 tablespoon paprika
- 1 tablespoon turmeric

Directions:

Peel the onion and dice it. Put the diced onion in a saute pan and add olive oil. Roast the diced onion until golden brown. Then pour the fish stock into the slow cooker. Peel the shrimp and chop the celery stalk. Put the turmeric, paprika, diced onion, ground thyme, salt, corn kernels, black peas, chopped dill, and celery stalk in the slow cooker. Peel the potatoes and cut them into cubes. Add the potato cubes in the slow cooker and close the lid. Cook the soup on HIGH for 3 hours. After this, add the peeled shrimp. Cook the soup for 20 minutes on HIGH. Ladle the shrimp soup in the bowls and serve.

Nutrition: calories 190, fat 2.8, fiber 4, carbs 29, protein 13

Cayenne Pepper Snapper

Prep time: 20 minutes | Cooking time: 6 hours | Servings: 7

Ingredients:

- 1 tablespoon cayenne pepper
- 1 jalapeno pepper
- 1 sweet pepper
- 1 yellow onion
- 1 tablespoon coriander leaves
- 3-pounds snapper
- 1 teaspoon cilantro
- ½ teaspoon paprika
- 1 teaspoon ground coriander
- ¼ cup lemongrass
- 1 tablespoon kosher salt
- 1 tablespoon minced garlic
- 1 cup water
- 2 oz lemon wedges
- ½ teaspoon sesame oil

Directions:

Peel and wash the snapper carefully. Combine the coriander leaves, cilantro, paprika, ground coriander, lemongrass, and kosher salt together. Stuff the snapper with this mix. After this, rub the fish with the minced garlic. Put the lemon wedges in the snapper as well. Then pour olive oil in the slow cooker bowl. Remove the seeds from the sweet pepper. Chop the jalapeno and yellow onion. Cut the sweet pepper into strips. Then put the vegetables over the snapper. Add the water and close the lid. Cook the snapper on LOW for 6 hours. When the time is over, transfer the vegetables to serving plates. Discard all the cooked greens and put the fish on the vegetables. Serve the fish immediately.

Nutrition: calories 218, fat 3.2, fiber 1, carbs 5, protein 41

Salmon Pie

Prep time: 25 minutes | Cooking time: 9 hours | Servings: 8

Ingredients:

- 10 oz yeast dough
- 1 teaspoon olive oil
- 1-pound salmon
- 1 tablespoon lemon juice
- ¼ cup cream cheese
- 6 oz Cheddar cheese shredded
- 1 tablespoon oregano
- 1 teaspoon salt
- 2 large eggs
- 1 cup onion, diced

Directions:

Brush the parchment with the olive oil and put it in the slow cooker. Roll the dough and put it in the slow cooker too. Beat the eggs in the bowl and whisk. Combine the whisked eggs with the lemon juice, cream cheese, oregano, salt, and diced onion. Chop the salmon and add it to the whisked egg mixture. Then pour the fish mixture into the rolled dough. Cover the pie with the shredded cheese and close the lid. Cook the salmon pie for 9 hours on LOW. When the pie is cooked, it will have a golden brown surface. From the slow cooker and cut into pieces. Serve warm.

Nutrition: calories 237, fat 10.1, fiber 3, carbs 11, protein 24

Slow Cooker Rosemary Trout

Prep time: 10 minutes | Cooking time: 4 hours | Servings: 4

Ingredients:

- 4 tablespoons fresh rosemary
- 1 lime
- 1 cup fish stock
- 1-pound trout filler
- 1 teaspoon kosher salt
- 1 teaspoon ground black pepper
- 1 teaspoon minced garlic
- 2 tablespoons butter

Directions:

Put the butter in the slow cooker. Then put the trout fillet in as well. Sprinkle the fillet with the kosher salt, minced garlic, and ground black pepper. Chop the lime and sprinkle over the fish. Then chop the rosemary and combine it with the fish stock. Pour the rosemary liquid in the slow cooker and close the lid. Cook the fish on LOW for 4 hours. When the fish is soft, it is cooked. Remove it from the rosemary liquid and transfer the fish to the serving plates. Serve it.

Nutrition: calories 239, fat 13.9, fiber 1, carbs 3, protein 25

Garlic Sole

Prep time: 18 minutes | Cooking time: 4 hours | Servings: 8

Ingredients:

- 3-pounds sole
- 1 cup garlic
- 1 cup cream cheese
- ¼ cup butter
- 1 tablespoon kosher salt
- 1 teaspoon paprika
- 1 teaspoon ground black pepper
- 1 tablespoon turmeric
- 1 teaspoon sage

Directions:

Combine the kosher salt, paprika, ground black pepper, turmeric, and sage together in the bowl. Stir the mixture. Then add the sole and rub the fish with the spices on both sides. Peel the garlic and smash it. Combine the smashed garlic with the cream cheese and whisk carefully. Toss the butter in the slow cooker and melt on HIGH for 10 minutes. Then add the cream cheese mixture and cook on HIGH for 20 minutes more. After this, add the spiced sole and close the lid. Cook the dish on LOW for 3.5 hours. Then check if the sole is soft and flakey. Serve it!

Nutrition: calories 291, fat 17.8, fiber 1, carbs 8, protein 25

Tuna Dip

Prep time: 15 minutes | *Cooking time: 3.5 hours* | *Servings: 9*

Ingredients:

- 1-pound tuna, canned
- 1 onion, diced
- 4 tablespoons butter
- 1 cup cream cheese
- 5 oz Cheddar cheese
- 1 teaspoon turmeric
- 1 teaspoon ground black pepper
- ½ teaspoon nutmeg

Directions:

Melt butter in the slow cooker on HIGH for 15 minutes. Add the diced onion and cook it on HIGH for 15 minutes more. Then grate the Cheddar cheese. Add the grated cheese and cream cheese in the slow cooker. Add canned tuna, turmeric, ground black pepper, and nutmeg. Mix and close the lid. Cook the dip on LOW for 3 hours. After this, close the slow cooker lid and stir the mixture well. Transfer the prepared dip in the serving bowl and chill it until room temperature. Stir the mixture frequently during the chilling to keep it soft. Serve with your favorite chips or corn tortillas.

Nutrition: calories 204, fat 14.7, fiber 0, carbs 4.52, protein 14

Cream Tuna Casserole

Prep time: 20 minutes | *Cooking time: 8 hours* | *Servings: 12*

Ingredients:

- 8 oz wild mushrooms, chopped
- 8 oz noodles, cooked
- 1-pound tuna, canned
- 3 potatoes, peeled and sliced
- 1 cup cream
- 7 oz Parmesan shredded
- 1 carrot, peeled, grated
- ½ cup green peas, frozen
- 1 tablespoon salt
- 1 teaspoon ground ginger
- ½ teaspoon ground coriander
- ½ teaspoon cilantro
- 1 tablespoon oregano
- 1 teaspoon olive oil
- 1 cup fresh dill, chopped
- 1 cup water

Directions:

Pour the olive oil in a skillet and add the mushrooms. Roast the mushrooms on medium heat for 6 minutes. Stir them frequently. Put the mushrooms in the slow cooker. Make a layer of the sliced potatoes over the roasted mushrooms. Sprinkle the potato layer with the grated carrot. Mash the canned tuna and combine it with the cheese. Make a layer of the noodles in the slow cooker. Then sprinkle the casserole with the green peas. Add the salt, ground coriander, ground ginger, oregano, and cilantro. Put the tuna-cheese mixture in the slow cooker and flatten it well. Then sprinkle the casserole with the chopped dill. Add the cream and water and close the lid. Cook the casserole on LOW for 8 hours. After this, open the slow cooker lid and let the casserole chill until room temperature.

Nutrition: calories 296, fat 5.8, fiber 5, carbs 44.39, protein 19

Stuffed Trout
Prep time: 20 minutes | Cooking time: 4 hours | Servings: 5

Ingredients:
- 16 oz whole trout, peeled
- ½ cup sweet corn
- ¼ cup rice, cooked
- 1 sweet pepper, chopped
- 1 tablespoon salt
- 1 teaspoon thyme
- 1 teaspoon ground black pepper
- ½ teaspoon paprika
- 1 tablespoon olive oil
- 1 tablespoon sour cream
- ¼ cup cream cheese
- 3 lemon wedges
- 2 tablespoons chives

Directions:
Combine the sweet corn and cooked rice together. Add the chopped sweet pepper. Then sprinkle with the chives and salt. Stir the mixture well. Combine the thyme, ground black pepper, paprika, sour cream, olive oil, and cream cheese together. Put the trout on the foil and rub it with the cream cheese mixture carefully. Then fill the fish with the rice mixture. Put the lemon wedges over the trout and wrap it in the foil. Close the slow cooker lid and cook the fish for 4 hours on HIGH. When the fish is cooked, remove it from the slow cooker and transfer directly to serving plates.

Nutrition: calories 255, fat 13.9, fiber 2, carbs 13.57, protein 22

Mushroom and Seabass Ragout
Prep time: 20 minutes | Cooking time: 8 hours | Servings: 8

Ingredients:
- 6 oz shiitake mushrooms
- 8 oz wild mushrooms
- 9 oz cremini mushrooms
- 2 white onions
- 1 tablespoon balsamic vinegar
- 1-pound seabass, boneless
- 1 tablespoon ground celery
- 1 teaspoon salt
- 1 teaspoon ground nutmeg
- 2 tablespoons sliced garlic
- 3 carrots, chopped
- 1 tablespoon butter
- ½ teaspoon sage
- 2 cups water
- 3 tablespoons fresh dill
- 1 tablespoons fresh celery

Directions:
Chop the shiitake mushrooms, wild mushroom, and cremini mushrooms. Sprinkle the mushrooms with the balsamic vinegar, ground celery, and salt. Put the mushrooms in the slow cooker and add the butter. Cook the mushrooms on LOW for 1 hour. After this, chop the seabass and add the chopped seabass in the slow cooker. Add the balsamic vinegar, ground nutmeg, sliced garlic, chopped carrot, sage, fresh dill, and fresh celery. Stir with a spatula and pour in the water. Close the slow cooker lid and cook the ragout for 7 hours on LOW. When it is done, stir it gently and serve.

Nutrition: calories 313, fat 5, fiber 9, carbs 55.86, protein 20

Salmon Miso Soup

Prep time: 15 minutes | Cooking time: 3 hours | Servings: 9

Ingredients:

- 5 cups fish stock
- 3 cups water
- 2 tablespoons miso paste
- 10 oz salmon fillet
- 4 oz carrot, peeled, choped
- 1 white onion, peeled, chopped
- 1 tablespoon fresh dill, chopped
- 6 oz tofu, chopped
- 1 teaspoon salt
- ½ teaspoon brown sugar
- ½ teaspoon ground coriander

Directions:

Sprinkle the salmon fillet with the salt and ground coriander. Pour the fish stock into the slow cooker and add the prepared salmon fillet. Add the vegetables in the slow cooker too and close the lid. Cook the salmon on LOW for 2 hours. Meanwhile, combine the water with the miso paste and whisk until miso paste is dissolved. When the salmon is cooked, add the miso paste water and tofu cheese in the slow cooker. Sprinkle with the brown sugar and close the lid. Cook the soup on HIGH for 1 hour. After the time is done, check if the salmon and vegetables are cooked. Ladle the miso soup into the serving bowls and serve it.

Nutrition: calories 148, fat 7.9, fiber 2, carbs 5.82, protein 15

Sweet Shrimps with Fresh Dill

Prep time: 10 minutes | Cooking time: 40 minutes | Servings: 4

Ingredients:

- 4 tablespoons fresh dill
- ¼ cup pineapple juice
- 2 tablespoons sugar
- 3 tablespoons mango puree
- 1 tablespoon butter
- 1-pound shrimp
- 1 teaspoon ground ginger
- ½ teaspoon lemon juice
- 1 tablespoon tomato juice
- 1 cup water
- ½ teaspoon sage

Directions:

Peel the shrimp and put them in the slow cooker. Add water and sage and close the lid. Cook the shrimp on HIGH for 20 minutes. Meanwhile, melt the butter and combine with the mango puree, sugar, pineapple juice, ground ginger, lemon juice, and tomato juice. Chop the fresh dill and add it to the sweet liquid. When the time is done on the shrimp, strain the shrimp and return them back to the slow cooker. Add the sweet dill liquid and stir the shrimp. Close the slow cooker lid and cook the seafood for 20 minutes more or until the shrimps are totally pink and cooked. Serve the shrimps with the sweet remaining hot sauce.

Nutrition: calories 192, fat 5.4, fiber 2, carbs 12.18, protein 24

Orange Fish
Prep time: 20 minutes | Cooking time: 3 hours | Servings: 7

Ingredients:
- 3 oranges, peeled, chopped
- 2-pound cod, peeled
- 1 tablespoon honey
- 1 garlic clove, peeled, sliced
- 1 teaspoon ground white pepper
- ½ teaspoon paprika
- 1 teaspoon chili flakes
- ½ teaspoon salt
- 2 tablespoons lemon juice
- 1 teaspoon olive oil
- ½ teaspoon honey

Directions:
Sprinkle the cod with the ground white pepper, paprika, chili flakes, and salt. After this, sprinkle the fish with the lemon juice, olive oil, and 1 tablespoon honey. Combine the chopped oranges and sliced garlic together. Add the ½ teaspoon of honey. Stir carefully. Stuff the fish with the orange mix and wrap in the foil. Then place the wrapped fish in the slow cooker and close the lid. Cook the cod on HIGH for 3 hours. Then discard the foil and serve the cod.

Nutrition: calories 141, fat 1.4, fiber 2, carbs 11.74, protein 21

Salmon Chili
Prep time: 21 minutes | Cooking time: 3.5 hours | Servings: 8

Ingredients:
- 1-pound salmon
- 7 oz shrimps
- 1 tablespoon salt
- 1 cup tomatoes, canned
- 1 teaspoon ground white pepper
- 1 tablespoon tomato sauce
- 2 onions
- 1 cup carrot, chopped
- 1 can red beans
- ½ cup tomato juice
- 1 cup fish stock
- 1 teaspoon cayenne pepper
- 1 cup bell pepper, chopped
- 1 tablespoon olive oil
- 1 teaspoon coriander
- 1 cup water
- 6 oz Parmesan, shredded
- 1 garlic clove, sliced

Directions:
Put the canned tomatoes in the slow cooker. Add the ground white pepper, tomato sauce, chopped carrot, and red beans. Add tomato juice, fish stock, and cayenne pepper, chopped bell pepper, coriander, water, and sliced garlic clove. Dice the onions and add them in the slow cooker bowl too. Close the slow cooker lid and cook the ingredients for 3 hours on HIGH. Meanwhile, pour the olive oil in the slow cooker. Peel the shrimps and chop the salmon. Add the seafood in the olive oil and roast the mixture on the medium heat for 3 minutes. Stir it gently with a spatula. Add the seafood mixture to the slow cooker and stir. Close the lid and cook the chili on HIGH for 30 minutes more. Let the cooked chili cool slightly and serve.

Nutrition: calories 281, fat 7.9, fiber 4, carbs 22.52, protein 30

Slow Cooker Fish Cakes
Prep time: 15 minutes | Cooking time: 5 hours | Servings: 12

Ingredients:
- 1-pound trout
- 6 oz mashed potato
- 1 carrot, grated
- ½ cup fresh parsley
- 1 teaspoon salt
- ½ cup panko bread crumbs
- 1 egg, beaten
- 1 teaspoon minced garlic
- 1 onion, grated
- 1 teaspoon olive oil
- 1 teaspoon ground black pepper
- ¼ teaspoon cilantro

Directions:

Mince the trout and combine it with the mashed potatos. Sprinkle the mixture with the grated carrot, salt, minced garlic, grated onion, ground black pepper, and cilantro. Mix well and add the egg. Chop the parsley and add it to the fish mixture. Add the panko bread crumbs and stir it well. Pour the olive oil in the slow cooker. Make 12 small balls from the fish mixture and flatten them to make small cakes. Put the fish cakes in the slow cooker and close the lid. Cook the dish on LOW for 5 hours. Flip the fish cakes to the other side after 2.5 hours of cooking. Serve the fish cakes hot.

Nutrition: calories 93, fat 3.8, fiber 1, carbs 5.22, protein 9

Trout Croquettes
Prep time: 18 minutes | Cooking time: 3 hours | Servings: 8

Ingredients:
- 14 oz trout fillet
- 3 tablespoons Worcestershire sauce
- 7 tablespoons flour
- 2 eggs
- 1 tablespoon Italian Seasoning
- 1 teaspoon salt
- 1 teaspoon ground black pepper
- 6 oz rice, cooked
- 3 tablespoons milk
- 1 teaspoon paprika
- 2 tablespoons sesame oil

Directions:

Grind the trout fillet and put it in a big bowl. Add Worcestershire sauce, flour, Italian seasoning, salt, ground black pepper, cooked rice, milk, and paprika. Then beat the eggs into the bowl. Transfer the mixture to a blender and blend until smooth. Make the croquettes from the fish mixture. Spray the slow cooker bowl with the sesame oil inside and put the fish croquettes there. Close the lid and cook the fish croquettes for 3 hours on HIGH. When the croquettes are done, transfer them to the serving plate and chill.

Nutrition: calories 186, fat 9.6, fiber 1, carbs 10.24, protein 14

Thai Fish Cakes

Prep time: 10 minutes | Cooking time: 6 hours | Servings: 10

Ingredients:

- 6 oz squid
- 10 oz salmon fillet
- 2 tablespoons chili paste
- 1 teaspoon cayenne pepper
- 2 oz lemon leaves
- 3 tablespoons green peas, mashed
- 2 teaspoons fish sauce
- 2 egg white
- 1 egg yolk
- 1 teaspoon oyster sauce
- 1 teaspoon salt
- ½ teaspoon ground coriander
- 1 teaspoon sugar
- 2 tablespoons butter
- ¼ cup cream
- 3 tablespoons almond flour

Directions:

Grind the squid and salmon fillet and place them in a bowl. Sprinkle the seafood with the chili paste and cayenne pepper. Chop the lemon leaves and add them to the seafood mixture. After this, add the mashed green peas and fish sauce. Combine the egg whites and egg yolk in another bowl and whisk it. Put the whisked egg mixture into the seafood mixture. Add the oyster sauce, salt, ground coriander, sugar, and almond flour. Take a spoon and mix the seafood mixture until it is smooth. Put the butter and cream in the slow cooker. Close the lid and cook it on LOW for 1 hour. Meanwhile, make the mini cakes from the fish mixture. Put the fish cakes in the slow cooker and close the lid. Cook the dish for 5 hours on LOW. When Thai fish cakes are cooked, put them on serving plates and sprinkle with the cream sauce. Serve it hot.

Nutrition: calories 112, fat 6.7, fiber 1, carbs 2.95, protein 10

Harissa Cod

Prep time: 25 minutes | Cooking time: 7 hours | Servings: 6

Ingredients:

- 2 tablespoons harissa, dried
- 17 oz cod
- 1 teaspoon salt
- 1 tablespoon minced garlic
- 1 tablespoon sour cream
- ¼ cup soy sauce
- 1 tablespoon oyster sauce
- 1 teaspoon chili paste
- 1 teaspoon cilantro
- 1 red onion
- 1 cup fish stock
- ½ cup canned tomatoes
- 1 tablespoon harissa sauce
- 4 tablespoons orange juice

Directions:

Combine the dried harissa, salt, minced garlic, sour cream, soy sauce, oyster sauce, chili paste, cilantro, fish stock, harissa sauce, and orange juice in the bowl. Whisk well. Put the canned tomatoes in the slow cooker. Then put the cod over the canned tomatoes. Peel the onion and slice. Sprinkle the cod with the sliced onion. Pour the fish stock in the bowl as well. Add the whisked harissa mixture and close the slow cooker lid. Cook the fish on LOW for 7 hours. Then remove the fish gently from the slow cooker and chill for 10 minutes. If the fish is too spicy, serve it with the cream sauce.

Nutrition: calories 116, fat 2.9, fiber 1, carbs 7.4, protein 15

Shri Lanka Mackerel Cutlet

Prep time: 30 minutes | Cooking time: 2 hours | Servings: 14

Ingredients:

- 16 oz mackerel fillet
- 1 cup mashed potato
- 1 chili pepper
- 1 cup onion, grated
- 1 teaspoon minced garlic
- ¼ teaspoon ground ginger
- 1 oz curry powder
- 1 teaspoon salt
- 4 oz tomato sauce
- 1 teaspoon ground thyme
- 4 teaspoons lime juice
- 3 large eggs
- 1 cup bread crumbs
- 1 teaspoon chives
- 1 tablespoon onion powder

Directions:

Grind the chili pepper and combine it with the mashed potato. Mince the mackerel fillet and add in the mashed potato. Sprinkle the mashed potato mixture with the grated onion, minced garlic, ground ginger, curry powder, salt, ground thyme, lime juice, chives, and onion powder. Mix the mackerel mixture with a spoon carefully. After this, form into small round cutlets. Whisk the beaten eggs and dip the cutlets in the egg. Then coat the cutlets in the bread crumbs. Put the cutlets in the slow cooker and sprinkle them with the tomato sauce. Close the lid and cook the cutlets for 2 hours on HIGH. When the cutlets are cooked, leave them for 30 minutes. Serve!

Nutrition: calories 83, fat 2, fiber 2, carbs 7.67, protein 8

Corn Fish Balls

Prep time: 25 minutes | Cooking time: 8 hours | Servings: 11

Ingredients:

- 1 cup sweet corn
- 5 tablespoons fresh dill, chopped
- 1 tablespoon minced garlic
- 7 tablespoons bread crumbs
- 2 eggs, beaten
- 10 oz salmon
- 2 tablespoons semolina
- 2 tablespoons canola oil
- 1 teaspoon salt
- 1 teaspoon ground black pepper
- 1 teaspoon cumin
- 1 teaspoon lemon zest
- ¼ teaspoon cinnamon
- 3 tablespoons almond flour
- 3 tablespoons scallion, chopped
- 3 tablespoons water

Directions:

Combine the sweet corn with the fresh dill. Add the minced garlic, beaten eggs, semolina, salt, ground black pepper, cumin, lemon zest, cinnamon, almond flour, scallion, and mix well. Chop the salmon and add it to the mixture. After this, make the balls from the fish mixture and coat them in the bread crumbs. Pour water and canola oil in the slow cooker. Add the corn fish balls and close the lid. Cook the fish balls for 8 hours on LOW, stirring them every hour. Serve the prepared corn fish balls hot.

Nutrition: calories 201, fat 7.9, fiber 2, carbs 22.6, protein 11

Trout Piccata

Prep time: 10 minutes | Cooking time: 45 minutes | Servings: 4

Ingredients:

- 4 oz dry white wine
- 1-pound trout fillet
- 2 tablespoons capers
- 3 tablespoons olive oil
- 3 tablespoons flour
- 1 teaspoon garlic powder
- 1 teaspoon dried rosemary
- 1 teaspoon oregano
- 1 teaspoon cilantro
- 1 tablespoon fresh dill, chopped
- 1 teaspoon ground white pepper
- 1 teaspoon butter

Directions:

Pour olive oil in the slow cooker. Then add the trout. Sprinkle the trout fillet with the garlic powder, dried rosemary, oregano, cilantro, and ground white pepper. Close the lid and cook the fish on HIGH for 30 minutes. Turn it into another side after 15 minutes of cooking. Meanwhile, combine the dry wine and flour together. Mix it until smooth. Pour the dry wine into the slow cooker. Add capers and butter. Then sprinkle the fish with the chopped fresh dill and close the lid. Cook the fish for 15 minutes more on HIGH. After this remove the fish from the liquid and serve.

Nutrition: calories 393, fat 25.9, fiber 1, carbs 8, protein 32

Salmon Fingers

Prep time: 25 minutes | Cooking time: 3 hours | Servings: 8

Ingredients:

- 2 large eggs
- 1 cup panko bread crumbs
- 1 tablespoon turmeric
- 1 tablespoon butter
- 13 oz salmon fillet
- 1 teaspoon salt
- 1 teaspoon ground black pepper
- ¼ cup chickpeas, canned
- 1 teaspoon onion powder
- 2 tablespoons semolina
- ¼ teaspoon ginger

Directions:

Beat the eggs in the bowl and mix them with the help of the mixer. Then add turmeric, salt, ground black pepper, semolina, and onion powder. Add ginger and mix the mixture up. Grind the salmon fillet and blend with the canned chickpeas. Add the prepared salmon and chickpeas into the egg mixture and mix well. Form medium logs (fingers) from the fish mixture. Then sprinkle every fish finger with the bread crumbs. Melt the butter and pour it in the slow cooker. Then put the fish fingers inside the bowl and close the lid. Cook the fish finger on HIGH for 3 hours. Flipping them after 1.5 hours of cooking. Serve the fish finger immediately or wrap them in the parchment to store.

Nutrition: calories 149, fat 6.5, fiber 1, carbs 9.72, protein 12

Lime Flounder

Prep time: 18 minutes | Cooking time: 8 hours | Servings: 9

Ingredients:

- 3-pounds flounder, peeled
- 1 lime
- ½ cup lemon juice
- 1 tablespoon sugar
- 1 teaspoon ground ginger
- 1 teaspoon ground cumin
- ½ teaspoon ground coriander
- 1 teaspoon ground celery root
- 2 teaspoons olive oil
- 1 teaspoon garlic, sliced
- 1/4 teaspoon nutmeg
- 1 teaspoon chili flakes

Directions:

Slice the lime and stuff inside the flounder. Put the stuffed flounder in the foil. Then sprinkle it with the lemon juice. Combine the sugar, ground ginger, ground cumin, ground coriander, ground celery root, nutmeg, and chili flakes in the bowl. Rub the flounder with the spices. After this, sprinkle the fish with the sliced garlic and olive oil. Wrap the flounder in the foil carefully and put it in the slow cooker. Cook the fish on LOW for 8 hours. Then discard the foil from the fish and put it on serving plates. Serve it!

Nutrition: calories 113, fat 3.6, fiber 2, carbs 11, protein 10

Snapper with Mushrooms

Prep time: 20 minutes | Cooking time: 6 hours | Servings: 6

Ingredients:

- 1 cup sour cream
- 1 onion, diced
- ¼ cup almond milk
- 1 teaspoon salt
- 7 oz cremini mushrooms
- 1 teaspoon ground thyme
- 1 tablespoon ground paprika
- 1 teaspoon ground coriander
- 1 teaspoon kosher salt
- 1 tablespoon lemon juice
- 1 teaspoon butter
- 1-pound snapper
- 1 teaspoon lemon zest

Directions:

Chop the snapper roughly. Sprinkle the chopped snapper with the ground thyme, ground paprika, ground coriander, kosher salt, lemon juice, and lemon zest. Mix the fish up well and leave it for 10 minutes to marinate. After this, put the butter in the slow cooker and add the chopped snapper mixture. Then slice the cremini mushrooms and combine them with the diced onion. Put the mushroom mixture over the chopped snapper. Then pour in the sour cream and almond milk. Close the lid and cook the dish on LOW for 6 hours. Stir the dish after 3 hours of cooking. When the fish is cooked, stir it one more time and serve.

Nutrition: calories 248, fat 6.3, fiber 5, carbs 31.19, protein 20

Carp Soup

Prep time: 15 minutes | Cooking time: 6 hours | Servings: 10

Ingredients:

- ¼ cup millet
- 8 cups water
- 1-pound carp, peeled, chopped
- 1 teaspoon black peas
- 1 teaspoon cilantro
- ¼ cup fresh parsley
- 1 tablespoon garlic, sliced
- 1 carrot, chopped
- 1 tablespoon salt
- 1 teaspoon ground celery root
- 1 teaspoon ground black pepper

Directions:

Put the millet in the slow cooker and add water. Sprinkle the chopped carp with the cilantro and ground celery root. Mix it carefully and transfer to the slow cooker. Then add the sliced garlic, ground black pepper, chopped carrot, and salt. Chop the fresh parsley and add it in the slow cooker too. After this add the black peas and close the lid. Cook the carp soup for 6 hours on LOW. When the soup is cooked, ladle it into the serving bowls. Add the sour cream if desired and serve.

Nutrition: calories 83, fat 2.8, fiber 1, carbs 5.07, protein 9

Spicy Perch

Prep time: 25 minutes | Cooking time: 4.5 hours | Servings: 6

Ingredients:

- 14 oz perch, peeled
- 1 teaspoon cayenne pepper
- 1 chili pepper, chopped
- 1 onion, peeled and diced
- 3 garlic cloves, sliced
- 1 teaspoon ground ginger
- 1 teaspoon cilantro
- 1 tablespoon harissa paste
- 1 teaspoon curry paste
- 1 teaspoon olive oil
- 3 tablespoons fish sauce
- 3 tablespoons water

Directions:

Rub the perch with the cayenne pepper, ground ginger, cilantro, harissa paste, and curry paste. Then fill the perch with the sliced garlic, diced onion, and chopped chili pepper. Combine the olive oil and fish sauce in a bowl. Add the water and whisk. Put the foil in the slow cooker and transfer the perch there. Sprinkle the fish with the fish sauce liquid and wrap it in the foil carefully. Close the lid and cook the fish on HIGH for 4.5 hours. When the fish is cooked, remove it from the slow cooker. Let it sit for 15 minutes in foil and then serve!

Nutrition: calories 88, fat 1.5, fiber 1, carbs 4, protein 14

Stuffed Squid
Prep time: 20 minutes | Cooking time: 7 hours | Servings: 4

Ingredients:
- 1-pound squid tubes
- 2 oz capers
- 1 cup tomatoes, chopped
- 1 teaspoon salt
- 1 teaspoon cayenne pepper
- 1 teaspoon ground black pepper
- 1 teaspoon butter
- 1 tablespoon tomato paste
- 1 garlic clove, chopped
- 1 cup chicken stock
- 6 oz ground chicken
- 1 teaspoon cilantro

Directions:
Combine the chopped tomatoes, salt, cayenne pepper, ground black pepper, butter, capers, chopped garlic clove, ground chicken, and cilantro in the bowl. Mix well. Fill the squid tubes with the ground chicken mixture. Sprinkle the squid tubes with the tomato paste and put them in the slow cooker. Add the chicken stock and close the lid. Cook the stuffed squid on LOW for 7 hours. Stir the squid tubes frequently during the cooking. When the dish is cooked, let it cool slightly. Slice it with the help of the knife and serve.

Nutrition: calories 216, fat 7, fiber 1, carbs 10.1, protein 28

Halibut with Peach
Prep time: 25 minutes | Cooking time: 1 hour | Servings: 6

Ingredients:
- 16 oz halibut fillet
- 4 tablespoons peach puree
- 2 peach, pitted
- 1 teaspoon salt
- 1 teaspoon turmeric
- 1 teaspoon white sugar
- 1 tablespoon sour cream
- ½ teaspoon ground white pepper
- 3 oz tangerines
- 1 tablespoon maple syrup
- 1 teaspoon oregano
- 1 teaspoon olive oil
- 1 teaspoon garlic, sliced
- ½ teaspoon sage

Directions:
Peel the peaches and chop them. Combine the chopped peaches with the peach puree. Add salt, turmeric, white sugar, and sour cream. Mix the puree mixture carefully. Then rub the halibut fillet with the ground white pepper, maple syrup, oregano, and stir it. Pour the olive oil into a saute pan. Add sliced garlic and sage. Roast it for 1 minute on high heat. Then add the halibut and roast it for 45 seconds on high heat on each side. Put the peach puree mixture in the slow cooker. Add the roasted halibut and all the remaining oil from the pan. Close the lid and cook the fish on LOW for 1 hour. Serve it!

Nutrition: calories 198, fat 11.7, fiber 1, carbs 11.82, protein 12

Glazed Sesame Salmon
Prep time: 20 minutes | Cooking time: 1.5 hours | Servings: 7

Ingredients:
- 5 tablespoons brown sugar
- 2 tablespoons sesame seeds
- 1 tablespoon balsamic vinegar
- 1 tablespoon butter
- 3 tablespoons water
- 1 teaspoon salt
- ½ teaspoon ground black pepper
- 1 teaspoon ground paprika
- 1 teaspoon turmeric
- ¼ teaspoon fresh rosemary
- 1 teaspoon olive oil
- 21 oz salmon fillet

Directions:
Combine the salt, ground black pepper, ground paprika, turmeric, and fresh rosemary in the bowl and grind the spices together. Sprinkle the salmon fillet with the spices on both sides. Pour the olive oil into the pan and roast the salmon on high heat for 3 minutes or until you get a crunchy crust. Meanwhile, put the brown sugar and sesame seeds in the slow cooker. Add the balsamic vinegar and butter. Sprinkle the mixture with water and cook it on HIGH for 30 minutes, stirring it frequently to not let the sugar burn. Then add the salmon fillet and cook it on low for 1 hour more. Stir the salmon fillet to glaze it on every side. Serve the cooked salmon hot.

Nutrition: calories 170, fat 9.9, fiber 1, carbs 1.43, protein 18

Japanese Style Cod Fillet
Prep time: 15 minutes | Cooking time: 1.5 hours | Servings: 9

Ingredients:
- 24 oz cod fillet
- 2 tablespoons miso paste
- 3 oz pickled jalapeno
- 2 tablespoons oyster sauce
- ¼ cup soy sauce
- ¼ cup fish stock
- 1 teaspoon sesame oil
- ½ teaspoon chili flakes
- ¼ teaspoon cayenne pepper
- 1 tablespoon sugar

Directions:
Chop the pickled jalapeno. Combine the miso paste with the oyster sauce, soy sauce, fish stock, and sesame oil. Add the chili flakes, cayenne pepper, and sugar. Whisk with the help of the fork to make the miso paste dissolve. Then brush the cod fillet with the miso paste sauce. Put the cod fillet in the slow cooker and sprinkle with the remaining sauce. Add the chopped pickled jalapeno pepper and close the lid. Cook the fish on LOW for 1.5 hours. When the fish is cooked, transfer it to a plate and shred gently with a fork. Sprinkle the fish with the slow cooker fish sauce and serve immediately.

Nutrition: calories 95, fat 2.5, fiber 1, carbs 4.81, protein 13

Slow Cooker Crab
Prep time: 15 minutes | Cooking time: 1 hour | Servings: 6

Ingredients:
- 15 oz crab
- 6 oz fennel bulb
- 1 lemon
- 1 tablespoon kosher salt
- 1 tablespoon oyster sauce
- 1 teaspoon black peas
- 6 cups water
- 1 tablespoon fresh parsley, chopped
- 1 oz bay leaf
- 4 oz shallot, peeled

Directions:
Put the crab in the slow cooker bowl. Chop the fennel bulb and shallot roughly. Put the vegetables in the slow cooker. Add the kosher salt, black peas, and water. Then add the bay leaf and close the lid. Cook the crab on HIGH for 1 hour or until it is cooked. The crab will change to be red. Meanwhile, squeeze the lemon juice and combine it with the chopped fresh parsley. Add the oyster sauce and stir. When the crab is cooked, peel it to get the crab meat out. Put the crab meat in the serving bowl and sprinkle it with the oyster sauce mixture. Serve immediately!

Nutrition: calories 103, fat 1.3, fiber 3, carbs 9.78, protein 14

Light Lobster Soup
Prep time: 10 minutes | Cooking time: 3.5 hours | Servings: 6

Ingredients:
- 5 cups fish stock
- 1 tablespoon paprika
- ½ teaspoon powdered chili
- 1 teaspoon salt
- 8 oz lobster tails
- 6 oz Cheddar cheese, shredded
- 1 teaspoon ground white pepper
- 1/3 cup fresh dill
- 1 tablespoon almond milk
- 1 garlic clove, peeled
- 3 potatoes

Directions:
Pour the fish stock into the slow cooker bowl. Peel the potatoes and cut into cubes. Put the potato cubes in the slow cooker. Add the powdered chili, paprika, salt, ground white pepper, almond milk, and peeled garlic cloves. Close the lid and cook the liquid for 2 hours on HIGH. Meanwhile, chop the fresh dill. When the time is done, add the fresh dill and lobster tails. Close the lid and cook the soup on HIGH for 1.5 hours more. Ladle the prepared soup into the bowls and sprinkle with the shredded cheese.

Nutrition: calories 261, fat 4.8, fiber 5, carbs 37.14, protein 19

Flounder Casserole

Prep time: 20 minutes | Cooking time: 6 hour | Servings: 11

Ingredients:

- 8 oz rice noodles
- 2 cups chicken stock
- 12 oz flounder fillet, chopped
- 1 cup carrot, cooked
- ½ teaspoon ground black pepper
- 2 sweet peppers, chopped
- 3 sweet potatoes, chopped
- 2 tablespoons butter, melted
- 3 tablespoons chives
- 4 oz shallot, chopped
- 7 oz cream cheese
- 5 oz Parmesan, shredded
- ½ cup fresh cilantro, chopped
- 1 cup water

Directions:

Sprinkle the slow cooker bowl with the melted butter. Then put the chopped flounder fillet in the bottom of the slow cooker. Sprinkle with the chopped carrot. Then make a layer of the chopped sweet potatoes and sweet peppers. Add the chives and chopped shallot. Crush the rice noodles and add them to the slow cooker. Sprinkle the mixture with the fresh cilantro. Combine the water, ground black pepper, chicken stock, and whisk. Pour the liquid into the slow cooker along with the cream cheese. Cover the casserole with the shredded cheese. Close the lid and cook it on LOW for 6 hours. When the casserole is cooked, let it cool slightly then serve!

Nutrition: calories 202, fat 9.1, fiber 2, carbs 19.86, protein 11

Fish Tacos

Prep time: 20 minutes | Cooking time: 2 hours | Servings: 6

Ingredients:

- 9 oz mackerel fillet
- 1 teaspoon salt
- ¼ cup fish stock
- 1 teaspoon butter
- 1 teaspoon paprika
- ½ teaspoon ground white pepper
- 6 corn tortillas
- ¼ cup salsa
- 1 teaspoon minced garlic
- ½ teaspoon mayo

Directions:

Rub the mackerel fillet with the salt, paprika, butter, ground white pepper, minced garlic, and mayo. Put the fish in the slow cooker. Add the fish stock and close the lid. Cook the fish on LOW for 2 hours or until the mackerel is cooked. Meanwhile, spread the corn tortilla with the salsa carefully. When the mackerel fillet is cooked, remove it from the slow cooker and shred. Then sprinkle it with 2 teaspoons slow cooker liquid. Put the shredded mackerel fillet in the corn tortillas and wrap them up.

Nutrition: calories 120, fat 2.4, fiber 3, carbs 14.37, protein 11

Dill Crab Cakes

Prep time: 21 minutes | Cooking time: 1 hour | Servings: 12

Ingredients:

- 12 oz crab meat, canned
- 4 tablespoons fresh dill
- 1 teaspoon salt
- ½ teaspoon cilantro
- 1 tablespoon turmeric
- 3 tablespoons almond flour
- ¼ cup mashed green peas
- 1 teaspoon olive oil
- 1 large egg
- 1 teaspoon lemon juice

Directions:

Put the canned crab meat in a blender. Add the fresh dill, salt, cilantro, turmeric, and almond flour. After this, add the mashed green peas, beat the egg, and sprinkle the mixture with the lemon juice. Pulse for 2 minutes or until you get a smooth dough. Make balls from the crab meat mixture and flatten them into the shape of cakes. Pour the olive oil in the slow cooker. Put the crab cakes in the slow cooker. Close the lid and cook the crab cakes for 1 hour on HIGH. Turn them into another side after 30 minutes of cooking. Remove the excess fat from the cakes and serve.

Nutrition: calories 45, fat 1.5, fiber 1, carbs 2.3, protein 6

Desserts

Easy Chocolate Cake

Prep time: 20 minutes | Cooking time: 3.5 hours | Servings: 8

Ingredients:

- 1 cup skim milk
- 2 cups brown sugar
- 1 cup cocoa powder
- 1 teaspoon baking soda
- 1 tablespoon vinegar
- ¼ teaspoon salt
- 2 cups flour
- 3 eggs
- 1 tablespoon caster sugar

Directions:

Beat the eggs in the mixer bowl and add the skim milk, salt, and baking soda. After this, add the vinegar and whisk. Then sift the flour into the egg mixture. Add the brown sugar and cocoa powder. Mix it carefully until you get a smooth dough. The texture of the dough should be like sour cream. Cover the slow cooker bowl with the parchment and pour the cocoa dough there. Close the lid and set the LOW regime. Cook the chocolate cake for 3.5 hours. Check if the cake is cooked by inserting a toothpick into the cake- if it comes out clean, it is done! Then remove it from the slow cooker or cook it for 30 minutes more (depending on the level of readiness of the cake. Chill the chocolate cake and sprinkle it with the caster sugar.

Nutrition: calories 419, fat 5.4, fiber 4, carbs 89.43, protein 10

Fruit Cobbler

Prep time: 10 minutes | Cooking time: 4 hours | Servings: 5

Ingredients:

- 1 cup cream
- 1 teaspoon cinnamon
- 7 oz biscuit mix
- ¼ cup sugar
- 6 oz bananas
- 4 oz peach, pitted
- 1 teaspoon vanilla extract

Directions:

Peel the bananas. Chop the bananas and peaches roughly and put them in the slow cooker bowl. Sprinkle the fruit with the sugar, vanilla extract, and cinnamon. Add the biscuit mix and mix well. Then pour the cream in the bowl and close the lid. Cook the fruit cobbler on LOW for 4 hours or until it is done. Transfer the fruit cobbler into the ramekins. Add vanilla ice cream if desired.

Nutrition: calories 356, fat 12.1, fiber 4, carbs 60.64, protein 5

Ginger Giant Cookies

Prep time: 15 minutes | Cooking time: 7.5 hours | Servings: 3

Ingredients:

- 5 tablespoons butter
- 1 tablespoon ground ginger
- 1/3 cup sugar
- 1 teaspoon vanilla extract
- 1 cup flour
- ½ teaspoon baking soda
- 1 teaspoon lemon juice
- 1 egg
- 3 tablespoons cream
- 3 tablespoons chocolate chips

Directions:

Combine the ground ginger with sugar, vanilla extract, baking soda, lemon juice, and cream. Then add the flour and beat in the egg. When the mixture starts to become a dough, add the chocolate chips and continue to knead the dough with your hands until the chocolate chips are well blended. Separate the dough into 3 parts. Roll each part out on a clean work surface, about ¼ of an inch thick. Use a round cookie cutter to punch out large circles. Then cover the bowl of the slow cooker with the parchment and place the first circle of the dough inside. Cook the first cookie on the HIGH for 2.5 hours. Then remove the cookie from the slow cooker and chill. Place the second cookie in the slow cooker and cook it. Repeat the same steps with the third cookie dough. Serve the giant ginger cookies chilled.

Nutrition: calories 556, fat 26.2, fiber 2, carbs 70.6, protein 9

Sweet Monkey Bread

Prep time: 15 minutes | Cooking time: 3 hour | Servings: 7

Ingredients:

- 5 tablespoons maple syrup
- 2 tablespoons brown sugar
- 7 eggs
- 13 oz cinnamon rolls
- ½ teaspoon cinnamon
- 1 tablespoon white sugar
- 5 tablespoons butter
- ¼ teaspoon ground cardamom

Directions:

Chop the cinnamon rolls and put them in a bowl. Sprinkle the chopped cinnamon rolls with the maple syrup, brown sugar, cinnamon, butter, and ground cardamom. Mix well. Beat the eggs in a separate bowl. Put the chopped cinnamon roll mixture in the slow cooker. Sprinkle it with the whisked eggs and stir gently with a   fc spatula. Close the lid and cook the monkey bread for 3 hours on HIGH. Then remove the monkey bread from the slow cooker and sprinkle it with the white sugar. Serve it!

Nutrition: calories 437, fat 26.6, fiber 1, carbs 37.65, protein 12

Pecan Brownies

Prep time: 16 minutes | Cooking time: 5 hours | Servings: 8

Ingredients:

- 6 oz cocoa powder
- 3 oz dark chocolate
- 1 teaspoon baking powder
- 1 tablespoon lemon juice
- ¼ cup pecan
- 1 cup flour
- ½ cup skim milk
- 2 eggs
- 1 tablespoon butter
- 1 teaspoon vanilla extract

Directions:

Crush the dark chocolate carefully. Combine the crushed dark chocolate with the cocoa powder and baking soda. Crush the pecan and add them to the chocolate mixture. Then add flour and stir it. Beat the eggs in a separate bowl. Whisk them with the skim milk and vanilla extract. Melt the butter and add it to the skim milk mixture. Combine the dry mass with the liquid mass together. Then cover the slow cooker bowl with parchment. Put the chocolate dough in the slow cooker and flatten it. Close the lid and cook the brownie for 5 hours on LOW. When the pecan brownie is cooked, remove it gently from the slow cooker and let it chill well. Cut it into the serving pieces. Serve it!

Nutrition: calories 280, fat 11.4, fiber 4, carbs 35.26, protein 9

Peanut Muffins

Prep time: 16 minutes | Cooking time: 5 hours | Servings: 8

Ingredients:

- ¼ cup peanut, crushed
- 1 tablespoon peanut butter
- 3 tablespoons butter
- 1/3 teaspoon salt
- ½ teaspoon baking soda
- 1 tablespoon lemon juice
- 1 teaspoon vanilla extract
- 1 egg
- ½ cup heavy cream
- 1 ½ cup flour
- 4 tablespoons sugar
- ¼ teaspoon lemon zest

Directions:

Melt the peanut butter and butter. Combine the ingredients together. Add salt, baking soda, lemon juice, and vanilla extract. Then beat the egg into the mixture and add the heavy cream. Add sugar and lemon zest and mix it with the help of the hand mixer. When the liquid is smooth, sift the flour in and continue to mix it until you get a smooth batter. Then pour the batter into silicone cupcake molds. Fill only 1/3 space of the mold. Put the muffins in the slow cooker and close the lid. Cook the muffins on HIGH for 5 hours. Check if the muffins are cooked and remove them from the slow cooker. Remove the muffins from the silicon molds and chill them. Serve!

Nutrition: calories 236, fat 12, fiber 1, carbs 26.13, protein 6

Spoon Cake

Prep time: 21 minutes | Cooking time: 4 hours | Servings: 6

Ingredients:

- 1-pound cake mix
- 5 oz water
- 7 oz peaches, canned, drained
- 4 large eggs
- 4 tablespoons butter, melted
- 8 tablespoons coconut
- 4 tablespoons walnuts, crushed
- 1 teaspoon lemon zest
- 4 tablespoons sugar
- 1/3 cup peach juice
- 3 teaspoons coconut
- 1 tablespoon butter, unsalted, melted
- 4 tablespoons peanut, crushed

Directions:

Chop the canned peaches and combine them with the 8 tablespoons coconut, crushed peanuts, lemon zest, and water. Mix and add the cake mix. Stir it carefully and pour into the slow cooker. Close the lid and cook the spoon cake for 4 hours on HIGH. Meanwhile, make the glaze for the spoon cake by combining the peach juice, caster sugar, 3 teaspoons coconut, melted unsalted butter, and crushed peanuts. Mix the glaze until you get a sauce texture. When the spoon cake is cooked, put it in the serving bowls. Sprinkle each serving with the prepared glazed sauce generously. Serve it!

Nutrition: calories 577, fat 24, fiber 3, carbs 83.17, protein 10

Lemon Curd

Prep time: 20 minutes | Cooking time: 2.5 hours | Servings: 4

Ingredients:

- 4 large eggs
- 1 cup sugar
- 1 teaspoon lime zest
- 6 tablespoons butter, unsalted
- ½ cup lemon juice

Directions:

Beat the eggs in the bowl and whisk them with 1 cup of the sugar. When you get a smooth lemon colored mixture, add the lime zest and half of the lemon juice. Mix it for 20 seconds more. After this, add the unsalted butter and all the remaining lemon juice. Whisk it gently and put into the slow cooker. Set the slow cooker regime on LOW and cook the lemon curd for 2.5 hours. Stir it frequently so it does not burn. When the lemon curd has a thick sauce texture, it is cooked. Pour it into the big bowl and chill well. Stir it during the chilling time to time.

Nutrition: calories 312, fat 21.9, fiber 0, carbs 27.78, protein 3

Pumpkin Cake Bombs

Prep time: 25 minutes | Cooking time: 3 hours | Servings: 6

Ingredients:

- 4 tablespoons pumpkin puree
- ½ teaspoon ground cardamom
- ¼ teaspoon ground cinnamon
- 1 cup flour
- 1 egg
- ¼ cup milk
- 3 tablespoons almond flour
- 1 tablespoon lemon juice
- ¼ cup sugar
- 2 tablespoons bread crumbs
- ½ tablespoon sesame oil
- 1 tablespoon honey, for serving

Directions:

Beat the egg in a bowl and add the pumpkin puree, ground cardamom, ground cinnamon, milk, almond flour, lemon juice, and sugar. Blend with a hand blender. Then sift the flour into the bowl and blend it for 2 minutes more. You should get a soft but not sticky dough. Then make medium balls from the pumpkin dough. Sprinkle the pumpkin balls with the bread crumbs. Brush the slow cooker bowl with the sesame oil. Put the pumpkin balls in the slow cooker and close the lid. Cook the desert for 3 hours on HIGH. Then chill the pumpkin cake bombs until room temperature and sprinkle them with the honey. Serve them immediately.

Nutrition: calories 213, fat 6.5, fiber 2, carbs 32.24, protein 7

Fragrant Cinnamon Apples

Prep time: 15 minutes | Cooking time: 2 hours | Servings: 5

Ingredients:

- 1-pound red apples
- 1 tablespoon cinnamon
- 3 tablespoons brown sugar
- 3 tablespoons lemon juice
- 2 tablespoons butter
- 1 tablespoon flour
- 1/3 teaspoon ground anise
- 2 teaspoons whipped cream, for serving

Directions:

Wash the red apples carefully and cut them into the halves. Then remove the seeds from the apples. Slice the prepared apple halves roughly and place them in the slow cooker. Sprinkle the apple slices with the lemon juice and add butter. Then combine the brown sugar, flour, and ground anise in the shallow bowl. Sprinkle the apples with the brown sugar mixture and close the lid. Cook the apples for 2 hours on HIGH. Mix the apples carefully with a spoon after 1 hour of cooking. When the cinnamon apples are cooked, they will be very tender. Chill them slightly and serve.

Nutrition: calories 110, fat 5.3, fiber 3, carbs 15.98, protein 1

Cherry Pudding

Prep time: 21 minutes | Cooking time: 4 hours | Servings: 5

Ingredients:

- 4 tablespoons cherry jam
- 2 cups milk
- 2 tablespoons cornstarch
- 1 tablespoon flour
- 6 tablespoons white sugar
- 1 teaspoon vanilla extract
- 2 tablespoons butter
- 4 egg yolks

Directions:

Combine the milk with the cherry jam and whisk with a fork. Then reserve 5 tablespoons of the cherry milk and pour the rest in the slow cooker. Add the butter and vanilla extract in the slow cooker. Whisk the white sugar and egg yolks until they are lemon colored. Put the whisked egg yolk mixture in the slow cooker and stir it. Close the lid and cook it on HIGH for 1 hour. Stir it frequently. Combine the remaining cherry milk with the cornstarch and flour and whisk. After 1 hour of cooking, add the cornstarch mixture slowly and stirring constantly. Stir the liquid 1 minute more and close the lid. Cook the pudding on LOW for 4 hours more. Chill the pudding and serve!

Nutrition: calories 177, fat 12.1, fiber 0, carbs 11, protein 6

Almond Dump Cake

Prep time: 20 minutes | Cooking time: 4.5 hours | Servings: 3

Ingredients:

- 7 oz cake mix
- 1 cup almond, crushed
- 3 tablespoons almond flour
- ¼ cup butter, unsalted
- ½ cup water
- 5 tablespoons white sugar
- 1 teaspoon vanilla extract
- 1 teaspoon lemon zest

Directions:

Melt the butter and combine it with the almond flour and white sugar. Add vanilla extract and lemon zest. Add the cake mix and stir it carefully. Add the water and stir into a very thick batter. Then crush the almonds and put the crushed almonds in the slow cooker bowl. Dump the cake mix mixture in the slow cooker and close the lid. Cook the dump cake for 4.5 hours on LOW. When the cake is cooked, transfer it to a big serving plate. Chill the dump cake and serve it.

Nutrition: calories 428, fat 20.8, fiber 1, carbs 56.93, protein 4

Apple Pie Dip

Prep time: 15 minutes | Cooking time: 3 hours | Servings: 4

Ingredients:

- 2 cups apples
- 1 can caramel sauce
- 1/3 teaspoon lemon zest
- 1 teaspoon lemon juice
- ½ teaspoon ground cinnamon
- 1 tablespoon apple pie seasoning
- ½ teaspoon ground ginger
- ½ teaspoon ground cardamom
- 1 tablespoon butter

Directions:

Peel the apples and discard the seeds. Chop the apples into the small pieces. Sprinkle the apple pieces with the lemon juice and the lemon zest. Stir the mixture and put it in the slow cooker. Add the ground cinnamon, ground ginger, and ground cardamom. Mix the apple mixture with a spatula. Add butter and caramel sauce. Add the apple pie seasoning. Close the slow cooker lid and cook the dip for 1 hour on HIGH. Stir well then cook the apple pie dip for 2 hours more on LOW. Let the prepared apple pie dip chill well. Serve it or keep in the fridge.

Nutrition: calories 248, fat 7.1, fiber 2, carbs 46.74, protein 3

Fudge Cake

Prep time: 18 minutes | Cooking time: 5 hours | Servings: 6

Ingredients:

- 9 oz sugar
- 6 oz flour
- 4 oz cocoa powder
- 1 teaspoon baking soda
- 1 tablespoon vinegar
- 1/3 teaspoon salt
- 5 oz milk
- 3 tablespoons butter
- 1 teaspoon vanilla extract
- 6 oz chocolate chips
- 1 cup water, boiled

Directions:

Combine the sugar, flour, cocoa powder, and baking soda in the bowl. Add vinegar and salt. Stir the dry mixture gently with a fork. Then add the milk and vanilla extract. Add butter. Use the hand blender to mix into a smooth batter. Cover the slow cooker bowl with parchment and pour the batter inside. Sprinkle the dough with the chocolate chips and boiled water. Do not stir the dough and close the lid. Cook the fudge cake for 5 hours on HIGH. Serve it warm.

Nutrition: calories 549, fat 13.9, fiber 3, carbs 98.19, protein 8

Classic Apple Pie

Prep time: 20 minutes | Cooking time: 3 hour | Servings: 6

Ingredients:

- 1 box yellow cake mix
- 1 teaspoon ground cinnamon
- 1 teaspoon vanilla extract
- ½ cup white sugar
- 2 eggs
- ½ teaspoon nutmeg
- 1 cup apples, chopped
- 4 tablespoons butter
- ¼ cup sour cream

Directions:

Beat the eggs in the bowl. Add the ground cinnamon and vanilla extract. Then add the white sugar and nutmeg. Add butter and sour cream. Use a hand mixer to blend. Add the yellow cake mix and blend with a spoon. Add the chopped apples and stir the dough gently. After this, cover the slow cooker bowl with the baking paper and put the apple pie dough. Make your palms wet and flatten the dough to make it flat. Close the slow cooker lid and cook the apple pie for 3 hours on LOW. When the apple pie is cooked, chill it slightly so it is still a little bit warm. Cut the apple pie into pieces and serve it. Serve the apple pie with the ice cream balls if desired.

Nutrition: calories 527, fat 20, fiber 2, carbs 79.61, protein 8

Charlotte

Prep time: 15 minutes | Cooking time: 5 hours | Servings: 8

Ingredients:

- 6 eggs
- 1 cup flour
- 1 cup apples
- 1 cup sugar
- 1 cup flour

- 1 teaspoon vanilla extract
- 1 teaspoon butter
- 1 teaspoon powdered sugar
- 1 pinch fresh mint

Directions:

Separate the egg whites and egg yolks. Start to whisk the egg yolks. When the egg yolks are fluffy, add the sugar and continue to whisk it until you get a bright yellow color. Add the vanilla extract. Then whisk the egg whites carefully until you get stiff peaks. Add the flour and stir it gently with a silicone spatula. Then combine the egg yolk mixture and the egg white mixture together. Stir it carefully. Slice the apples. Butter the slow cooker bowl and pour the batter inside. After this, add the sliced apples and close the lid. Cook the Charlotte for 5 hours on LOW. Check if the Charlotte is cooked and remove it from the slow cooker. Chill it well. The Charlotte may deflate as it cools. Cut into pieces and sprinkle with the powdered sugar and fresh mint.

Nutrition: calories 296, fat 8.7, fiber 1, carbs 43.51, protein 10

Cinnabons Pie

Prep time: 25 minutes | Cooking time: 3 hours | Servings: 6

Ingredients:

- 1 teaspoon fresh yeast
- 2 cup flour
- 1 egg
- 4 oz whey
- ½ teaspoon salt
- 1 teaspoon white sugar

- 1 cup sugar, brown
- 1 cup butter
- 5 tablespoons ground cinnamon
- 1 teaspoon vanilla extract
- 1 can condensed milk
- ½ teaspoon olive oil

Directions:

Preheat the whey to room temperature and combine it with the fresh yeast. Whisk it until the fresh yeast is dissolved. Then beat the egg into the whey mixture. Add the salt and white sugar. Add the flour and knead into a soft non-sticky dough. Cover the prepared dough with a towel and leave it in a warm place to let the dough to rise. Then roll the dough into a big flat square. Combine the brown sugar and ground cinnamon together. Spread the rolled dough with the butter. Then sprinkle the dough with the cinnamon-sugar mixture well. Roll the dough in a long log. Then make a snail from the dough log. Cover the slow cooker bowl with the baking paper, brush it with the olive oil, and put the cinnamon snail inside. Cook the cinnabons pie for 3 hours on HIGH. When the cinnabons pie is cooked, transfer it to the plate and sprinkle it with the condensed milk. Serve!

Nutrition: calories 667, fat 40.1, fiber 6, carbs 71.65, protein 7

Walnut Pudding Cake

Prep time: 25 minutes | Cooking time: 5.5 hours | Servings: 5

Ingredients:

- 1 teaspoon canola oil
- ½ cup walnuts, crushed
- 5 oz heavy cream
- 1 teaspoon instant coffee
- 5 tablespoons coconut flour
- 4 eggs
- ½ teaspoon vanilla extract
- 4 tablespoons sugar
- 1 cup milk
- 1 tablespoon cornstarch

Directions:

Brush the slow cooker with the canola oil inside. Then whisk the heavy cream until it is slightly fluffy. Combine the whisked heavy cream with the instant coffee and stir it carefully. Add the vanilla extract and sugar. Beat the eggs in a separate bowl and whisk them lightly. Then combine them with milk and cornstarch. Stir it until smooth. Add the coconut flour in the cream mixture. Stir it carefully. Add the crushed walnuts. Combine the egg mixture with the cream mixture and whisk it with the help of a hand whisker. Pour the pudding mixture into the slow cooker. Close the lid. Cook the pudding for 5.5 hours on Low. When the time is done, stir the pudding carefully and chill it till the room temperature. Then stir it gently again and serve.

Nutrition: calories 327, fat 26, fiber 1, carbs 13.64, protein 11

Carrot Muffins

Prep time: 20 minutes | Cooking time: 6 hours | Servings: 6

Ingredients:

- 1 cup carrot, grated
- 1 cup cream cheese
- 1 cup flour
- 3 tablespoons sugar
- 2 tablespoons butter
- 1 egg
- ½ teaspoon baking soda
- 1 teaspoon apple cider vinegar
- 1 tablespoon dark chocolate, grated

Directions:

Put the cream cheese, sugar, butter, baking soda, and apple cider vinegar in the bowl. Mix it gently with a fork. Then add the flour and beat the egg. Use the hand mixer to make a smooth batter. Add the grated carrot and stir it gently. Then fill the ½ part of every silicon muffin mold with the prepared carrot batter and put them in the slow cooker. Cook the carrot muffins for 6 hours on HIGH. Chill the grated muffins and remove them from the silicone molds.

Nutrition: calories 288, fat 18.2, fiber 1, carbs 24.46, protein 7

Baked Apple Slices

Prep time: 25 minutes | Cooking time: 2 hours | Servings: 5

Ingredients:

- 5 red apples
- 6 oz Parmesan cheese, grated
- 2 tablespoons white sugar
- 1 teaspoon nutmeg
- ½ teaspoon anise star
- 1 teaspoon vanilla extract
- 1 teaspoon honey
- 2 teaspoons butter
- 1 pinch salt
- 5 ice cream scoops, for serving, if desired

Directions:

Discard the seeds from the apples and slice them roughly. Put the white sugar, nutmeg, anise star, vanilla extract, honey, butter, and salt in the slow cooker bowl. Close the slow cooker lid and melt it on HIGH for 1 hour. Stir the sweet mixture every 15 minutes. Then toss the apple slices in the slow cooker and coat them with the sweet hot liquid with a spatula. Close the lid and cook it for 40 minutes on HIGH. Then make a layer of the grated cheese over the sliced apples and cook the dish for 20 minutes more on HIGH. Transfer the hot apple slices in to serving bowls/plates. Add the ice cream scoops if desired and serve it hot.

Nutrition: calories 294, fat 11.9, fiber 5, carbs 36.3, protein 10

Simple Lava Cake

Prep time: 15 minutes | Cooking time: 3 hours | Servings: 6

Ingredients:

- 1 package cake mix
- 1 tablespoon sesame oil
- ½ cup water
- 3 tablespoons sugar
- 4 eggs
- 1/3 cup chocolate chips
- 1 cup milk
- 1 cup chocolate pudding
- ½ teaspoon vanilla extract
- 3 tablespoons maple syrup

Directions:

Put the cake mix in the bowl. Beat in the eggs. Add the water. Sprinkle it with sugar and whisk the mixture. Then combine the milk and chocolate pudding. Add the vanilla extract and maple syrup. Add the chocolate chips. Combine the cake mix mixture and milk mixture together to make the homogenous batter. Spray the slow cooker bowl with the sesame oil. Pour the lava cake dough in the slow cooker. Cover the slow cooker with the parchment and then close the lid. Cook the lava cake on LOW for 3 hours. Then serve the lava cake immediately.

Nutrition: calories 505, fat 12.8, fiber 1, carbs 85.2, protein 13

Caramel Cake

Prep time: 20 minutes | Cooking time: 3 hours | Servings: 7

Ingredients:

- 14 oz yellow cake mix
- 7 oz vanilla caramel
- 4 large eggs
- 8 oz water, boiled
- 4 tablespoons caster sugar
- ½ teaspoon canola oil
- 1 tablespoon butter, unsalted
- 1 teaspoon ground nutmeg
- ¼ teaspoon ground anise

Directions:

Beat the eggs in a bowl. Add the vanilla caramel and caster sugar. After this, add the boiled water and yellow cake mix. Add butter and ground nutmeg. Then sprinkle the ingredients with the ground anise and mix until you get a smooth batter Pour the canola oil into the slow cooker. Then add the caramel dough into the slow cooker. Close the slow cooker lid and cook the cake for 3 hours on HIGH. Chill the caramel cake and serve it. Sprinkle the caramel cake with the condensed milk if you'd like a very sweet dessert.

Nutrition: calories 436, fat 15.1, fiber 2, carbs 70.96, protein 5

Tapioca Pudding

Prep time: 8 minutes | Cooking time: 6.5 hours | Servings: 10

Ingredients:

- 4.2 oz tapioca
- 3 cup milk
- 4 tablespoons white sugar
- 3 large eggs
- 1 teaspoon vanilla sugar

Directions:

Combine the tapioca, milk, white sugar, and vanilla extract in the slow cooker bowl. Beat the eggs in a bowl. Pour the whisked egg mixture in the slow cooker and stir the milk mixture with a spoon gently. Close the lid and cook the pudding for 6.5 hours on LOW. Then chill the prepared tapioca pudding and serve it. Taste it!

Nutrition: calories 108, fat 4, fiber 0, carbs 14.45, protein 3

Super Tasty Banana Dip

Prep time: 1 5 minutes | Cooking time: 5 hours | Servings: 5

Ingredients:

- 1-pound banana
- 1 cup cream
- 4 oz peaches
- 1 tablespoon butter
- ½ cup sugar, brown
- 1 teaspoon vanilla extract
- 1 tablespoon cherry juice
- 1 tablespoon cornstarch
- 2 tablespoons water

Directions:

Peel the bananas and chop them. Chop the peaches. Combine the ingredients with the cream. Add butter, brown sugar, vanilla extract, cherry juice, cornstarch, and water. Put the mixture in a mixing bowl and mix it for 3 minutes on the high speed. After this, pour the banana mixture in the slow cooker. Close the lid and cook it for 5 hours on LOW. Stir the banana dip after 3 hours of cooking gently. Serve the banana dip at room temperature.

Nutrition: calories 486, fat 13.3, fiber 10, carbs 96.08, protein 5

Sweet Wild Rice

Prep time: 15 minutes | Cooking time: 4 hours | Servings: 3

Ingredients:

- 3 tablespoons caramel
- 1 cup wild rice
- 3 tablespoons sugar
- 1 teaspoon vanilla extract
- 3 cups milk
- 1 teaspoon fresh ginger, piece
- 1 oz cinnamon stick
- 2 tablespoons butter

Directions:

Put the wild rice in the slow cooker. Add the vanilla extract and milk. Stir the wild rice gently. Then add a piece of the fresh ginger, and cinnamon stick. Close the lid and cook the wild rice for 3 hours on HIGH. Then remove the cinnamon stick and piece of the fresh ginger from the slow cooker. Add the butter and caramel in the slow cooker and stir it until the caramel and butter are dissolved. Close the lid and cook the wild rice on LOW for 1 hour more. Then open the slow cooker lid and let the wild rice chill naturally. Put the wild rice in the bowls and serve it warm.

Nutrition: calories 548, fat 20.5, fiber 9, carbs 77.78, protein 17

Coconut Pie

Prep time: 25 minutes | Cooking time: 3.5 hours | Servings: 8

Ingredients:

- 5 eggs
- 1 cup milk
- 1 cup flour
- 1 cup coconut flakes
- 1/3 cup white sugar
- 1 teaspoon baking soda
- ½ cup whipped cream
- ½ cup strawberries
- 1 tablespoon lemon juice
- 1 teaspoon lemon zest
- 1 teaspoon vanilla sugar
- 1 teaspoon butter, unsalted

Directions:

Beat the eggs in the bowl and add the milk. Whisk the liquid until smooth. Add the coconut flakes, white sugar, baking soda, lemon juice, and vanilla sugar. Stir the mixture with a fork. Then sift the flour into the mixture and make the batter. Butter the slow cooker bowl. Put the batter there and close the lid. Cook the coconut pie for 3.5 hours on HIGH. Meanwhile, slice the strawberries and combine them with the whipped cream. When the coconut pie is cooked, chill it until the pie is cooled. Then spread it with the whipped strawberry mixture.

Nutrition: calories 260, fat 15.2, fiber 2, carbs 21.98, protein 9

Bread Cake with Oranges

Prep time: 20 minutes | Cooking time: 6 hours | Servings: 6

Ingredients:

- 8 oz white bread
- 2 eggs
- 2 egg yolks
- ½ cup sugar, brown
- 2 oranges
- 3 tablespoons condensed milk
- 1 teaspoon ground ginger
- 2 oranges
- 1 teaspoon nutmeg
- 4 tablespoons butter
- ¼ cup cream cheese
- ¼ teaspoon baking spray
- 3 tablespoons flour

Directions:

Chop the white bread into the cubes. Peel the oranges and chop them. Then whisk the eggs and egg yolks. Add the brown sugar and mix the egg with a mixer for 1 minute. Add the condensed milk and ground ginger. Add the chopped oranges. Then sprinkle the mixture with the nutmeg, butter, cream cheese, and flour. Spray the slow cooker bowl with the baking spray. Put the chopped white bread cubes in the slow cooker. Then pour the egg mixture into the slow cooker and close the lid. Cook the bread cake for 6 hours on LOW. When the cake is cooked, chill it and put on a serving plate. Chill it fully and slice.

Nutrition: calories 352, fat 17.2, fiber 6, carbs 37.77, protein 13

Strawberry Pavlova

Prep time: 20 minutes | Cooking time: 3 hours | Servings: 6

Ingredients:

- 8 egg whites
- 2 cups white sugar
- 5 tablespoons corn flour
- 1 cup strawberry
- 1 cup whipped cream
- ¼ teaspoon lemon juice

Directions:

Whisk the egg whites until you get stiff peaks. Then add the white sugar and continue to whisk the egg whites for 1 minute more. After this, add the corn flour and lemon juice. Mix well. Then put the parchment in the slow cooker bowl. Pour the egg white mixture into the slow cooker. Close the lid and cook "Pavlova" for 3 hours on HIGH. Meanwhile, wash the strawberries and chop them. When the egg white crust is cooked, chill it well and only after this transfer in the serving plate. Spread it with the whipped cream. Then cover the cake with the chopped strawberries.

Nutrition: calories 278, fat 21, fiber 3, carbs 16.72, protein 8

Blueberry Bread Pudding

Prep time: 20 minutes | Cooking time: 4 hours | Servings: 7

Ingredients:

- 10 oz white French bread
- 1 cup milk
- 4 eggs
- ½ cup sugar
- 3 tablespoon prunes, chopped
- ½ cup blueberries
- 1 tablespoon almond flour
- 1 teaspoon cornstarch
- 2 tablespoons cream cheese
- 1 teaspoon butter
- 1 tablespoon vanilla extract

Directions:

Combine the blueberries with the sugar and blend them carefully. Then chop white French bread and toss it in the slow cooker vessel. Beat the eggs in a mixing bowl. Add the whisked eggs to the slow cooker. Then sprinkle the bread with the blended blueberries. Chop the prunes. Add the chopped prunes in the slow cooker. After this, add the almond flour, cornstarch, cream cheese, butter, and vanilla extract. Mix the bread mixture with a wooden spatula to make it smooth and close the lid. Cook the pudding for 4 hours on HIGH. When the blueberry bread pudding is cooked, chill it fully. Then remove it from the slow cooker bowl and serve.

Nutrition: calories 191, fat 9.1, fiber 1, carbs 19.26, protein 7

Cocoa Bars
Prep time: 25 minutes | Cooking time: 3.5 hours | Servings: 8

Ingredients:
- 1 cup cocoa
- 1 cup flour
- 1 cup butter
- 1 teaspoon baking powder
- 1 tablespoon lime juice
- 2 teaspoons lemon zest
- ½ cup pecan, crushed
- ¼ teaspoon olive oil
- 2 tablespoons dried apricots, chopped

Directions:
Combine the cocoa, flour, baking powder, lemon zest, crushed pecans, and chopped dried apricots in the bowl. Melt the butter and add the melted butter and lime juice to the cocoa mixture. Make a soft but non-sticky dough and knead it with your hands. Then wrap the dough in the plastic wrap and put it in the fridge for 10 minutes. When the dough is little bit firm, remove it from the fridge and roll in the shape of the slow cooker bowl surface. Cover the slow cooker bowl with baking paper. Put the prepared cocoa dough in the slow cooker and cut it into the bars with the help of the knife. Then close the slow cooker lid. Cook the cocoa bars for 3.5 hours on HIGH. Check if the cocoa bars are cooked and remove them from the slow cooker gently to not damage them. Serve the cocoa bars warm with milk.

Nutrition: calories 338, fat 29.2, fiber 4, carbs 21.75, protein 4

Peach Caramel
Prep time: 20 minutes | Cooking time: 2.5 hours | Servings: 5

Ingredients:
- 1 cup peach, pitted
- 1 cup sugar, brown
- 1 tablespoon butter
- ¼ teaspoon cinnamon
- 4 tablespoons white sugar

Directions:
Peel the peaches and chop them. Blend the peaches to a puree. Combine the peach puree with the brown sugar. Put the peach mixture in the slow cooker bowl. Add the white sugar and cinnamon. Cook the mixture on HIGH for 30 minutes. When the sweet mixture starts to melt, add the butter. Whisk it carefully and continue to cook the caramel on LOW for 2 hours more. Stir it every 30 minutes. When the caramel is cooked, it will have a thick but smooth texture. Chill to room temperature and serve.

Nutrition: calories 143, fat 2.8, fiber 1, carbs 30.82, protein 0

Apples with Granola Filling
Prep time: 18 minutes | Cooking time: 5 hours | Servings: 5

Ingredients:
- ½ cup granola
- 5 apples
- 3 tablespoons cream cheese
- 2 tablespoons sugar
- 1 egg
- 2 tablespoons coconut flakes
- 1 teaspoon butter
- ½ teaspoon vanilla extract
- 1 tablespoon raisins

Directions:
Cut the apple tops off and remove the flesh from the apples. Combine the granola, cream cheese, sugar, coconut flakes, butter, vanilla extract, and raisins together in the bowl. Beat the egg in the granola mixture and mix it up. Then fill the apples with the granola mixture and cover the apples with the apple tops. Put the apples in the slow cooker and close the lid. Cook the apples on LOW for 5 hours. When the apples are cooked, open the lid and chill them. Transfer the chilled apples with granola filling to plates. Taste it!

Nutrition: calories 186, fat 6.5, fiber 5, carbs 31.4, protein 3

Orange Upside down Cake

Prep time: 20 minutes | Cooking time: 4 hours | Servings: 8

Ingredients:

- 3 oranges
- 6 oz butter, unsalted
- 1 teaspoon ground ginger
- ½ cup sugar
- 4 eggs, beaten

- 3 cups flour
- 1 cup skim milk
- 1 teaspoon baking powder
- 1 teaspoon vinegar
- ½ teaspoon sesame oil

Directions:

Peel the oranges and slice them. Combine the unsalted butter with the sugar, beaten eggs, flour, skim milk, baking powder, and vinegar. Spray the slow cooker bowl with the sesame oil and make a layer of the sliced oranges. Then pour the prepared batter in the slow cooker and close the lid. Cook the cake for 4 hours on HIGH. Check if it is cooked and put the prepared cake upside down on the serving plate. Chill it well. Slice the prepared orange cake and serve it.

Nutrition: calories 473, fat 23, fiber 4, carbs 56.2, protein 11

Oatmeal Crumble

Prep time: 15 minutes | Cooking time: 5 hours | Servings: 4

Ingredients:

- 1 cup oatmeal
- 1 cup pears
- 1 teaspoon salt
- 1 cup white sugar
- 1 tablespoon ground cinnamon

- 2 tablespoons butter
- 3 tablespoons almond flour
- 4 tablespoons raisins
- ¼ teaspoon turmeric
- 1/3 cup water

Directions:

Chop the pears and combine them with the oatmeal. Stir it and add the salt and white sugar. After this, add the ground cinnamon and almond flour. Sprinkle the mixture with the raisins and turmeric. Mix it with a spoon. Then chop the butter and put it in the slow cooker bowl. After this, put the oatmeal mixture in as well. Add water and stir it gently. Close the slow cooker lid and cook the crumble on LOW for 4 hours. Mix the crumble carefully with a spoon and cook it for 1 hour more on HIGH. Transfer the prepared crumble in the serving bowls. Serve it warm.

Nutrition: calories 281, fat 17.6, fiber 7, carbs 36.92, protein 6

Brewed Coffee Pie

Prep time: 20 minutes | Cooking time: 6 hours | Servings: 8

Ingredients:

- 4 tablespoons brewed coffee
- 2 cup flour
- 2 eggs
- 1 cup almond milk
- 1 teaspoon baking powder
- 1 tablespoon instant coffee

- 1 tablespoon cocoa powder
- 1 teaspoon lemon juice
- 1 cup sour cream
- 4 tablespoons sugar
- ½ cup sugar, brown
- 2 kiwi

Directions:

Beat the eggs in a mixing bowl. Add the brewed coffee and baking powder. Then add the lemon juice, sour cream, and brown sugar. Mix well. Cover the slow cooker bowl with parchment. Transfer it to the slow cooker and close the lid. Cook the pie for 6 hours on LOW. Meanwhile, combine the cocoa powder and instant coffee together. Stir the dry mixture. Peel the kiwi and mash them with the help of a fork. When the pie is cooked, remove it from the slow cooker and spread the surface with the smashed kiwi mixture. Then sprinkle it with the instant coffee mixture. Cut the pie into pieces and serve it immediately.

Nutrition: calories 261, fat 6.2, fiber 1, carbs 44.7, protein 7

Vanilla Cream Pie

Prep time: 25 minutes | Cooking time: 7 hours | Servings: 8

Ingredients:

- 2 cups cream
- ½ cup white sugar
- 6 eggs
- 1 teaspoon butter
- 1 cup flour
- 1 cup whipped cream
- 2 bananas
- 1 tablespoon vanilla extract

Directions:

Combine the cream with the white sugar. Beat the eggs in the cream mixture and whisk it well. Then add flour and butter. Sprinkle the mixture with the vanilla extract and mix it up with the help of the hand mixer. When you get a smooth batter, pour it into the slow cooker bowl. Close the lid and cook the pie for 7 hours on LOW. Meanwhile, slice the bananas and combine them with the whipped cream. Stir the cream mixture until homogenous. When the cream pie is cooked, let it chill very well. Cut the cream pie into 2 parts crosswise and spread every part of the pie with the whipped cream mixture. Then connect the two parts of the pie and slice it into pieces.

Nutrition: calories 366, fat 27.7, fiber 1, carbs 17.76, protein 11

Graham Cookies Bars

Prep time: 35 minutes | Cooking time: 3 hours | Servings: 6

Ingredients:

- 9 oz graham cookies
- 1 cup lemon juice
- ¼ cup sugar
- 3 tablespoons butter
- 1 tablespoon cornstarch
- 1 teaspoon vanilla extract
- 1 tablespoon caster sugar
- 4 egg yolks
- 1 egg
- ¼ teaspoon baking spray

Directions:

Crush the graham cookies gently and put them in a blender. Add the butter and blend it until you get a smooth dough. Then whisk the egg yolks with the sugar and caster sugar. Add the vanilla extract and beat the egg in the mixture. Whisk it until smooth and add the lemon juice and the cornstarch. Put the prepared lemon mixture in the slow cooker and cook it on LOW for 3 hours. Stir it every 30 minutes. When the mixture is thick, it is cooked. Meanwhile, cover a square form with plastic wrap and put the graham dough inside. Flatten it well to make a flat, firm crust. When the lemon mixture is cooked, chill it well. Pour the lemon mixture over the cookies crust and put the pie in the fridge. Chill it for 25 minutes. Then cut the dish into bars and serve.

Nutrition: calories 371, fat 21.6, fiber 1, carbs 38, protein 8

Chopped Strawberry Pie

Prep time: 30 minutes | Cooking time: 7 hours | Servings: 8

Ingredients:

- 1 cup butter
- 1 cup flour
- ½ cup sugar
- 1 cup strawberry
- 4 tablespoons sugar, brown
- 1 teaspoon vanilla extract
- 2 tablespoons almond flour
- 1 teaspoon ground cinnamon

Directions:

Cut the butter and combine it with the flour using your hands. Then add the almond flour and ground cinnamon. Mix it well to get a smooth, sticky dough. Wrap the dough in the plastic wrap and put it in the freezer for 10 minutes. Meanwhile, chop the strawberries and put them in the blender. Add the sugar and brown sugar. Then add the vanilla extract and blend the strawberries until they have the texture of jam. Remove the dough from the freezer and chop it into the tiny pieces. Then separate the chopped dough into 2 parts. Put the first part of the dough in the slow cooker. Then cover it with the strawberry blended mixture. After this, add the second part of the chopped dough and close the lid. Cook the pie for 7 hours on LOW. When the pie is cooked, chill and slice.

Nutrition: calories 310, fat 23.4, fiber 1, carbs 23.94, protein 2

Citron Bars

Prep time: 25 minutes | Cooking time: 4 hours | Servings: 10

Ingredients:

- 6 tablespoons sugar
- 9 tablespoons butter
- 1 ½ cup flour
- 7 oz lemon curd

- 1 tablespoon lemon zest
- ¼ teaspoon olive oil
- 1 large egg, beaten
- 1 teaspoon vanilla extract

Directions:

Melt the butter until it is soft but not liquid. Combine the soft butter with the flour and sugar. Add lemon zest and the large egg. After this, sprinkle it the mixture with the vanilla extract and stir. When the mixture starts to come together, start to knead the dough with your hands. When the dough is done, roll it in the shape of the slow cooker bowl. Then spray the slow cooker bowl with the olive oil inside. Put the prepared dough in the slow cooker bowl. Then spread the dough with the lemon curd and close the slow cooker lid. Cook the citron mixture for 4 hours on HIGH. Remove it from the slow cooker and cut the prepared dough into bars.

Nutrition: calories 191, fat 11.2, fiber 1, carbs 20.69, protein 2

Sweet Apple Butter

Prep time: 10 minutes | Cooking time: 6 hours | Servings: 6

Ingredients:

- 1-pound sweet apples
- 6 oz white sugar
- 2 oz cinnamon stick

- ¼ teaspoon salt
- ¼ teaspoon ground ginger

Directions:

Peel the apples and chop the fruits into the small pieces. Then put the apples in the slow cooker bowl. Sprinkle the fruits with the white sugar and add the cinnamon stick. After this, add salt and ground ginger. Do not stir the mixture and close the slow cooker. Cook the apples on HIGH for 3 hours stirring every 30 minutes. Blend the apples until you get s buttery texture. Close the slow cooker lid again and cook it on LOW for 3 hours more. When the apple butter is cooked, it has light brown color. Chill the apple butter well and enjoy it.

Nutrition: calories 222, fat 14.1, fiber 9, carbs 27.15, protein 3

Cocoa Candies

Prep time: 25 minutes | Cooking time: 2.5 hours | Servings: 11

Ingredients:

- 6 tablespoons, peanuts
- 8 oz dark chocolate
- ¼ cup cocoa powder

- 4 tablespoons chocolate chips
- 3 tablespoons heavy cream

Directions:

Roast the peanuts carefully and then crush them. Put the roasted chopped peanuts in the slow cooker bowl. Crush the dark chocolate and put it in the slow cooker too. After this, add the cocoa powder and chocolate chips. Sprinkle the mixture with the heavy cream and close the lid. Cook the chocolate mixture on LOW for 2.5 hours. After this, stir the mixture with a wooden spatula. Prepare the silicone candy molds. Pour the melted chocolate mixture into the prepared silicon molds. Transfer the candies to the fridge and keep them there until they are firm candies.

Nutrition: calories 229, fat 15.8, fiber 3, carbs 19.02, protein 5

Summer Melon Pudding

Prep time: 15 minutes | Cooking time: 3.5 hours | Servings: 7

Ingredients:

- 1 tablespoon cornstarch
- 1 tablespoon flour
- 1-pound melon
- 5 bananas
- 1 cup cream
- ½ cup white sugar
- 1 teaspoon vanilla extract
- 3 tablespoons semolina
- 1 tablespoon butter

Directions:

Peel the bananas. Chop the banana and melon and put them in the blender. Blend the fruits and transfer them to the slow cooker bowl. Sprinkle the mixture with the flour. White sugar, vanilla extract, semolina, and butter. Mix and add the cream. Stir it carefully and close the slow cooker lid. Cook the pudding on LOW for 3.5 hours. When the pudding is cooked, stir it gently again. Transfer the pudding to serving bowls. Taste it!

Nutrition: calories 236, fat 11.5, fiber 3, carbs 32.82, protein 4

Latte Cake

Prep time: 25 minutes | Cooking time: 7 hours | Servings: 7

Ingredients:

- ½ cup pumpkin puree
- 3 cups flour
- 4 eggs
- 1 cup sugar, brown
- ½ cup coconut milk
- 4 tablespoons olive oil
- 3 tablespoons espresso powder
- 2 tablespoons maple syrup
- 1 tablespoon vanilla extract
- 4 tablespoons liquid honey
- ¼ teaspoon cooking spray

Directions:

Beat the eggs in the pumpkin puree and whisk it. Sprinkle the pumpkin puree with the brown sugar and espresso powder. Stir until the espresso powder is dissolved. After this, add the coconut milk and olive oil. Sprinkle the mixture with the maple syrup, vanilla extract, and liquid honey. Whisk it and sift the flour into the mix. Then use a hand mixer and mix the dough to make it smooth. Spray the slow cooker bowl with the cooking spray inside and put the dough in. Close the slow cooker lid and cook the latte cake on LOW for 7 hours. Leave the cake in the slow cooker for 15 minutes more with the lid open. Remove the cake gently so as to not crush it and leave it until it is cooled fully. Slice the dessert and serve it.

Nutrition: calories 538, fat 22, fiber 2, carbs 71.97, protein 14

Peach Crisp

Prep time: 20 minutes | Cooking time: 3.5 hours | Servings: 6

Ingredients:

- 1-pound peaches, pitted
- ¼ cup sugar
- 4 tablespoons lemon juice
- 1 teaspoon vanilla extract
- 5 oz oats
- 1 teaspoon baking soda
- 1 teaspoon vinegar
- 1/3 cup flour
- 3 tablespoons butter
- 1 teaspoon ground ginger
- ½ teaspoon pumpkin pie seasoning

Directions:

Slice the peaches. Butter the slow cooker bowl carefully and put the sliced peaches inside. Then sprinkle the sliced peaches with the sugar and lemon juice. Add vanilla extract. In the bowl combine the oats, baking soda, vinegar, flour, ground ginger, and pumpkin pie seasoning. Mix the oat mixture carefully. Put the oats mixture over the sliced peaches and close the lid. Cook the crisp on HIGH for 1.5 hours. After this, open the slow cooker lid and stir the mixture gently. Then close the slow cooker lid and cook the peach crisps for 2 hours more on HIGH. When the dish is cooked, stir it carefully with a spatula and transfer to serving bowls/plates.

Nutrition: calories 212, fat 7.6, fiber 5, carbs 41.26, protein 5

Milk-Chocolate Fondue

Prep time: 10 minutes | Cooking time: 4 hours | Servings: 5

Ingredients:

- 1 pinch salt
- 1 cup milk chocolate chips
- 1 cup dark chocolate chips
- ½ cup milk

- 1 tablespoon butter
- ¼ teaspoon nutmeg
- 2 teaspoons maple syrup

Directions:

Put the milk chocolate chips and dark chocolate chips in the slow cooker bowl. Add butter, milk, nutmeg, and maple syrup. Do not stir the chocolate mixture and close the slow cooker lid. Cook the fondue on LOW for 4 hours. Stir carefully once the chocolate is melted. When the time is done, whisk the fondue and serve it.

Nutrition: calories 571, fat 28.7, fiber 0, carbs 74.85, protein 7

Raspberry Sponge

Prep time: 25 minutes | Cooking time: 7 hours | Servings: 8

Ingredients:

- 4 eggs
- 1 cup sugar
- 1 cup flour
- 1 teaspoon vanilla extract
- 1 cup raspberry

- 1/3 cup sugar, brown
- 1 tablespoon butter
- ¼ teaspoon nutmeg
- 1 tablespoon cornstarch

Directions:

Separate the egg yolks and egg whites. Whisk the egg yolks with the cup of sugar and egg whites separately to stiff peaks. After this, add the flour in the whisked egg yolk mixture. Add vanilla extract. Then add nutmeg and cornstarch in the egg yolk mixture. Fold in small portions of the egg whites into the egg yolk mixture until they are all combined. Then combine the raspberries and brown sugar together in the blender. Blend it well. Put the raspberry mixture in the dough and stir until smooth. Then brush the slow cooker bowl with the butter and pour the batter inside. Close the lid and cook the raspberry sponge on LOW for 7 hours. When the time is over, check the readiness of the pie with a toothpick. Chill it until the sponge is cooled and slice it into the serving pieces.

Nutrition: calories 234, fat 6.5, fiber 6, carbs 37.51, protein 6

Puff Pastry Pears Boards

Prep time: 25 minutes | Cooking time: 3 hours | Servings: 8

Ingredients:

- 4 pears
- 4 teaspoons brown sugar
- 1 teaspoon vanilla extract
- 8 oz puff pastry

- 3 tablespoons butter
- ½ teaspoon cooking spray
- 1 egg yolk
- 1 teaspoon cinnamon

Directions:

Wash the pears carefully and cut them into the halves. Then remove the pear seeds gently. Roll the puff pastry and cut it into 8 parts. Then make the shape of the pear from every puff pastry piece. After this, rub the puff pastries with the butter. Sprinkle them with the cinnamon. Put the pear half in every puff pastry piece. Whisk the egg yolk and brush the pears. Cover the slow cooker bowl with the parchment and spray it with the cooking spray. Put the puff pastry pears in the prepared slow cooker and close the lid. Cook the dessert on HIGH for 3 hours. Then chill and serve the dessert with honey if desired.

Nutrition: calories 238, fat 15.9, fiber 3, carbs 21.95, protein 3

Banana Foster

Prep time: 15 minutes | Cooking time: 4 hours | Servings: 4

Ingredients:

- 1-pound banana
- 3 oz butter
- 1 cup white sugar
- 2 teaspoons rum
- 1 teaspoon ground cinnamon
- 3 tablespoons coconut flakes
- ½ teaspoon vanilla extract
- 4 tablespoons almond, crushed

Directions:

Peel the bananas and chop them. Toss the chopped bananas in the slow cooker bowl. Add the white sugar, rum, ground cinnamon, coconut flakes, vanilla extract, and crushed almonds. Stir gently. Close the slow cooker lid and cook the banana foster for 4 hours on LOW. When the sugar is dissolved, stir it carefully one more time and transfer to serving plates. Serve the dessert with the whipped cream.

Nutrition: calories 689, fat 30.7, fiber 13, carbs 109.32, protein 6

Vanilla Crème Brulee
Prep time: 25 minutes | Cooking time: 3 hours | Servings: 4

Ingredients:

- 1 tablespoon vanilla extract
- 1 cup sugar
- ½ cup heavy cream, whipped
- 7 egg yolks

Directions:

Whisk the egg yolks carefully and combine them with the heavy cream and sugar. Keep whisking the mixture until the sugar is dissolved. After this, add the vanilla extract and stir it carefully with the help of the plastic spatula. Then wrap several ramekins in foil. Pour the 1 cup of the water in the slow cooker bowl. Then pour the egg yolk mixture into the ramekins. Put the ramekins in the slow cooker. Close the slow cooker lid and cook the Crème Brule for 3 hours on LOW. After this, chill the dessert well.

Nutrition: calories 254, fat 13.5, fiber 0, carbs 26.84, protein 5

Tangerine Pie
Prep time: 21 minutes | Cooking time: 4.5 hours | Servings: 6

Ingredients:

- 8 oz tangerines
- 1 teaspoon baking soda
- 1 tablespoon vinegar
- 1 cup sour cream
- 1 cup flour
- ¼ teaspoon salt
- 5 tablespoons white sugar
- 1 teaspoon vanilla extract
- 2 eggs
- 1 teaspoon butter

Directions:

Peel the tangerines and separate them into pieces. Then butter the slow cooker bowl. Line the tangerine pieces in the slow cooker. Combine the baking soda, flour, and salt. In a separate bowl, combine the sour cream, vinegar, and beaten eggs. Whisk the mixture. After this, add the dry mixture to the wet mixture and whisk to get a smooth and soft batter. Pour the prepared batter in the slow cooker to cover the tangerines. Close the slow cooker lid and cook the pie for 4.5 hours on HIGH. Then check if the pie is cooked and remove it upside down onto a plate. Let it chill carefully and slice it.

Nutrition: calories 201, fat 8.7, fiber 1, carbs 23.21, protein 7

Lemon Pie with Cardamom
Prep time: 20 minutes | Cooking time: 7 hours | Servings: 6

Ingredients:

- 3 lemons
- 1 teaspoon ground cardamom
- 5 eggs
- 1 cup whey

- ½ cup cottage cheese
- 2 cups flour
- 1 teaspoon baking powder
- 1 tablespoon lemon juice
- 1 cup sugar
- 1 teaspoon lime zest
- 2 teaspoons ground ginger

Directions:

Slice the lemons. Beat the eggs in a bowl and whisk them. Add the whey, cottage cheese, baking powder, lemon juice, sugar, lime zest, ground cardamom, and ground ginger. Whisk the mixture until homogenous. Then add flour and knead the dough. Add the sliced lemons and stir the dough with a spoon. Cover the slow cooker bowl with the baking paper. Put the prepared lemon dough in the slow cooker and close the lid. Cook the lemon pie for 7 hours on LOW. Let the prepared pie chill well. Serve it!

Nutrition: calories 363, fat 9.5, fiber 1, carbs 54.92, protein 14

Caramel Apples

Prep time: 8 minutes | Cooking time: 4 hours | Servings: 6

Ingredients:

- 6 gala apples
- 8 oz caramel, package
- 5 tablespoons water
- 3 tablespoons walnuts, crushed

Directions:

Wash the gala apples carefully and cut them into 2 parts. Remove the seeds. Toss the apple halves in the slow cooker bowl. Add the caramel and water. Mix gently and close the slow cooker lid. Cook the apples on LOW for 3 hours. After this, sprinkle the mixture with the crushed walnuts and stir. Close the slow cooker lid and cook it for 1 hour more on LOW. Then let the caramel apples chill well. Enjoy the dessert!

Nutrition: calories 307, fat 12, fiber 5, carbs 47.17, protein 4

Raisin Bars

Prep time: 15 minutes | Cooking time: 3.5 hours | Servings: 8

Ingredients:

- ¼ cup raisins
- 1 cup oat flour
- 1 egg
- 4 oz banana, mashed
- 5 oz milk
- 1 tablespoon flax meal
- 1 teaspoon ground cinnamon
- ½ teaspoon baking soda
- 1 tablespoon lemon juice
- 1 tablespoon butter
- 1 tablespoon flour

Directions:

Beat the egg in the bowl and whisk it. Combine the whisked egg with the mashed banana. Add the raisins and oat flour. Then add the milk and flax meal. After this, sprinkle the mixture with the ground cinnamon, baking soda, lemon juice, and flour. Mix the mixture and knead the dough. Butter the slow cooker bowl and make a big ball from the raisin mixture and put it in the slow cooker. Push the raisin ball with your palms to make a flat layer in the slow cooker. Cut the dough into bars and close the lid. Cook the raisin bars on LOW for 3.5 hours. Let the chill in the slow cooker for 2 hours then serve the dessert or wrap it in the parchment to save for later.

Nutrition: calories 152, fat 3.7, fiber 2, carbs 26.74, protein 4

Cocoa Rice Pudding

Prep time: 20 minutes | Cooking time: 3 hours | Servings: 3

Ingredients:

- 3 tablespoons coconut flakes
- 1 cup rice
- 1 cup almond milk
- 1 teaspoon vanilla extract
- 1 tablespoon butter
- 2 teaspoons sugar
- 1 tablespoon dried apricots, chopped

Directions:

Put the coconut flakes in the slow cooker. Add the rice. Sprinkle the ingredients with the vanilla extract, sugar, and add the milk. Stir it gently and close the lid. Cook the rice pudding for 3 hours on LOW. Meanwhile, chop the dried apricots. When the time is done, sprinkle the rice pudding with the chopped apricots and butter. Mix it carefully until the butter is dissolved. After this, close the slow cooker lid and leave the pudding for 10 minutes more. Serve it!

Nutrition: calories 182, fat 7.6, fiber 1, carbs 25.5, protein 3

Cheesecake

Prep time: 25 minutes | Cooking time: 3 hours | Servings: 8

Ingredients:

- 2 cups cream cheese
- ½ cup sour cream
- 5 eggs
- 8 oz graham cookies
- ½ cup butter, melted
- 1 cup sugar
- 1 teaspoon vanilla extract
- 1 teaspoon lemon zest

Directions:

Combine the cream cheese and sour cream together in a big mixing bowl. Sprinkle the mixture with the sugar, lemon zest, and vanilla extract. Beat the eggs into the mixture with a hand mixer. Meanwhile, crush the graham cookies well and combine them with the melted butter. Knead into a dough with your hands. Cover the cheesecake mold with the parchment. Then put the graham cookies dough inside to form the crust. Take the foil and make into the shape of a snail. Pour 1 cup of water in the slow cooker and put the foil snail in the bowl. Then pour the mixed cream cheese mixture over the graham cookies crust. Put the mold in the slow cooker on the foil snail. Close the slow cooker lid and cook the cheesecake for 3 hours on LOW. Chill it well then

Nutrition: calories 551, fat 39.2, fiber 1, carbs 38.36, protein 12

Thick Hot Chocolate

Prep time: 9 minutes | Cooking time: 2 hours | Servings: 3

Ingredients:

- 2 cups milk
- 6 oz. condensed milk
- ½ cup chocolate chips
- 1 cup heavy cream, whipped
- 1 teaspoon cinnamon

Directions:

Pour the milk, condensed milk, chocolate chips, heavy cream, and cinnamon in the slow cooker. Whisk gently and close the slow cooker lid. Cook the hot chocolate for 2 hours on LOW. Stir the hot chocolate during the cooking every 30 minutes. When the hot chocolate is cooked, pour it into the glasses. Serve it immediately.

Nutrition: calories 440, fat 29.7, fiber 1, carbs 34.97, protein 10

Indian Pudding

Prep time: 21 minutes | Cooking time: 7 hours | Servings: 6

Ingredients:

- 4 oz. corn meal
- 10 oz. milk
- ¼ teaspoon salt
- 2 oz. butter
- 1 egg

- 2 oz. molasses
- 1 teaspoon vanilla extract
- 1/3 teaspoon ground ginger
- 3 tablespoons dried apricots, chopped

Directions:

Spread the slow cooker bowl with the butter and close the lid. Cook it on HIGH for 10 minutes. Meanwhile, combine the cornmeal and milk together. Add the salt and vanilla extract. After this, add the ground ginger and whisk until smooth. Then beat the egg in a bowl and whisk it. Add the molasses and stir. Combine the two mixes and whisk well. Then put the mix into the prepared slow cooker bowl. Sprinkle it with the dried apricots. Close the slow cooker lid and cook the pudding for 7 hours on LOW. When the pudding is cooked, stir it gently. Serve it in bowls and

Nutrition: calories 234, fat 11.2, fiber 1, carbs 28.97, protein 5

Huge Coffee Cinnamon Roll

Prep time: 25 minutes | Cooking time: 4 hours | Servings: 4

Ingredients:

- 3 tablespoons butter
- 3 tablespoon ground cinnamon
- 1 tablespoon instant coffee powder
- 1 teaspoon vanilla extract
- 3 tablespoons sugar, brown
- ½ teaspoon yeast

- ¼ cup whey
- ½ cup flour
- ¼ teaspoon salt
- 1 teaspoon white sugar
- 1 egg yolk
- ½ teaspoon canola oil

Directions:

Combine the yeast with the whey and white sugar. Whisk it until the yeast is dissolved. After this, add salt and flour. Sprinkle it with the vanilla extract and knead into a smooth dough. Roll the dough. Combine the ground cinnamon, butter, instant coffee powder, and brown sugar in the bowl and churn it. Spread the rolled dough with the ground cinnamon mixture. Spray the slow cooker bowl with the canola oil. Roll the dough into the shape of the snail. Whisk the egg yolk and brush the cinnamon roll. Put the cinnamon roll in the slow cooker and close the lid. Cook the dessert on HIGH for 4 hours. When the dessert is cooked, chill it well. Serve it!

Nutrition: calories 203, fat 10.8, fiber 4, carbs 24.52, protein 3

Slow Cooker Figs

Prep time: 15 minutes | Cooking time: 6 hours | Servings: 8

Ingredients:

- 3 oz. lemon
- 1-pound figs
- 5 oz. water

- 2-pound sugar
- 1 teaspoon cinnamon
- ½ teaspoon ground ginger

Directions:

Remove the flesh from the figs and mash it with the help of the fork. Put the fig's flesh in the slow cooker. Add water, sugar, and cinnamon. Then sprinkle the mixture with the ground ginger. After this, wash the lemon carefully and slice it. Add the sliced lemon in the slow cooker and stir the fig's mix. Close the slow cooker lid and cook it on LOW for 4 hours. After this, open the slow cooker lid and blend the mixture with a hand mixer. Then close the lid again and cook the figs for 2 hours more on LOW. Transfer the prepared figs into glass jars and chill well. Taste it!

Nutrition: calories 586, fat 0.6, fiber 6, carbs 150.43, protein 2

Poppy Sweet Pie

Prep time: 16 minutes | *Cooking time:* 6 hours | *Servings:* 6

Ingredients:

- 5 tablespoons poppy seeds
- 3 egg
- 1 cup cream cheese
- 1 cup flour
- 1 teaspoon baking soda
- 1 cup sugar
- 1 tablespoon orange juice
- 1 teaspoon butter
- 3 tablespoons heavy cream
- 1 pinch salt

Directions:

Beat the eggs in a bowl. Add the cream cheese and continue to mix with a hand mixer. Then add the baking soda and sugar. Mix for 1 minute on the high speed. After this, add the orange juice, butter, and heavy cream. Sprinkle the mixture with the salt and mix until you get a smooth batter. Add the poppy seeds and stir the batter with a spoon. After this, cover the slow cooker lid with the parchment and pour the batter inside. Close the slow cooker lid and cook the poppy sweet pie for 6 hours on LOW. When the pie is cooked, chill it well and then remove it from the slow cooker bowl. Slice it and serve!

Nutrition: calories 395, fat 22.9, fiber 2, carbs 37.01, protein 11

Conclusion

The slow cooker is the kitchen tool that can help you cook healthy food in an easy way. It is simple to use and require no special training or extra culinary skills. You can make almost anything inside the slow cooker! And cleanup is easy as well.

The slow cooker does not need any special, expensive detergents or brushes, all you need is dish soap, vinegar, baking soda and some water. Just unplug the slow cooker and remove the bowl and clean with dish soap and water. Another way to cook the slow cooker bowl is to combine the baking soda with the vinegar and make a smooth liquid paste. Then brush the slow cooker bowl with the baking soda mixture and rinse it with the water.

One important rule is to not put the wet slow cooker bowl back in the machine. It can cause rust and electric shock while using it- wait until it is dry!

There are no special rules about using the slow cooker- you can use it however you see fit to make almost any meal! You can be sure that it is one of the most convenient and useful pieces equipment for a big family with children, for the couples and just for anyone who is busy and does not have time for a long cooking process! You are going to absolutely love your slow cooker! Time to start cooking!

Printed in Great Britain
by Amazon